CAMB[RIDGE TEXTS IN THE]
HISTORY O[F POLITICAL THOUGHT]

BAXTER
A Holy Commonwealth

CAMBRIDGE TEXTS IN THE
HISTORY OF POLITICAL THOUGHT

Series editors

RAYMOND GUESS

Lecturer in Social and Political Sciences, University of Cambridge

QUENTIN SKINNER

Professor of Political Science in the University of Cambridge

Cambridge Texts in the History of Political Thought is now firmly established as the major student textbook series in political theory. It aims to make available to students all the most important texts in the history of western political thought, from ancient Greece to the early twentieth century. All the familiar classic texts will be included but the series does at the same time seek to enlarge the conventional canon by incorporating an extensive range of less well-known works, many of them never before available in a modern English edition. Wherever possible, texts are published in complete and unabridged form, and translations are specially commissioned for the series. Each volume contains a critical introduction together with chronologies, biographical sketches, a guide to further reading and any necessary glossaries and textual apparatus. When completed, the series will aim to offer an outline of the entire evolution of western political thought.

For a list of titles published in the series, please see end of book.

RICHARD BAXTER

A Holy Commonwealth

EDITED BY

WILLIAM LAMONT

Professor of History
University of Sussex

CAMBRIDGE
UNIVERSITY PRESS

Published by the Press Syndicate of the University of Cambridge
The Pitt Building, Trumpington Street, Cambridge, CB2 1RP
40 West 20th Street, New York, NY 10011-4211, USA
10 Stamford Road, Oakleigh, Melbourne 3166, Australia

First published 1994

Printed in Great Britain at the University Press, Cambridge

A catalogue record for this book is available from the British Library

Library of Congress cataloguing in publication data

Baxter, Richard, 1615–1691.
A holy commonwealth / Richard Baxter; edited by William Lamont.
p.   cm. – (Cambridge texts in the history of political
thought)
Includes bibliographical references and index.
ISBN 0 521 40518 1 (hc) – ISBN 0 521 40580 7 (pb)
1. Great Britain – Politics and government – 1649–1660.
2. Political science – Early works to 1800.   3. Church and state.
4. Divine right of kings.   I. Lamont, William M. (William
Montgomerie)   II. Title.   III. Series.
JN 196 1659.B33 1984
941.06'3 – dc20   93–8970 CIP

ISBN 0 521 40518 1 hardback
ISBN 0 521 40580 7 paperback

Contents

Contents

Introductory preface

In editing this text for the modern reader certain principles were followed. Baxter's 'Theses' were retained in their entirety; the additional comments upon each only when they added fresh material. The omissions were indicated in the conventional way. There are arguments for and against retaining the original spelling, but it was decided in this case not to modernise it. Nevertheless there are many obvious original printer's errors which it would have been pedantic to preserve – e.g. 'everlasti*u*g' for 'everlasting' – and these have been silently corrected, rather than choosing to impose a rather wearying (for the reader) repetition of '*sic*'. Either Baxter, or his printer, got confused with the numbering. There are sometimes, for instance, 1, 2 and 4, and the 3 has been forgotten. Again the decision was taken to correct silently. Italicising in the seventeenth century was not an exact art. The bulk of the text has, therefore, been printed in ordinary roman type, and italicisation has been retained only for genuine emphasis, for foreign words and quotations, and for titles of books. Although many of the original typographical conventions have been preserved, along with the spelling, these have not been observed when they are outside the modern typesetter's apparatus. Where the original printer had used 1, 2, 3 in lists of numbered points, an arabic 1 (instead of a roman numeral) is used to begin the series of numbers. The original punctuation has been retained, except when to do so obfuscates the meaning. Baxter's contents pages have been removed from the body of the text and are incorporated, in abbreviated form, in the main contents page for this edition of the book. There is a discrepancy between the actual chapter headings for the text and the original contents pages: nothing substantive, however, is involved and so the new contents pages now follow the chapter headings in the text rather than those set out in the old contents pages. Chapter 6 has two distinct sections: 'Of the several sorts of Commonwealths' and 'Of the objective or material differences of Government'. In the text, they become two separate chapter headings, although not numbered as such. The decision here has been taken to retain the two sections as parts of the one chapter, since to renumber the chapters would be to depart too much from the original, and would make cross-checking with the original the more cumbersome for the reader. In all these difficult decisions, a compromise has been struck between the desire to retain the original text as far as possible with the desire to ensure as much ease and accessibility for the reader as can be achieved. The 'Meditations' which Baxter added to the text, dated April 25, 1659, has been added on to the contents pages, after Chapter 13. An appendix to the text contains the Preface to Baxter's later work, *The Life of Faith*, in which he formally repudiated *A Holy Commonwealth*.

The Cambridge University Press has an enviable record for the help which it gives its authors. This is the second occasion on which I have had the pleasure of working with Jean Field as my copy-editor. The demands imposed by the tricky decisions, described above, made this a fiercer assignment by far than on the previous occasion, and my debt to her is therefore all the greater. She has been a most skilful and sensitive guide. Lastly, I would like to acknowledge (not for the first time) the professional skill, in producing a typescript of beauty from my illegible hand, of my invaluable secretary, Anne Woodbridge.

William Lamont
University of Sussex

Introduction

A Holy Commonwealth is Richard Baxter's invisible masterpiece. It is high time that it was made more visible. It was written in 1659, but its author disowned it publicly in 1670. This did not save the work from being part of a great book-burning by repressive authorities in 1683. Baxter's *A Holy Commonwealth* was in good company there, alongside Hobbes's *Leviathan* and Milton's writings.

This is to flatter Baxter. He is not in the same league as Hobbes or Milton. His book is a curiously constructed work, which begins with a number of high-minded generalities, and only relatively late in the text gets down to discussing the practical alternative ways of governing the country. There is a very important chapter on resistance theory, in which he draws upon the writings of William Barclay, Thomas Bilson and Hugo Grotius to show the exceptional circumstances in which a ruler should be disobeyed. The last chapter is in the form of a confessional: the application of these theories to his own personal reasons for disobeying Charles I in 1642. A careful reading of the text, we shall see, will show that there is a logic to the whole, and if he ends with a personal apologia, rather than some grand summing-up statement of political theory, we have to remember that it is an *unfinished* treatise. Before Baxter could finish his work, it was overtaken by events.

The major political event was the overthrow of Richard Cromwell's Protectorate. *A Holy Commonwealth* is a love poem to Richard Cromwell. It is not dedicated to him (although a companion book written a few months earlier, *A Key for Catholicks*, was); however, everything in the treatise hinges upon the support that Richard

Cromwell's Protectorate could give to clergymen like Baxter. When Richard Cromwell fell, the measure of Baxter's disappointment is felt in the resigned note of his epilogue, entitled 'Meditations' (written on 25 April 1659), and in his naming of the guilty parties in the bitter introductory prefaces he added at the same time.

How had Baxter come to such a dependence? It was not predictable from his earlier career. He was born in 1615 in Shropshire, had become a salaried preacher in Kidderminster in Worcestershire on the eve of the Civil War, and had fought for Parliament between 1642 and 1647 before resuming his Kidderminster ministry. This was the profile of a Puritan Parliamentarian, but hardly that of a zealot. It is clear indeed that his service as an Army chaplain left him with a lasting distaste for radical sectarians, of whom he originally saw Oliver Cromwell as chief. He opposed the execution of the King and he refused an oath of allegiance to the new Commonwealth. How did he come to write the pro-Cromwell *A Holy Commonwealth* a decade later?

There are many interesting features about the book. It contains one of the frankest explanations offered by a contemporary of why he took up arms in the Civil War, and one which is at variance with the later explanations which he offered in his memoirs. That delicate Puritan juggling act, between the pressures to obey magistracy and to disobey ungodliness, is rarely seen to better advantage than in some of the middle chapters of this book. The subtle interplay between civil magistracy and clerical discipline is explored in profound depth. Yet the overwhelming advantage of the book is *contextual*. He belongs, in this book, to the genre of what one historian, Judith Shklar, has happily called 'action-minded utopists'. Baxter claimed that he wrote the book to confute James Harrington's *Oceana* (1656). This is not a claim to be taken too seriously. Harrington's ideas come late in the text and are dealt with perfunctorily. But Baxter and Harrington are alike in offering detailed reform proposals, model constitutions, *which they expected to see put into practice*. They had reason to do so. Kings, Lords, Bishops – all had been swept away by 1649. Reform was on the agenda. There was confusion by 1659 at the centre: various constitutions had been adopted and then discarded. We know that Harrington's followers were active in promoting his ideas in Oliver Cromwell's Second Protectorate Parliament. Similarly, Baxter's reforms in *A Holy Commonwealth* are of a piece with the private advice he was giving to friendly MPs like Colonel Harley and John Swinfen. Baxter, like Harrington three years earlier, indeed like Winstanley, founder of the Digger communal experiment, seven years earlier, looked to Oliver Cromwell as the instrument of reform. This marked some change from the earlier sullen postures I have described. There were two main explanations for this change. One was the success of Baxter's ministry at Kidderminster: to the end of his days they were accounted by him as the happiest time of his life. The godly discipline which he had established there was the basis for his hopes of a 'holy Commonwealth'. Moreover, it was a model which had proved exportable. It became the basis, in its turn, for the Ministerial Associations of like-minded clerical disciplinarians, first within Worcestershire and then transmitted on a county basis across the entire nation. Oliver Cromwell provided the stable context for such reforms: gratitude alone would dictate some reappraisal of former attitudes to the Protector. There was, however, a second reason. John Howe, Baxter's Puritan ministerial friend, became Oliver Cromwell's chaplain, and this provided the vital link to the Protector himself. Baxter could (and did) push in private correspondence with Howe those ideas which would surface in his public writings. When Oliver Cromwell died, John Howe continued to serve as his son's chaplain. Richard Cromwell was, for Baxter, an even better candidate as the godly magistrate than his father had been; there was nothing in *his* personal slate to be wiped clean.

For Baxter to set out in 1659 to justify a 'holy commonwealth' was, then, anything but fantastic or quixotic. He believed that England was on the verge of becoming a 'theocracy'. The way Baxter uses that word is not the way that either contemporaries or later historians would use it. The word normally connotes clerical control over the laity. That is not what Baxter means, as will be seen from a careful reading of the text. He believed that magistracy could and should become holy; Henry VIII's botched Reformation had signally failed to bring this about but he would ensure a partnership between magistrate and pastor which certainly did not mean one was superior to the other. If 'theocracy' is a potentially confusing word for the reader, so too is Baxter's use of the word 'religious' when applied to wars. He meant by such a word in its English context the hijacking of the noble Parliamentary cause by religious zealots late in the Civil War. That noble cause, however, as we shall see, was anything but secular

secular in our sense of the word. Men had legitimately, Baxter argued, taken up arms to defend themselves against Papists (who operated with the connivance of a fellow-travelling crypto-Papist, Charles I). That, says Baxter, is not religion but simple self-preservation. This argument, put forward by Baxter in 1659, would be repeated by him in 1688: he was terribly anxious that people should not think that a necessary defensive action against James II meant that Parliament had committed itself to a 'religious' war.

The text which is reproduced here is not the gargantuan original. Baxter was a very repetitive writer, and it has been relatively easy to compress his ideas without violating the sense. He was anxious not to give himself false airs, and says that in writing *A Holy Commonwealth* he was not setting out to compose 'a Treatise of Politicks', thus underlining again the practical nature of the reforming proposals contained in that work. Instead he said he would lay down 'a few Political Aphorismes'. His term for these 'Aphorismes' is 'Theses'. In the event they number 380, scattered across twelve chapters. They have been reproduced here for the first time in a modern edition in their entirety. Explanatory commentaries on each 'Thesis' have only been retained when they add to the original and not (as is often the case) when they are only repetitive padding. As well as the twelve chapters which contain the 'Theses', this edition reproduces (again with omissions indicated in the conventional way) the thirteenth personal chapter, the equally personal 'Meditations' at the end, and the introductory 'Preface', 'Addition to the Preface', and excerpts from a Jesuit's writings.

The proposition offered here is that in this new sinewy form the reader should be able to reconstruct the logic of the piece as a whole. Let us therefore recreate his strategy as far as we can. He begins with a 'Preface' (which, of course, is added to the text afterwards) which is addressed to those wreckers in the Army who have overthrown Richard Cromwell. Here he actually states points to be developed at length later in the work itself. We are told that 'subjects are not allowed to resist'; even a Nero must be obeyed; the clerical profession is maligned in the present political climate; 'masked infidels or Papists' are making snares for unsuspecting Protestants; the people are not the source of power; Parliaments *could* become holy, if correct reforms are introduced. He states in the preface that the book had been written 'while the Lord Protector (prudently, piously, faithfully, to his immortall Honour, how ill soever you have used him) did exercise the Government'. Then he writes an additional preface which swipes at Sir Henry Vane's *A Healing Question* (1656). What Vane calls 'the good old cause' is, according to Baxter, liberty of conscience (the open door to Popery) and the renunciation of the magistrate's power in spiritual matters. James Harrington, in his *Oceana* (1656), had rightly wanted England to become a Commonwealth, not Vane's godly élite, but Harrington's own anti-clericalism made him equally suspect. Baxter, writing in 1659, saw both men's works of that year as reproducing their respective weaknesses. Baxter claimed to hold a balance between these two extremes in *his* work: 'Holy' (because, *pace* Harrington, he began with God); 'Commonwealth' (because, *pace* Vane, he recognised that a nation was something more than its armed saints). The Popish Plot, finally, was condemned from the Papists' own writings.

The chapter-headings, with their Theses, show how the cumulative argument is developed. Chapter 1 (Theses 1–8) starts with the proposition that 'There is a God that is mans Creator'. Chapter 2 (Theses 9–23) argues that 'God is the Soveraign Ruler of Mankind'. Chapter 3 (Theses 24–34) describes 'the Constitution of Gods Kingdome' and Chapter 4 (Theses 35–44) 'the Administration of the Universal Kingdom'. Chapter 5 discusses 'a subordinate Commonwealth in General' (Theses 45–64), and Chapter 6 (Theses 65–100) 'the several sorts of Commonwealths'. Here he avoids the question of the legality of the title 'Protector' (Baxter had refused to take the Engagement to the Commonwealth in 1650), but calls popular government the worst form of government, and monarchy 'most suited to a moderate Government' the best. This is not quite, however, the resounding commitment to monarchy against Harringtonian democracy which he would claim, after the Restoration, had been the driving force behind his work. In the second part of chapter 6 (Theses 101–20) he would discuss 'the Objective or Material Differences of Government', and in Chapter 7 (Theses 121–89) 'the Foundation efficient and conveying causes of Power'. Chapter 8 is a discussion of 'the best form of Government and Happyest Commonwealth' (Theses 190–209). Here he makes clear that by 'Happyest' he means 'holiest': the 'public Good' and 'the pleasing of God' are his twin criteria for defining 'holiness'. Or, more pithily (Thesis 192): 'The more Theocratical, or truly Divine any Government is, the better it is.' This sounds like a covert plea for something like Scottish Presbyterianism, but that was not Baxter's intention. Like many English Puritans, he felt that the Scots took too much power from the magistrate in order to give it to the ministry; only at the end of his life would he concede that he had been over-suspicious in that respect. His idea of 'theocracy' was one in which the magistrate retained the full panoply of powers which went back in England to the Reformation, but harnessed them to an alliance with a ministry which for its part kept a tight spiritual control over its parishioners.

James Harrington makes his first major appearance in the book in the eighth chapter, and late on even there (Thesis 208). This is important in the light of Baxter's own claim to have written his book to defeat *Oceana*. Baxter became convinced by his own experiences in the 1650s that a holy commonwealth was imminently realisable. Thus the disdainful allusion to Harrington's 'jingles' expresses something of the impatience of a pragmatic politician with the theoretician. So Chapter 9 shows 'how a Common-wealth may be reduced to this Theocratical temper, if it have advantages, and the Rulers and People are willing' (Theses 210–44). Here are articulated most keenly his worries about a secular magistrate who devolves too many of his proper coercive powers into the hands of the clergy. These powers are themselves adumbrated in the next two chapters: Chapter 10, 'the Soveraigns Power over the Pastors of the Church, and of the difference of their Offices' (Theses 245–70) and Chapter 11, 'the Soveraigns Prerogatives, and Power of Governing by Laws and Judgement' (Theses 271–316).

The last two chapters turn from magistrate and pastor to subject. Chapter 12, 'Of due Obedience to Rulers, and of Resistance' (Theses 317–80), is the heart of the book. He begins conventionally enough with Romans 13, and the subject's submission to the higher powers. He moves from there, by the most careful gradations, to that extreme, *almost* unthinkable (and unsayable) exceptional case, when the subject is forced for preservation of self to resist the ruler/madman who invades his own realm. He cites Barclay, Bilson and Grotius as his authorities. Although he doesn't always differentiate very clearly between the positions of these three, he does (correctly) identify them all as teachers of *obedience*. The Theses end here, but not the book, for his last chapter is his personal apologia: why these counsels to subjects in general have specific relevance to one subject in particular, and that one himself. Chapter 13, 'Of the late Warres', explains why Baxter fought for Parliament in the Civil War, and why if necessary he would do so again. He fights on the grounds set out for him by Barclay, Bilson and Grotius. This is not the explanation he offered in the memoirs he wrote after the Restoration, and it becomes critically important in evaluating historical explanations of the origins of the Civil War to determine what weight should be given to it. The 'Meditations' appended to the work after the collapse of Richard Cromwell's Protectorate are moving in their restraint: the bile is siphoned off into the 'Prefaces', written, of course, at the same time.

A Holy Commonwealth is an *immediate* work, with all the disadvantages that entails. His wife always regretted that he didn't take more time over his work, to give it more polish. When we look at the text, even in this abbreviated form, we can see that she had a point. It is not that the work has no internal logic (as we now see), nor that it ducks the great theoretical issues (see Chapter 12), but that it is a rushed response to immediate events (hence the disjunction in mood between text on the one hand, and the two 'Prefaces' and 'Meditations' on the other). However, for the historian this immediacy has itself a compensatory element. The odd oscillation of moods between hope and fear tells us much about the psychology of 1659.

There was nothing fortuitous about Baxter's choice of title for his most important work. He knows the implications this title carries: 'ordinarily the same persons are fit to be members of Church and Commonwealth'. That would sound like Vane's godly élitism: a revolution of the saints. After all, the majority are ungodly: that is the trouble with democracy. However, Baxter's 'Holy Commonwealth' or 'National Church' (his preferred term for the same concept in 1691) is not minority rule. This is because of Baxter's recognition that the Church has not only its 'members within' but those without. His Kidderminster success had been built upon the catechising of his parishioners. This was no less important in his County Associations of Ministers and ultimately in their extension across the nation. There was a 'ripening' process by which 'catechumens' were brought into Church membership. Beyond them, more distantly, were those who had been excommunicated and neighbouring infidels who still came under the aegis of a true 'National Church'. A 'Christian Commonwealth' owned none as *Civis* but he who was fit to be a Church member, yet there were many 'meer subjects' who were nevertheless entitled to look to the State for the protection of their lives and possessions. Vane's holiness dissolved commonwealths; Harrington's commonwealth denied holiness. Baxter squared the circle.

Baxter, reared on English Protestant reverence for a magistrate-led Reformation, was not blind to its defects. Coleridge, steeped in Baxter's thought, offered his own 'National Church' in 1829, which was based not on what the Reformation was but on what *it should have been*. That 'should have been' was the theme of Edward VI's 'Commonwealth' preachers: social justice, new schools and universities, a Welfare State, hospitals, ministerial discipline over Church members; the programme in fact that Baxter outlined to similarly minded correspondents throughout the 1650s. It is no accident that the twelfth chapter of *A Holy Commonwealth* concludes with the lament: 'How sad a blow was it to England that Edward the Sixth was so soon taken away!'

The trouble with one of these correspondents, John Humfrey, was that *his* thinking had stopped with Henry VIII. He might invoke the term 'National Church' along with Baxter (and even suggest that it would make a good title for the next Baxter book), but it did not have the same resonance for him that it had for Baxter. Baxter knew what Humfrey's Erastianism lacked:

> You should not have left out the word [Christian] when you allways distinguish the *Commonwealth* from the *Church*. A *Christian Commonwealth* that is *No Church* is as grosse a Contradiction, as an Army that are no Soldiours, or a Kingdome that are no Men.

He then adds that he wishes that the world had 'more such Nationall Churches as New England is (if a Province may be called a Nation)'. He knew all about New England from, among others, John Eliot, the missionary who was converting the native Indians to Christianity. The excited correspondence of the two men – for there were parallels in the problems posed by American heathens and Kidderminster reprobates – throughout the 1650s would result in two near-identical titles, published in the same year of 1659: Baxter's *Holy Commonwealth* and Eliot's *Christian Commonwealth*.

So much for the hopes. But the time of greatest hope for English Protestants was, paradoxically, also the time of greatest dread. As long as Richard Cromwell was in power, hope prevailed: after April

1659 the balance swung the other way. To see what fuelled Baxter's fears, it is worth looking more closely at the Prefaces he wrote after Richard had fallen. The first address is to the Army who had destroyed Richard. In this Preface he believes that the rot had set in earlier, by 1646. It was in the preceding summer that he became a chaplain in the Parliamentary Army and met at first hand the radical antinomian preachers. These were the men (as he would argue later in his memoirs) who turned the Civil War into a 'War for Religion', and destroyed the legitimacy of Parliament's case. This, as has been said, has caused some confusion. Baxter did not like 'Wars for Religion' at any time in his life. He thought it quite inappropriate as a description of the revolt against James II in 1688. When applied to the English Civil War it has led some to think that, if Baxter believed that it only *became* a religious war later, it must earlier have been exclusively about constitutional disagreements. That is not, however, what Baxter is saying in the twelfth and thirteenth chapters of *A Holy Commonwealth*. He is saying that a legitimate self-preservative action took place against an alien invader, even if it was debased later to serve sectarian ends. In 1691 he argued that exactly the same self-preservative forces which justified Parliament in 1642 were at work against James II. What fuelled that self-preservative drive *on both occasions* was less a concern for mixed monarchy (he blamed Richard Hooker repeatedly for encouraging populist theories of government) than a concern for Protestantism.

Why was Protestantism in danger in 1659, just as it had been when Irish Papists launched their rebellion in October 1641? In the earlier period the Catholics' threat had been a direct one; in the later period, they worked under the cover of 'masks'. Quakers, antinomians, Fifth Monarchy Men, 'Vanists' – what were they but the 'visors' put on by Papist conspirators? The second preface assaults Vane in those terms. When two months after *A Holy Commonwealth*, a clerical correspondent, William Mewe, wrote to Baxter with the hope that he could lead the reconcilers, and undeceive 'the more Eminent Persons in power who have taken upp so strong and strange a Prejudice against our Function', he made an error. He cited a personal relationship with Vane which went back twenty-six years. Baxter was incredulous. Writing back in August 1659, he asked if Mewe seriously believed that an apology for the ministry would ensure the backing of Vane. Baxter was unyielding: 'Sir HV will not be reconciled by a thousand apologies.' Then he added this significant comment: 'I never came in danger till I set against the papists. They do all, that are seene in nothing.' Vane was a masked Papist. Read Adam Contzen (and Baxter dutifully went on to supply juicy excerpts) to see, out of their own writings, how Jesuits tricked Protestants. There were two developments within Protestantism which benefited Popery. One was the growth of sectarianism. Not only Vane was guilty here. John Owen, the leading Independent minister, was also a spiritual heir of the 1646 Army wreckers. Men like him threatened the ecumenical hopes of the Ministerial Association movement. John Howe had warned Baxter about this as early as May 1658, and the Declaration of Independent ministers at their Savoy Conference on 12 October 1658 struck a fatal blow at Church unity. The 'deeper discoverie' demanded of communicants in that resolution was far more stringent than Baxter's requirement in his Ministerial Associations of a profession of outward faith: 'how low then hath this laid our hopes of Reconciliation', Baxter wrote in manuscript at the time. He believed that Owen and like-minded ministers had personally collaborated with Fleetwood and the Army plotters to destroy Richard Cromwell: a belief written into the manuscript of his posthumously published memoirs, and promptly edited out of these again by his literary executor, Matthew Sylvester.

There was a second Protestant development which could only help the advance of Popery. That was the popularity of 'Grotian' views in the English episcopate. In the year before *A Holy Commonwealth* appeared Baxter had published his fullest exposé of their plot, *The Grotian Religion Discovered*. Hugo Grotius was a Dutchman whom Baxter admired for his theology (the Arminianism of his *Catholick Theologie* owed much to Grotius), his political theory (obedience tempered by self-preservation), his ecumenical spirit (reflected in Baxter's correspondence with John Durie) and his views on the Papacy (not Antichrist). He had one fault, but that was monstrous. He thought that Protestant union with Rome was possible on modified terms. The modification was 'French', not 'Italian', in conception: a recognition of conciliar, not papal, supremacy; but for Baxter this concession was worthless. Catholicism, whether 'French' or 'Italian', meant the 'revolt to a foreign jurisdiction'.

Even more clearly than in the thirteenth chapter of *A Holy Commonwealth*, Baxter applied this insight to the English Civil War in his companion piece of 1659, *A Key for Catholicks*. When the second edition came out in 1674 the incriminating argument was missing. Charles I, he had written in the 1659 edition, was not a 'flat Papist', but he had become a Grotian fellow-traveller. The 'Italian' Papists were actually afraid of 'King Charles and the Grotian designe', and therefore they were the men who engineered his execution under the 'visor' of Army radicals. Baxter's source for this conspiracy theory was the old anti-Catholic bloodhound, William Prynne, but the implications drawn by the two men are very different. For Prynne this was the decisive personal step on the road back to royalism: he believed that Charles I had expiated his past sins and errors by dying as a Protestant martyr. Henceforth, Prynne, 'the Cato of his age' according to one royalist admirer, would be deep in Cavalier plots against the Cromwellian Protectorate. For Baxter, however, the King was less Protestant Martyr than 'French'-Catholic-Victim. At least that made him the enemy of 'Italian' Popery; and so a more venial offender? In 1691 Baxter would say that if 'our fate' was to become Papist, 'I love the French Church much better than the Italian.' However, he added this significant rider: 'I more fear the French Papists than the Italians.' Why? Because they were more plausible. The Italians cried up toleration (a patently bogus plea); the French didn't. The Italians cried up Pope against Crown; the French didn't. Baxter was not even worried about 'their Mass, and other Corruptions' they had in common; what was critical was their common allegiance to a 'foreign Jurisdiction'. 'Must we be Frenchified?' was his question to fellow Protestants in 1691; but he had asked the same question in 1642.

These arguments are boldly maintained in his 1659 *Holy Commonwealth*, but nowhere else, it may be objected. That is not true: they are maintained, in private letters (despite the dangers here too with the censor) and in manuscript notes throughout the period after the Restoration. So we have a schizophrenic Baxter in the years after 1660. There is the abject public penitent, whose *Holy Commonwealth* becomes *non-scriptum*. There is a rather different Baxter, the private man, as revealed from the unprinted sources. For example, in 1673 when he is doing his public breast-beating in *A Christian Directory* he is privately telling a young man, Edmund Hough, who wants to write a history of the Civil War, to read his *Holy Commonwealth*: the book which three years earlier he had revoked. And while *A Christian*

Directory discourages clergymen from meddling in things they don't understand, Baxter tells Hough that commentators had erred in relying *too much* on the Bible, and not enough on the political theory of Grotius, Bilson and Barclay! He exulted in private at the guarded terms, even of his disowning of *A Holy Commonwealth*: some well-wishers indeed scolded him for not going further than he had. The Oxford Convocation charges, which made *A Holy Commonwealth* in 1683 an arsenal for popular sovereignty or conquest theory, were plainly absurd. There was one charge (the twenty-seventh proposition) they attributed to him which, however, did have point: 'King Charles the First made war upon his Parliament, and in such a case, the King may not only be resisted, but he ceaseth to be King.' Baxter denied he said it, but he never renounced the subject's right of self-defence against a sovereign who invaded his own realm. Baxter quoted his revered Bilson here: 'none but a madman will do it'. But it is a form of madness for a Protestant King to sell his realm to 'Popery', whether of the 'French' or 'Italian' variety. Is this what Charles I had done? The critical date was October 1641: 'And when the Irish murdered two hundred thousand, it's like they would have destroyed a protestant nation if they could.' Its relevance to Charles I depended upon whether there was substance in the widely held view that he had secretly commissioned his friend, the Earl of Antrim, to lead the Irish Rebellion. Even at the end of his life Baxter was in two minds about the authenticity of the royal commission: (in manuscript in 1686) calling it *perhaps* a falsity; (in print in 1691) dismissing it as another Papist trick. Either way, it didn't help the sovereign very much. He was either accomplice or dupe. If the commission were a forgery, the very plausibility of the charge showed how much damage had already been done by the sovereign's drift to 'Grotianism'. In 1691 Baxter claimed to have known as early as 1660 that Charles II 'was as he Died' – a Catholic – and that Baxter's episcopal adversaries (Morley, Sheldon and Gunning) were aware of this fact. More shame on them, that they continued to flirt with 'Grotian' plans for reunion, which Baxter went on attacking in the 1670s. James II's wickedness is thus no aberration. His open Catholicism must be set against the long tradition of 'French' Catholicism going back to Charles I and Charles II. And so 1688 is not a 'War for Religion' any more than the English Civil War had been: Protestant self-defence was not 'religion' but common sense, in both cases. Baxter would say in 1691 (in manuscript) that 'the designe of K. Charles I and II' – which itself puts James II's shortcomings in a longer historical perspective – was to cast out 'the Puritan Protestants' in order 'that Papists might come in'. Even in 1691 he warned that 'the game is still going on'.

The game might be going on, but with different players. For the first time since 1659 England had Protestant rulers on the throne, and that made the crucial difference. Baxter's mood of 1691 is as upbeat as it was when he wrote *A Holy Commonwealth*, and for the same reason. Popery remained a constant menace, but England had the weapons to defeat it. They were the weapons of 1659: a Protestant magistrate and clerical discipline. For Richard Cromwell, read William III; for 'Holy Commonwealth', read 'National Church'. Baxter would refer back in 1689 to the 'true summary of the English policie in my *politicall Aphorisms*', and at last therefore pay tribute to the work he had been obliged formally to repudiate for the previous thirty years. During that time his public posture was one of regret at having *seemed to* slight monarchy. His secret regret about *A Holy Commonwealth*, we now see, was the opposite: that he had inadvertently wounded *the Protectorate*. In the manuscript of his memoirs he described his agony at having provoked his enemies to strike at Richard Cromwell, because Baxter's 1659 work had shown how close England was to becoming a 'holy commonwealth'. This was too much even for manuscript purposes in Restoration England, and Baxter crossed the passage out. But the conviction it expressed was a genuine one, and it went on gnawing at Baxter. A month after he had written his despairing 'Meditations' his confidant, John Howe, Richard Cromwell's chaplain, wrote to him 'of such persons as are now at the head of affaires will blast religion if God prevent not the designe you writ me of some time since to introduce infidelitie or Popery'. That design went on apace after the Restoration; only the providential events of 1688 prevented their fruition. In the black years after 1660 Howe (his biographer tells us) became very angry at contemporaries who wrote Richard Cromwell off as a weakling. There is something very touching about the fact that, when Howe was dying in 1705, he received a courtesy call from the old Protector. Baxter, of course, had been dead long before, but his *Holy Commonwealth* survives as the testament of this peculiar triangular relationship which had fostered hopes, for a brief time in 1659, that England would become a New Jerusalem.

Richard Baxter: a chronology

1615	Born in Rowton, Shropshire.
1638	Ordained as deacon, and headmaster of school at Dudley.
1640	Assistant master at Bridgnorth, Shropshire.
1641	Lecturer at Kidderminster, Worcestershire.
1642–5	Retreats to Gloucester and Coventry.
1645	Chaplain in Edward Whalley's regiment, in the Parliamentary Army.
1647	Collapse of health – loss of 'a Gallon of Blood by the Nose' – and convalescence at Rous-Lench in Worcestershire, where he begins in manuscript *The Saints Everlasting Rest*.
1649	*Aphorismes of Justification* (intended as appendix to that manuscript) becomes his first published work: a controversial Puritan defence of Arminianism.
1652	Meeting of fellow ministers in Worcester to begin the Association of Ministers.
1653	Publishes *Christian Concord*, which makes details of the Worcestershire agreement accessible to other counties.
1655	Wiltshire, Hampshire, Dorset, Somerset, Kent and Devon form Associations on the Worcestershire model.
1658	Publishes *The Grotian Religion Discovered*.
1659	Publishes *A Key for Catholicks* and *A Holy Commonwealth*.
1660	Restoration of monarchy; Baxter offered bishopric, but refuses.
1661	Prepares 'Reformed Liturgy' for Savoy Conference, but

deprived of his Kidderminster ministry. Married Margaret Charlton.

1669 Imprisoned for allegedly violating the Five Mile Act by 'conventicles' in Acton, and released probably through the influence of his friend, Sir Matthew Hale.

1670 Moves to Totteridge to join his friend from Gloucester days, John Corbet. Publishes formal retraction of *A Holy Commonwealth* in his *Life of Faith*.

1673 Publishes *A Christian Directory*: fourth section repudiates *A Holy Commonwealth*, and returns to London.

1674 Publishes second edition of *A Key for Catholicks*: much revised, and original dedication to Richard Cromwell dropped.

1675 Warrants issued for Baxter's arrest.

1681 Death of his wife.

1683 Oxford University Convocation order the burning of *A Holy Commonwealth* (along with writings of Milton, Hobbes and others).

1684 Publishes *Paraphrase on the New Testament*.

1685 Put on trial for sedition in that *Paraphrase* before Judge Jeffreys: found guilty and imprisoned.

1686 Composes millenarian manuscripts in prison before release.

1688 Welcomes Glorious Revolution as vindication of Civil War principles.

1691 Publishes *Against the Revolt to a Foreign Jurisdiction* and *Of National Churches* and writes (though not published until 1926) *The Poor Husbandman's Advocate*: all works which take up again the themes of his 1659 writings; dies in December.

1696 His memoirs published posthumously as *Reliquiae Baxterianae*, edited by his friend Matthew Sylvester.

Further Reading

The student of Baxter can begin best with the accessible, and easily read, *Autobiography* in the *Everyman* series edited by N.H. Keeble (1974). But these are memoirs written in a censor-ridden Restoration; they are selections originally made by J.M. Lloyd Thomas in the first *Everyman* edition of 1931 from *Reliquiae Baxterianae*, itself partially edited in 1696, posthumously, by his friend, Matthew Sylvester. Their royalism, and detachment from the Cromwells, should be taken with a pinch of salt, as will be clear from this edition of *A Holy Commonwealth* and the Introduction to it. There is a gap between the printed Baxter and the unprinted Baxter (as revealed in the magnificent archive collection of letters and manuscripts in Doctor Williams's Library, Gordon Square, London) which few have bridged. Three who have are: G.F. Nuttall, *Richard Baxter* (London, 1965), a short chronological narrative; N.H. Keeble, *Richard Baxter: Puritan Man of Letters* (Oxford, 1982), a literary reconstruction; William Lamont, *Richard Baxter and the Millennium*, now reprinted as the third volume of *Puritanism and the English Revolution* (Gregg Revivals, London, 1991), an analysis based upon Baxter's millenarian notes in prison in 1686. F.J. Powicke's two-volume biography – *A Life of the Reverend Richard Baxter* (London, 1924) and *The Reverend Richard Baxter Under the Cross* (London, 1927) – was a pioneering work in its time but rested too much on the printed sources. A more recent two-volume work, *Calendar of the Correspondence of Richard Baxter* (Oxford, 1991), edited by N.H. Keeble and G.F. Nuttall, is, however, a landmark in Baxter scholarship, precisely because the voluminous unprinted correspondence is at last made accessible to a wider public in a scholarly and digestible form. Excerpts from *A Holy Common-wealth* are reproduced in: R.B. Schlatter, *Richard Baxter and Puritan Politics* (Rutgers, N.J., 1957), pp. 68–124, along with some other useful snippets from Baxter's printed and unprinted material. Although the Baxter correspondence has now been calendared, the manuscript *Treatises* have not, and still need to be consulted in Doctor Williams's Library.

Biographical Notes

BARCLAY, WILLIAM (c. 1546–1608)
Educated at Aberdeen but moved to France in 1571. Used his position as university teacher to attack Jesuits and defend absolute monarchy. His most famous book, *De regno* (1600), attacked Catholic and Protestant theorists of resistance. That is why Baxter (along with Corbet and Humfrey) felt free to invoke his authority for the right of a whole people to defend itself in the exceptional circumstance of being attacked by a Prince who had taken leave of his senses.

BILSON, THOMAS (1547–1616)
Bishop, briefly, of Worcester in 1596 and then, for the rest of his life, of Winchester. Celebrated for two works: *The True Difference Between Christian Subjection and Unchristian Rebellion* (1585) and *The Perpetual Government of Christs Church* (1593). The first work was probably more quoted on the Parliamentary side in the English Civil War than any other source: Baxter is then not unusual in his deference to Bilson. But (as with Barclay) the comfort to those who quoted him lay in the recognition by a teacher of obedience that, *in extremis*, a madman must be restrained.

CORBET, JOHN (1620–80)
Baxter's closest friend from his Gloucester days, a Puritan minister who gave Baxter and his wife accommodation with him for three years when Baxter was trying to escape the consequences of the repressive Restoration legislation. His book on the Civil War, *An Historical Relation of the Military Government of Gloucester* (1645),

offers an explanation on why men took up arms for Parliament which is much along the lines of what Baxter was to say at greater length fourteen years later in *A Holy Commonwealth* (chapter xiii).

DURIE, JOHN (1596–1680)

The untiring advocate of Church unity who had the ear, at different stages in his long career, of men as diverse as Gustavus Adolphus, Archbishop Laud and Oliver Cromwell. In his correspondence with Baxter, he was an invaluable go-between: links between the Ministerial Associations (a development he warmly welcomed) and the Swiss Churches were discussed for instance by both men in 1658. Baxter's vision of a College for Conversion outlined in his *Life of Faith* drew inspiration from Durie's efforts to convert the Jews as well as from Eliot's efforts to convert the native Americans.

ELIOT, JOHN (1604–90)

A Cambridge graduate, who emigrated in 1631. His correspondence with Baxter was founded on agreement on doctrine (Eliot bore witness against the antinomian Anne Hutchinson in 1637, whose trial affected Baxter when he wrote *his* attack on antinomianism, *The Aphorismes of Justification*, 1649). But equally it was founded on a common evangelical impulse. Baxter was fascinated by Eliot's pioneer work in proselytising the native Americans, which he related to his own work among the parishioners of Kidderminster. Eliot's *Christian Commonwealth* (1659) and Baxter's *Holy Commonwealth* (1659) are thus fruits of a common impulse.

GROTIUS, HUGO (1583–1645)

Born in the United Provinces but, from 1619 until his death, first a prisoner, and then an exile from his native land. He was Swedish Ambassador in Paris from 1634 where, according to Baxter's informant the Earl of Lauderdale, he began his 'French Catholic' designs for Church unity. The exposure of these designs was to be Baxter's driving obsession, not only when he wrote *A Holy Commonwealth* and (in the previous year) *The Grotian Religion Discovered*, but indeed for the rest of his life. Their essence was the supremacy of Church councils; unlike the views of the 'Italian' Catholics, who exalted Pope above Crown. To Baxter they were a more plausible menace: they shared with the 'Italian' Catholics the intention to impose on England a foreign jurisdiction and had influential support in the English episcopate. Yet Baxter admired Grotius for his Arminian doctrine, his emphasis on natural law, and – with particular relevance to the English Civil War and later to 1688 – the recognition that the people, individually or collectively, could defend themselves against an intolerable tyrant (and, on this latter point, he linked Grotius consistently with Barclay and Bilson).

HALE, SIR MATTHEW (1609–76)

Educated at Magdalen Hall, Oxford and Lincoln's Inn, Hale became one of the most influential jurists of his age, and headed Cromwell's law-reform commission. He was to be a close friend of Baxter: his closeness to reform circles around the Protector made him a valued figure in Baxter's hopes for 'A Holy Commonwealth'. Later this would be translated in Baxter's career to the advocacy of a 'National Church', and to this end he would continue to quote Hale on the need for a *new* Act of Uniformity. Nevertheless it was only intervention by Hale which prevented Baxter suffering more than he did from the *old* Act of Uniformity, introduced as part of the Clarendon Code after the Restoration. Baxter believed that it was men like Hale and Selden who understood best what a 'commonwealth' meant.

HARRINGTON, JAMES (1611–77)

Educated at Trinity College, Oxford, and an attendant to Charles I before the regicide, to whom, according to Aubrey, he liked to expatiate on the merits of a 'Commonwealth'. Baxter claimed to have written his programme for a Commonwealth in reaction to Harrington's version, as set out in his *Oceana* (1656). There is no doubt that the thoroughgoing anti-clericalism of that work irritated Baxter, as did its reliance on paper contrivances, as Baxter saw them; but Harrington is only dealt with peripherally (and superficially) in the text of *A Holy Commonwealth*, and it is difficult to sustain Baxter's claims at the Restoration that it was intended as a defence of royalism against Harrington's republicanism.

HUMFREY, JOHN (1621–1719)

Educated at Pembroke College, Oxford, friend and frequent correspondent of Baxter, and ejected from his ministry at the Restoration. He had been ordained a Presbyterian minister in 1649; was reordained episcopally; defended his action and then renounced it; formed a congregational church in London. There was a purpose behind these zig-zags: which was to establish a broad-based National Church, which brought him into close relationship with Baxter. He suggested the title for Baxter's treatise on National Churches; he suggested that Baxter write the paraphrase on the New Testament (which led to his imprisonment); but behind the superficial agreements (and genuine friendship) lay a profound difference. Humfrey's 'National Church' was shorn of holiness: his belief (like Prynne's) in free admission to the Sacrament was at variance with Baxter's insistence on an outward profession of belief.

HOWE, JOHN (1630–1705)

Ejected minister, educated at Christ's College, Cambridge, who was as crucial in the spiritual sphere as Sir Matthew Hale was in the legal in persuading Baxter that Oliver and Richard Cromwell could deliver a New Jerusalem. This belief derived from knowledge of Howe's position as chaplain to both men, and the correspondence between Baxter and Howe shows how this intimacy was exploited for their reformist ends. Before his death, Howe was to confer privately with both William III and Richard Cromwell – the heroes of Baxter's 'National Church' and 'Holy Commonwealth' respectively.

LAWSON, GEORGE (1598–1678)

Presbyterian divine, supporter of Parliament in the Civil War, and friend of Baxter. After the Restoration, when publicly saying (after his own experience) that clergymen should not meddle in politics, Baxter made an exception for Lawson. He invariably (in private as well as public) praised Lawson's political acuteness; he enjoyed Lawson's attacks on Hobbes; but Lawson's anticipation of Locke's theory of the dissolution of government (which is perhaps now seen as his greatest distinction) was repudiated by Baxter as itself not being relevant to the situation he himself had faced, as outlined in *A Holy Commonwealth*, when he took up arms for Parliament.

NETHERSOLE, SIR FRANCIS (1587–1659)

Scholar, fellow and tutor of Trinity College, Cambridge; M.P. for Corfe Castle in 1624, 1625 and 1629; former secretary to the Electress Elizabeth of the Palatine and imprisoned in 1634 for his over-zealous championing of her cause. Baxter, trying to kill the *canard* that Presbyterians were for Parliament and Anglicans for the King in the Civil War, used to invoke Nethersole as the token 'Presbyterian/Royalist' (Richard Hooker's malign influence was cast on the other side). His own responses to Nethersole's Royalist overtures in the Interregnum were markedly frigid: a point glossed over in Baxter's Restoration tributes to Nethersole's royalism.

OWEN, JOHN (1616–1683)

The leading spokesman for Independency, Cromwell's chaplain in 1650, dean of Christ Church, Oxford, 1651–60 and Vice-Chancellor 1652–8, and collaborator with Fleetwood in the downfall of Richard Cromwell. Hopes for a union between Presbyterians and Independents after the Restoration foundered on the mistrust between Baxter and Owen. They disagreed over doctrine (Owen's Calvinism against Baxter's Arminianism); over church polity (Owen's restrictive admission to the Lord's Supper as against the more generous policy which underlay Baxter's Ministerial Associations); and finally over government (Baxter never forgave Owen for the part he played in destroying the Holy Commonwealth: comments to that effect were excised by Baxter's editor from his 1696 version of Baxter's memoirs).

POOLE, MATTHEW (1624–79)

Biblical commentator and ejected minister, he won fame among contemporaries for his 'Synopsis' of the critical labours of biblical commentators after the Restoration. During the Interregnum, corresponded excitedly with Baxter about the collation of 'Providences' – a task taken up in 1681 by their fellow-correspondent, Increase Mather, for his organisation of Massachusetts ministers. Interest in witchcraft and 'prodigies', and the need for their scientific investigation by experts, was a common interest of the three divines, and part of the mental background of *A Holy Commonwealth*.

PRYNNE, WILLIAM (1600–69)

Puritan pamphleteer and lawyer, apologist for Parliament in the Civil War but later Royalist, he had a formative influence on Baxter's thinking in the Interregnum. His revelations of Popish Plots profoundly altered Baxter's views of the monarchy, and became the basis for Baxter's own theory of a 'Grotian' conspiracy among the bishops.

But the differences as well as the sympathies should be stressed: Prynne's Erastianism was offensive to Baxter and they therefore quarrelled (as Baxter had with Humfrey) on the terms of admission to the Sacraments; Baxter was more cool than Prynne about the Royal Martyr, because of the distinction he made between 'French' and 'Italian' Popery; Prynne saw Oliver Cromwell as Richard III revived while Baxter saw him (and later his son) as the instrument of a 'Holy Commonwealth'.

SELDEN, JOHN (1584–1645)
The great Erastian, hebraist legalist who opposed the Crown in the 1620s and was a moderate Parliamentarian in the Civil War. He sat in the Westminster Assembly of Divines, and was a merciless destroyer there of clericalist pretensions. This should have put him firmly in the opposite camp to Baxter, except that Baxter recognised in both Selden and Erastus a respect for the civil magistracy, which runs through his own *Holy Commonwealth*.

VANE, SIR HENRY the younger (1613–62)
Former Governor of Massachusetts 1636–7, active Parliamentarian in the Civil War, in charge of naval affairs in the Rump Parliament and, though he had taken no part in Charles I's trial, executed for treason in 1662. Baxter abhorred Vane's *A Healing Question* (1656) for its advocacy of popular sovereignty and its denial of the magistrate's power in religion, fraudulently (in Baxter's eyes) claiming them both to be part of the 'good old cause'. Vane was bracketed with Harrington as the man who had provoked Baxter to write *A Holy Commonwealth*: his offence was compounded, in Baxter's view, by his being a 'masked' Papist.

A HOLY

Commonwealth,

OR

Political Aphorisms,

Opening

The true Principles of Government:

FOR

The Healing of the *Mistakes*, and Resolving
the *Doubts*, that most endanger and trouble
ENGLAND at this time: (if
yet there may be hope.)

And directing the Desires of sober Christians that
long to see the Kingdoms of this world,
become the Kingdoms of the Lord, and of his Christ.

Written by *Richard Baxter* at the invitation of
James Harrington Esquire.

With a Preface to them that have caused
our Eclipses since 1646.

And a Sounder Answer to the Healing Question.
And the *Jesuites* Method for restoring *Popery*.

London, Printed for *Thomas Underhill* and *Francis
Tyton*, and are to be sold at the Sign of the
Anchor and *Bible* in *Pauls* Churchyard; and at
the *Three Daggers* in *Fleet Street*, 1659.

PREFACE

To all those in the Army or elsewhere, that have caused our many and great Eclipses since 1646

Gentlemen,

Being summoned by Mr James Harrington Esquire, to give an account of my Political Principles, I found none at the Publication, so meet to receive it as your selves. Your practices assure me, that between Your Judgments and Consciences, and Mine, there is no little difference. And I think it not meet to differ in points, which our souls, and the Churches Peace depend on, without giving you the reasons of my Dissent. Some I understand are much offended, that I vindicate the honour of Providence, and the Protestant Religion, against the accusations of the Papists, by which they have made it odious abroad. But I am still of the Opinion, that the Honour of God, and the Gospel should be dearer to us, than the honour of those that sin against them: (and is so to every upright heart:) and that the truth of Events may be recorded, and History should be impartial, and Providence on both sides have its due. They that have not read such Books, as *The Scotish and English Presbytery discovered by a (pretended) French Divine, The Image of both Churches*[1] and other Revilers and Slanderers of the Church, and that know not the infamy that's cast on our names through most of the Christian world, are no fit Censurers of my words. While my hand may write I will never betray the Cause of Christ to Papists or Infidels, for fear of the displeasure of any that are culpable. And if I have thought that corruption tainted any of the Army, they thought so too that surprized them at Burford, that prosecuted Thompson and his Adherents, that

[1] Matthew Pattinson, *The Image of Both Churches* (Tornay, 1623).

3

shot some to death, imprisoned others, cashiered more (to pass by the rest.) Repentance doth not justifie sins, but confess and forsake it: Nor doth it hate the Reprover, but rather the Tempter, and the Flatterer, and cometh with love and submission to the light, which the impenitent evil doers hate, Job 3. 20, 21.

I desire you to believe, that it is not from a time-serving spirit, nor want of love to your immortal souls, or of faithfulness to my dearest ancient Friends, nor of deep compassion on the Land of my Nativity, that I meddle not here with reproof or Aggravation of your sin. But it is,

1. Because that Doctrine must go before Application: It's meet that the Light be first set up, which by its manifesting efficacy may bring sincere ingenious minds to self-reprehension, and freely to say more against themselves, then before they could endure to hear from others. And till this Light have discovered sinne, and humbled the soul, I find the most compassionate Reproofs do but exasperate, and seem reproaches; and all men are thought to hate the person that hate the sinne: Innocency and Penitence are much more patient, than guilt and impenitency are.

2. Because I find that self-conviction worketh in you, and hath brought you already to more confessions than Volumes of Arguments from me, were ever like to have procured. And when Nature hopefully begins a Cure, it must not be disturbed by violent Medicines. You have already discerned and confessed, that you contributed by your wanderings into unrighteous paths, to our discomposed State! and that a special presence of God was with that Parliament, which you then pull'd down, or forced out. The Officers of the Army in Scotland confess (as the Publick Intelligencer tells us, May 16) That 'Almost all the Assertors of a glorious Cause had manifestly declined it, by a defection of many years:' Adding, 'We cannot but acknowledg to our exceeding great sorrow and shame, that our selves, though we hope most of us through weakness and frailty, not out of design, have very much contributed to those provocations, which have caused God to depart from our Israel: and we could heartily wish, that even among those that help to make up your own number, there had not been an helping hand to this sad and deplorable work:' And therefore they beseech God 'To heal the backslidings of his people, and not to charge unto their account in this his day of their deliverance, their miscarriages while they were wandering in dark and slippery places,

after the imaginations of their own hearts.' Penitent Confessions will be some reparation of your honour. This much from another, in any of those many years, that you lived in the sinne, would by some have been called a second *Gangrena*,[2] and a *Scandalum magnatum*: It is but lately that it was proclaimed Treason, to say, that 'This Parliament is in being.' A man might have been hang'd then, for saying that which is now publickly Declared. And if you be indeed sincerely penitent, we are not only in Hope, but past all doubt, that God who hath shewed you the sinne of forcing out the last hundred and twenty Members, will shew you also the sinne of the Imprisoning and Secluding above an hundred and fourty at once, long before. Some of them I am acquainted with, and have reason to judg them to be men so eminently wise and holy, as to be unlikely to be the betrayers of the Commonwealth. The keeping out also these men since; the calling of the nominal Little Parliament, the Fabrication of an Instrument of Laws without a Parliament, and many other actions of these times, we doubt not but you will ere long repent of: Finding you in so fair a beginning, I shall not disturb or exasperate you now, by the aggravating, or so much as describing of your sinnes, or giving them the Names which the Laws of God and man do give them. Only may I be bold to intreat you, impartially and often to read over Rom. 13. 1 Pet. 2. 13, 14, 15, 16, 17. Numb. 16. 2 Pet. 2. Luke 12. 13, 14. Matth. 17. 24, 25, 27. 2 Tim. 3 and beg of God to help you to understand them; and fall not out with God and his holy Word.

And give me leave to lay one Argument before you, which may save you from all temptations to Impenitency, if from the (real or supposed) faults of Governours, or their difference of Judgment from you, you should ever be tempted to justifie your sin.

To resist or depose the Best Governours in all the world that have the Supremacy, is forbidden to Subjects on pain of damnation. But the Best Governours in all the world that have the Supremacy, have been resisted or deposed in England: I mean, 1. Them that you called the 'Corrupt Majority', or an hundred fourty and three imprisoned and secluded Members of the long Parliament, who as

---

[2] Thomas Edwards, *Gangraena* (London, 1646) Vol. 1, pp. 91–2, includes, in its enormous collection of anti-libertarian correspondence, a contribution from Baxter in 1645 to William Strong. The evidence for the attribution is to be found in: N.H. Keeble and G.F. Nuttall (eds.), *Calendar of the Correspondence of Richard Baxter* (Oxford, 1991), Vol. 1, p. 41 (although a different page reference is given).

the Majority had, you know what Power: and the remaining Members, that now sit again (so many of them as are living.) 2. The Powers that were last laid by. I should with great rejoycing give a thousand thanks to that man, that will acquaint me of one Nation upon all the Earth, that hath Better Governours in Sovereign Power (as to Wisdome and Holiness conjunct) than those that have been resisted or deposed in England. Now if it were never so clearly proved, that Subjects may resist and depose bad Sovereigns (of which you have my judgement afterward at large; yet the Best must be obeyed and excepted for Violation, or else none at all must be obeyed and excepted: (which is an opinion inconsistent with humane Societies, as well as with Christianity.) If a Heathen persecuting Nero must be obeyed, not only for wrath, but for Conscience sake, and that as a Minister (or Officer) of God, then certainly the Best on Earth must be obeyed, what ever faults you can charge upon them. If any understand not the truth of the Minor, let them first consider the men resisted, their parts, and principles, and practices, and then consider their Laws and publick endeavours to attain the principal ends of Government, and then enquire into the state of the best govern'd Nations in the world, and tell me whether England under their Government, were not like to have been more happy, than any one of all the Nations. If this convince not, (and dark eyes perceive not an Eclipse) stay till the effects of the late Eclipse do prove it in another manner.

Object. But the best Governours may destroy the Commonwealth by a particular Act, and there-in may be resisted.

Ans. They cannot be called the Best Governours that would destroy the Commonwealth. Would they have made it more unhappy than the Romane Empire under Nero? Or than the best Nation known this day on Earth? Every probable or possible danger, or every certain hurt or loss; is not the destruction of the Commonwealth. Nor are all things destructive to the Commonwealth that are judged so by dissenting Subjects. Either the Treachery and Destruction was controvertible or Notorious and past Controversie. If controvertible, the Trustees of the Nation, and not a party of Subjects are the Judges. If Notorious, why is it not discerned by all others, or by the most? Not only I, but twenty for one (as I have reason to believe) throughout the Nation, of men truly fearing God, are of another mind. Subjects are not allowed to resist; when ever they are confident that Rulers would destroy the Commonwealth: much less when they would but cross them in their opinions, or hurt them in their personal Interests. And least of all may they depose their Rulers.

O England! Hast thou forgot the Marian dayes! Hast thou no compassionate thoughts of the Nations of the Earth? Among whom the Power of Godliness is so rare? Shall the best of Governours, the greatest of Mercies, seem intollerable? Oh how happy would the best of the Nations under Heaven be, if they had the Rulers that our Ingratitude hath cast off.

Forbearing therefore such Reproofs as I imagine you cannot bear, will you bear with me, while I presume to wish for these few things, for the prevention of much worse to us and you: 1. I wish you may be tender of your Bretherens Consciences, and while Oaths or Engagements are doubtful to them in these unsettled times, that they may not become snares, either to our Magistrates, Ministers or People: Let not men too hastily be forced to engage to a Power that about a Moneth ago, it would have been judged Treason to acknowledg! Ungodly men of seared Consciences, will engage to any thing for their worldly ends! If you would not take in those into your trust, and shut out them that fear an Oath, or the violating of a Promise, then be not too forward with such Impositions. You know what Changes of the Government we have lately seen, since things were taken into your hands: such as I never read of before. Our old Constitution was King, Lords and Commons, which we were sworn, and sworn, and sworn again to be faithfull to, and to defend: The King withdrawing, the Lords and Commons ruled alone, though they attempted not the change of the Species of Government. Next this we had the Minor part of the House of Commons in the exercise of Sovereign Power, the corrupt Majority, as you called them, being cast out: and by them we had the Government changed, Regality and a House of Lords being cast off. Next this we had nothing visible, but a Generall and an Army. Next this we had all the whole Constitution and Liberties of the Commonwealth at once subverted: Certain men being called by the name of a Parliament, and the Sovereign Power pretended to be given them, and exercised by them, that never were chosen by the People, but by we know not whom (such a fact as I never heard or read that any King in England was guilty of, since Parliaments were known.) Next this, we had a Protector governing according to an Instrument, made by God knows who. After this we had a Protector Governing according to the Humble Petition and advice: (and sworn to both.) And now we are wheel'd about again. And would you have had all the Nation sworn or engaged to all these various forms, and that so suddenly, before they can feel well where they stand? Should you have desired us all to engage to that which you now disclaim yourselves, and to have followed you so sarre in that which you now Repent of as your sinne? The case is weighty! Incomperably beyond the Estates or Lives of particular men. Should we change so rashly, and continue in it six years impenitently, and then come off again, and say, We followed the Imaginations of our own hearts, what would you judge of us for our sinne, and for our lying in it so long? And what a miserable Nation would so guilty a Nation be? Verily if you believe that there is such a thing as Godliness and Conscience in us, you cannot expect in such quick and frequent turns as these, that all that love their souls should follow you. Especially when you are publishing your long mistakes; which should make you fearfull of forcing us to follow you again, and us to be your hasty followers. They that have been deceived, and so deceived, and so long deceived, and so confident in it, and so angry with them that told them of it, may be deceived again for ought we know. Should we be called to as frequent Engagements as you have made mutations in the Government, were it not the way to banish conscience out of the Land, and to teach men to swallow any thing that is offered, and to sinne till they believe that nothing is a sinne?

And consider how Ministers especially are dealt with. The Pamphlets that flatter you tell the world, that the Ministers no doubt will follow you any whether, and will alwaies be on the stronger side: yet others, (if not the same) proclaim, that we are seditious, turbulent, and unworthy of Protection, because we do in some things dissent. And thus they have laid such a snare for our reputations with you, that no man living can avoid. For we must assent or dissent, obey or disobey. If we follow you, we are called, base temporizers that love our bellys and Benefices better than our consciences. If we do not, we are called seditious, turbulent, Traytours, and what such tongues shall please. And this by men that heve seemed Religious, and forget what pathes themselves have trod. But man is not our finall Judge: We wait for his appearance that will pass the finall righteous sentence upon them and us.

Much less should it ever enter into your thoughts to require others, to justifie your former actions. While you are bewailing part your selves, enforce not others to justifie the rest. Even where Christianity is unknown, such a thing would be abhorred. Every man hath a soul to save or lose; and a conscience of his own, which will accuse him, for his own transgressions, and not for other mens. If your Works have been good, the Reward will be your own; and if you force men to own them, it will not procure them your Reward: If they do prove evill, why should the Nation, or any one that did not commit them, be drawn into the guilt! If you have saved a mans life, or saved the Nation, and I had no hand in it, would you not bear with my unhappy folly, if I glory that I had no hand in it, and say, It was no deed of mine? If you had destroyed a mans life, what reason had I or another to subscribe to it? Our Justification of your actions, is no Justification at the Barre of God, or of any well-informed conscience. Take heed of such Impositions, that more cruelly invade the Liberty of mens consciences than sober Turks or Heathens do attempt. What consciences would you bring before the Lord, and what Names would you leave to all Generations, if you should do such things as these, that have gone so farre, and ventured more than many lives, for Liberty of conscience? You know that honest men will not go against their consciences, what ever it cost them, when others will: And therefore unnecessary Engagements will strengthen the unconscionable, and engage you in a persecution of the best, and who will have the worst of that at last? Our quietnesse under the Lord Protector is much to be ascribed to his prudent shunning such engagements. The world is not so simple, but they can see what is aimed at, when unnecessary snares are laid before us. And no Army is so strong, or sure, but that an Army of the Prayers of persecuted Innocents may overcome them.

2. My second wish, is, That whatever be our difference in smaller things, you would prove true to the Interest of Christ in the Main, and not be ensnared by the masked Infidels or Papists of these times, to side with them against your Brethren, that are nearer to you. Do good if you would be esteemed good. He knoweth not Christianity, that doth not know, that the Interest of Christ doth much consist in the HOLINESSE and CONCORD of his Servants: and therefore in a HOLY and CONCORDANT MINISTRY: And in the restraint of the seducing enemies of Christ. If we see once the Doctrines of

Infidelity and Popery propogated (under what Name we do not much regard,) and the able, holy, concordant Ministry, begin to be undetermined, we shall soon know what you mean by it, and what it is that you are about. And if Gods Elect shall be put to cry to him night and day, will he not avenge them though he long delay? I tell you he 'will avenge them speedily', Luk. 18. 6, 7.

3. My third wish is but that our Parliaments may be Holy, and this ascertained from Generation to Generation, by such a necessary Regulation of Elections, as I have after here at large described: that all those that by wickednesse have forfeited their Liberties, may neither choose nor be chosen: but yet no Faction exalt themselves, and oppresse their Brethren on this pretence: that so both Promiscuous and Partiall Elections may be avoided, and we may become a Holy Nation, and a Kingdom of the Lord and of his Christ. And that none of the chosen Trustees of the People, may be deprived of their freedom at their entrance, by unnecessary Engagements; but if they find it needfull to the Nations good to restore a Regulated-well limited Prince, they may be as free as those of the contrary opinion.

If Honesty and Godlinesse be the things you aim at, you will find my Principles suited to your ends. And as I like not the Democratick formes, so am I not fond of any other, above the rest. That a succession of wise and godly men may be secured to the Nation in the Highest Power, is that which I have directed you the surest way to, in this Book, which if you will read, perhaps you may see the errour of those Principles, which have led you into Errours of Practice. I wrote it purposely for the use of the multitude of well-meaning People, that are tempted in these times to usurpe Authority, and meddle with Government before they have any call from God, or tollerable understanding of its Principles. I never intended it for learned men that are verst in Politicks; but for such as will be Practitioners before they have been Students. An impartiall reading I think may satisfie you, that neither the People as such, nor the Godly as such, are the Original of Authority, but that it must come from the Universal Sovereign; and I have shewed you the stream of its derivation.

I had thought here to have added some more Arguments against the Peoples being the Original of Power. As 1. Governing Power must be exercised in the Name of God: Magistrates are his Officers. But the People have no such celestial Power as to grant Commissions in the Name of God. They may choose or nominate the Person, but give not the Power. Our Charter enbleth the Burgesses to choose their Bayliff: but he is ridiculously ignorant, that will hence conclude, that the people or Burgesses are the Original, of his Power; or that know not that they never had it, but that it flows immediately from the Charter as the Instrument of the Sovereign who is the Giver of it. So whether Princes, Lords or Parliaments be Sovereigns, the People may choose or nominate the Persons, but the Charter of the universal King (in the Law of Nature or Scripture) is the immediate Instrument of the Authority, as being the act of that will of God which doth convey it.

2. If the People be naturally the Subject or Original of Sovereign Authority, then they must or may exercise that Authority themselves without Electing others to do it: But the consequent is false: the people may not exercise it (ordinarily) themselves. For every man knows that it is monstrous confusion, and morally impossible. How can the people of France, Spain, Hungary, Brittaine, much lesse of the Turkish Empire, all leave their Houses and Employments, and meet together to make Laws, where the Assemblies may consist of so many millions as cannot possibly consult. He seems distracted that is for such distracted Government.

If you Object, That the Romane People did personally Resolve, and so did Exercise their Sovereign Power?

I answer: No plainer Instance can be given to disprove your Doctrine. The Romane Citizens were a small Portion of the People of the Romane Empire. Did all the People of the Empire ever meet to Resolve on Laws? Or dare you say that Naturally the Inhabitants or Citizens of Rome alone were born the Original of Power, and Governours of the rest of the world? What difference between their Natural Right, and other mens?

And that the consequence is valid, (that the People may exercise the Power themselves if they have it) is evident from the true nature of this Power. For it is an office Power under God, and consisteth essentially in two parts: 1. An Obligation to Govern, making it a Duty. 2. A Right to Govern, warranting the Performance. Now he that is Obliged to Govern, sinneth if he do not; and he that hath a Right to Govern, may justly himself Govern. I confess, in many other cases, a man may have a thing to Give, which he hath not to Use: But it cannot be so here, because the very nature of the thing is referred immediately to Use. Governing is the Use of the Power: and the Power in question is a Power to Govern; and not only to choose a Governour; for that we are agreed of: and I will not suppose the Reader so ignorant, as not to see a difference between a Power to Rule, and a Power to Choose Rulers. (Popular Church Government is also concerned in the decision.)

3. If the people are naturally the Sovereign Power, then it is either All or Part: But neither All, nor Part, therefore. 1. It cannot be All conjunctly: because where all Govern, none are Governed; and so there being no Subjects, there can be no Sovereign: Nor can any be punished against his will, because the Malefactor is One of the All. Nor was ever such a thing yet existent in the world, as a Government exercised by All the People: it is a contradiction. If you say, It shall be exercised by a Part, then it is not the People, but only that Part of the People, that have the Power: It is plain, therefore that it is not Naturally in the People as such; for the Nature of that Part that Governeth is the same with the rest. Either the Governing Part is statedly determinate, or only temporarily. If statedly determinate, (as is a Senate, a Parliament, Lords, &c.) this is but a Part elected by the People; and as Electing a Governour, is not Governing; so a Power of Electing is not a Power of Governing. If the Ruling Part be temporarily determinate, (as is a Major Vote of the People themselves) this also must come but from the Election of the People: for by Nature an hundred and one are not the Governours of Ninety nine: or if they were, that would prove it but in Part of the People. Whoever therefore the People choose, whether King, Lords, Senates, Parliaments, or their own Major Part, it is but a Power of chooseing the Persons that they have, and not a Power of Governing.

But the late Transactions satisfie me, that you are far from believing the Power to be in the People; I would their part without violation might have rested in them whom the People Chose. But when I remember and look about me upon the present face of things, I am not in much fear of Popular Power, or Liberty either, for full and free Elections. Though the name do ring so much in my ears, and Mr. Harrington may think his work begun, I never lesse feared a free Commonwealth.

But there are two other Opinions, that have as much need of Confutation. One is, Whether the strength and Authority be not the same, and that strongest have not Right to Govern? But the Brutishnesse of the Affirmative I have after manifested. Then it would follow that a Thief or Pirate wants nothing but strength to justifie his actions, even before God. And that the Army is to Command the Generall, and the Common Souldiers must rule their Collonels and Captains because they are the stronger, and can master them if they will: And that no People are to be Ruled by ther Prince or Parliament, because they are the stronger. And that the Servants must command their Masters (if he have not an assistant strength,) and the Children when grown up must Rule the Aged Parents, &c. But wee'l leave this Authority which consists in strength to ravenous Beasts, and rapacious Birds, and to Tyrants, and Rebels against the Lord and all just Power.

The last Doubt with some is, Whether Godlinesse be not Authority, and the Saints the Rightfull Rulers of the World? This also I have after Answered. 1. If all Saints be Governours, then all the Subjects must be wicked; and then all Commonwealths must be wicked. 2. Every soul is commanded to be subject to the Highest Powers; even the Godly to the Heathen; and that not only for fear of wrath, but for Conscience sake, because they are Ministers, that is Officers of God. 3. The Godly must excell all others in Obedience; and be so far from aspiring after Government, that they must take it for their greatnesse to be the Servants of all; and must sit down at the lower end, and be humble and not exalt themselves, but imitate Christ in lowliness and meekness, that in his state of humiliation, saith, his 'Kingdom was not of this world', and asketh, 'who made him a Judge; or divider of Inheritances?' and himself paid Tribute Money to Heathen Governours. Godlinesse doth doubly dispose and oblige us to obey: And the Godly must eminently excell all others in their Obedience. Even the chosen Generation, the Royal Priesthood, the holy Nation, the peculiar People are commanded to submit themselves to every Ordinance of Man for the Lords sake, whether it be to the King as Supream, or unto Governours, as unto them that are sent by him for the punishment of evil doers, and for the praise of them that do well: For so is the will of God, that with well doing, we may put to silence the ignorance of foolish men. Servants must be subject to their Masters with all fear, not only to the good and gentle, but to the forward, 1 Pet. 2. 9, 13, 14, 15, 18. See more in Eph. 6, 1, to 9, &c; Col. 3. 22, to the end, &c; 2 Pet. 2, and Epistle of Jude, &c. To allow men to Rebell or resist Authority, because they are Godly (though their Rulers be ungodly) is to allow them to be ungodly or disobedient to God, because they are Godly: A palpable contradiction.

The predictions of the Power of the Saints do warrant none to usurpe a Power: no more then the prediction that the Kings of the Earth shall give up their Power to the Beasts, doth warrant them to do it. Predictions make not Duty, but Precepts; and Promises will not serve instead of Commissions or Donations, nor allow us to seize on the thing promised, before it's given to us. Nor doth the prediction or promise it self intend that Godlinesse shall be any mans Title to Government. For then (still) the Subjects must be all ungodly. Pride and not Godlinesse breeds the Vermine of such impious conceits, through the power of temptation by the Prince of Pride, and the Sun shine of Victory and prosperity, requiting God with Evil for Good.

> Object. But at least if strength and Godlinesse meet (and these encouraged by notable Providence giving success) do they not warrant the godly to defend their Liberties, though not to Govern?

Answ. So far to defend them, as other men may do: (that is, in the Cases mentioned near the end of this Book) but they are not disobliged from as much Obedience to the higher Powers, as is due from any others. They that Resist shall receive to themselves damnation. Much more they that pull them down.

> Object. But did not you Resist the King?

Answ. Prove that the King was the Highest Power, in the time of Divisions, and that he had Power to make that Warre, which he made, and I will offer my Head to Justice as a Rebell.

But yet though Godlinesse give men no Authority, yet as Freemen, we have a certain Liberty; and Wickednesse may forfeit this Liberty; and therefore I shall thus far close with you, that the Church and Commonwealth should be very near commensurate, and that proved ungodly persons should neither Choose nor be Chosen. Reduce elections to the faithfull, honest, upright men, and settle an impartiall way for the triall of them, and we all agree with you, and professe it to be the only, only, only way to our certain and perpetuated peace and happiness. And I must testifie, that I have reason to believe that

14

it was the desire of the Late Dissolved Parliament to have accomplished this: and that it was their full intent not to exclude Independants, Anabaptists, or any truly Godly men of sober lives, from the enjoyment of their Liberties.

But if now it be in the hearts of any to set up a party (or all the shreds of the Dividers conjoyned) instead of all that fear the Lord, and to cry up themselves as the Godly Party, and subdue their Brethren, and captivate those that are better then themselves. Let them expect a Munster issue,[3] and the Church expect a New-England Vindication. Dividing partiality will but shew your want of Charity, that is, of Sanctity. And if Saints that are no Saints, to procure Liberty of Conscience for them that have no Conscience, will go about to subjugate the Saints indeed, and the best informed, tenderest, Consciences, and take in the Loose, whose Consciences can swallow any Engagements, and turn with the times, the Lord will be the avenger, and will come in a day, when such wicked Servants little expect him, and will hew them in pieces, and give them their portion with Hypocrites, where there is weeping and gnashing of teeth. And we can as easily bear their Persecutions now, as they can bear the fire of Hell for ever. Their indignation against me as Censorious, will not free them from those Flames.

For my part, you may see the worst that I designed by this Book; which was written while the Lord Protector (prudently, piously, faithfully, to his immortall Honour, how ill soever you have used him) did exercise the Government: And for ought I know it was almost all Printed, before the Eclipse (only the Epistles, and the concluding Meditation, were written since.) And I have forborn to change any one word of it all, that you may see the worst of my Intendments, and that true Principles will stand in all times and changes, though to the shame of those changes that make bad times.

If you are now offended with my plain former or present expressions, beware lest it manifest your impenitency. I am as able to say that it proceeds from Love, as I am that I have Love within me. And remember how far I have gone with you in the War; and by that and my dearest Love to some of you, am more obliged to speak then many others, lest I be guilty of your sin. Shall an Arch-Bishop

---

[3] On the messianic reign of John of Leyden in Münster in 1535 – the exemplary warning to all conservatives thereafter – see Norman Cohn, *The Pursuit of the Millennium* (London, 1957), pp. 295–306.

Grindall speak so plainly to Queen Elizabeth, (when she would have diminished the number of Preachers,) and an Arch-Bishop G. Abbot deal so plainly with K. James about the Spanish match, as to tell him expresly that 'he laboured to set up that most damnable and Heretical Doctrine of the Church of Rome, the Whore of Babylon' and what would follow: and then bid him 'And now Sir do with me what you please.' (See Prin's Introduct. p. 40.[4]) and shall I be afraid of man whose breath is in his Nostrils? Yea of my old most intimate Friends? and so afraid as to be unfaithfull? I were then the most unexcusable wretch alive.

Hear the Word of the Lord and prove not disobedient: 'The Lord will judge you every one according to his waies. Repent and turn your selves from all your transgressions; so iniquity shall not be your ruine', Ezek. 18. 30. 'Turn ye to the Lord with all your hearts, with fasting, weeping, and with mourning: who knows if he will return and repent, and leave a blessing, &c.' Joel 2.12, 14. If God have special mercy for you, he 'will cause you to passe under the rod, and will bring you into the bond of the Covenant; and will purge out from among you the Rebels, and them that transgress against him', Ezek. 20.37, 38. Be not 'of those that rebell against the light that knows not the waies thereof, and abide not in the pathes thereof ', Job 24.13. 'Wash you, make you clean', &c. If ye be willing and obedient, ye shall eat the good of the Land: but if ye refuse and rebell, ye shall be devoured with the Sword, Isa. 1.16, 19, 20. Jer. 42. 18, 20. 'Righteousness exalteth a Nation, but sin is a reproach to any people', Prov. 14.34. 'Ye know not what spirit ye are of ', Luk. 9.55. 'The wrath of man worketh not the righteousnesse of God', Jam. 1.20. 'If ye have bitter envying and strife in your hearts, glory not, and lie not against the truth, this wisdom descendeth not from above, but is earthly, sensuall and devilish. For where envying and strife is, there is Confussion, and every evil work. But the wisdom that is from above, is firstly pure, then peaceable, gentle, and easie to be entreated, full of mercy and good fruits, without partiality, and without HYPOCRISIE; and the fruit of Righteousnesse is sown in peace of them that make peace', Jam. 2. 14, 18. 'Thus saith the Lord the holy one of Israel, In returning and rest shall ye be saved; in quietnesse and confidence shall be your strength; and ye would not', Isa. 30. 15. 'While they

---

[4] William Prynne, *Hidden Workes of Darkness Brought to Publike Light* (London, 1645).

promise you Liberty, themselves are the Servants of Corruption: For of whom a man is overcome, of the same is he brought in bondage', 2 Pet. 2. 19. 'Therefore now amend your waies and your doings, and obey the voice of the Lord your God, and the Lord will repent him of the evil that he hath pronounced against you. As for me, behold I am in your hand, do with me as seemeth good and meet unto you', Jer. 26. 13, 14. I beseech you patiently read over the Representation or Letter of the London Ministers, to the Lord Generall, Jan. 18. 1648.[5] and their Vindication,[6] and Mr. Nathaniel Ward's Petition of the Associated Counties, and his Religious Retreat sounded to a Religious Army.[7]

---

[5] *A Serious and Faithful Representation* (London, 1649) was the Presbyterian ministers' attempt to distance themselves from the trial of the King which provoked Milton's reply, *The Tenure of Kings and Magistrates* (London, 1649): on which, see A.E. Barker, *Milton and the Puritan Dilemma* (Toronto, 1942), p. 371.

[6] *A Vindication of the Ministers of the Gospel in, and about London, from the Unjust Aspersions upon Their Former Actings for the Parliament* (London, 1649).

[7] Nathaniel Ward: *To the High and Honourable Parliament of England now Assembled at Westminster* (London, 1648); *Religious Retreat Sounded to a Religious Army* (London, 1647).

An Addition to the Preface, being a Discussion of the *Answer* to the *Healing Question*.[8]

Because it is a matter of so great moment, that you pass not in impenitency to the Barre of God, (where you must all speedily appear) and that the many Thousands of this Nation, that never were actually guilty, may not make your sinnes (sinnes of such a dreadfull nature) to become their own by approbation; I thought it my duty to manifest the fallacy of all those Arguments, which I judged might most probably deceive you. And therefore supporting that thence you are likely to fetch matter of encouragement, I shall briefly discuss the wounding *Answer* to the *Healing Question*, so far as may concern your Consciences.

1. He placeth the Cause in two things; 1. p. 3, 4. 'To have and enjoy the Freedom (by way of dutifull compliance and condescension from all the parts and members of this society,) to set up meet persons in the place of Supream Judicature, and authority amongst them.' 2. p. 5, 6. 'Freedom in matters of Religion, or that concern the service and worship of God.'

The former is thus enlarged, p. 10. 'That the body of the good people in their military capacity and posture, are most properly Soveraign, and possesse their right of naturall Soveraignty.' And p. 11. 'Becoming one Civill or Politick Incorporation with the whole Party of honest Men, they do therein keep the Soveraignty, as Originally seated in themselves, and part with it only as by way of Deputation, and Representation of themselves, &c.'

---

[8] Sir Henry Vane, *A Healing Question* (London, 1656): reproduced in *Somers Collection of Tracts*, ed. W. Scott (London, 1811), pp. 303–13.

The second (Religious Liberty,) is (p. 5, 6, 7.) said to be that 'which the Nations of the world have right and title to by the purchase of Christs blood, who by virtue of his Death and Resurrection, is become the sole Lord and Ruler in and over the Conscience, &c. And that every one might give an account of himself in all matters of Gods Worship unto God and Christ alone, as their own Master unto whom they stand or fall in Judgment, and are not in these things to be oppressed, or brought before the judgment Seats of Men. For why shouldst thou set at naught thy Brother in the matters of his Faith and Conscience. and herein intrude into the proper Office of Christ, &c. By virtue of this Supream Law Sealed and Confirmed in the Blood of Christ to all Men, it is, that all Magistrates are to fear and forbear intermedling with giving Rule or interposing in those matters. — He is to be a Minister of Terror and Revenge to those that do evil in matters of outward practice, converse, and dealings dealing in the things of this life between man and man, for the cause whereof the Judicatures of men are appointed and set up. To exceed these limits is not safe, &c.' And p.7. he would have 'this restraint laid on the Supream Power, before it be erected, as a Fundamentall Constitution among others &c. and that it be acknowledged the Voluntary act of the Ruling Power, when once brought into a capacity of acting Legislatively, that herein they are bound up, and judge it their duty so to be, both in reference to God, the Institutour of Magistracy, and in reference to the whole body, &c.' So much of the Cause.

2. The Persons that he supposeth have this Soveraign Power, are sometimes said to be 'the Nations of the world' and 'all men whose souls Christ challenges a propriety in, to bring under his inward Rule in the service and worship of God', &c. And the ground of it is made to be Nature it self, sometimes it is 'The whole party, of Honest Men adhearing to this Cause', p. 3. 'And their right is double, 1. Naturall, 2. By the success of their Armes, this is restored': 'They have added to the naturall right which was in them before, the right of Conquest', p. 2. Sometimes it is 'the whole body of the People', that the right and freedom was, and is due to, p. 4. Sometimes 'the actions proceeding from hearts sincerely affected to the Cause, created in them a right, to be of an Incorporation and society by themselves, under the name of the Good Party. — These in Order to the maintaining of this Cause have stood by the Army, in defence and

support thereof, against all opposition whatever, as those that by the growing light of these times, have been taught and led forth in their experiences, to look above and beyond the Letter, form, and outward circumstances of Government, into the inward reason and spirit thereof, herein only to fix and terminate, &c.' p. 9. It is 'the whole Body of the adherents to this Cause', 'that in the several parts of the Nations, that must choose a General Council or Convention of Faithfull Honest and discerning Men', p. 20.

3. Lastly, 'The capacities wherein the persons then qualified have acted, have been very variable.—And very seldom, if ever at all so exactly, and in all points consonant to the Rule of former Laws and Constitutions of Government, as to be clearly and fully justified by them, any longer than the Law of successe and Conquest did uphold them, who had the inward warrant of Justice and Righteousnesse, to encourage them in such their actings. The utmost and last reserve which they have had, in case all other failed, hath been their military capacity; not only strictly taken for the standing Army, but in the largest sense, wherein the whole Party may (with the Army, &c.) associate themselves.'

I pretend not to an infallibility in the interpretation of these words; but that they may do your Consciences no harm, I shall first tell you what we Grant, and secondly wherein we dissent from what doth seem to be here expressed and emplyed, and the reasons of this dissent shall be annexed.

1. We Grant that the Peoples Consent is ordinarily necessary to the constitution of the Government, and that their freedom is taken from them, when this is denied them.

2. We believe that notorious wickednesse, and divers particular crimes, may forfeit this Freedom as to particular persons: And if the design of this Honourable Writer were, that 'all Honest men indeed without partiality and division', might have the liberty of choosing and being chosen, and none shut out, but those that are provided to have forfeited their liberty; we should concurre with great alacrity and joy (so be it, that oppression make not those scruples or differences of judgment to seem a forfeiture of our liberty, which are not.)

3. We Grant that the Consciences of men are out of the reach of the Magistrates judgment; further then they are manifested by their Words or Deeds: And we grant that the Unity and Peace of the Church, must not be laid on lower Controversies, but on the Essen-

tials of Religion, even of Faith and Communion: and that we must tolerate all tolerable differences among honest men: In well doing all men should be encouraged, In ill doing through mistakes, well meaning men must be tolerated, as far as Charity to Church and State, and to their own and others souls will bear it.

4. We believe that a Prudent Godly Magistracy, is so exceeding great a blessing to the Nation, (above any forms in wicked hands) that all lawfull means should be used to procure and secure it to us and our posterity.

But yet these following Propositions I shall manifest to be most certain truths.

> Prop. 1. The free Choice of Parliament men was a thing that on all hands was granted to be our due, and therefore could not be the Cause of the Warre.

The King granted it; and all Parties in our latter Divisions do assert it: so that it cannot be the matter of any New Cause neither, because we know not of any Adversaries that it hath considerable among us, unlesse those that chose the Little-nominall Parliament. Indeed by the Disuse of Parliaments, our Rights were violated: but the Peoples Right to a free Choice was still acknowledged.

> Prop. 2. That the People had right to choose a House of Commons, that should have the whole Soveraignty, or the whole Legislative Power, was none of the Old Cause.

For 1. No such thing was Asserted and Declared by the Parliament, when the Cause was stated, and the War begun. 2. They professed the contrary in their Declarations of the Cause, and in their Laws, which were Enacted by Authority of the King and Lords, as well as of the Commons. Read them, and this will be past all doubt. 3. And the Protestations and Covenant confirm it.

> Prop. 3. It was none of the Old Cause, to assert any proper Soveraignty in the People, either as People, or as Godly People.

For 1. No such thing was declared. 2. The Soveraignty was stated elsewhere. 3. It was only the Rights and Liberties of the People, and not their Soveraignty that was Declared for.

> Prop. 4. It was none of the Cause of our Warre, to change the Constitution of the Common wealth, into any other form than we found it in.

1. To assert, this were to lay all the guilt of the blood and miseries of the Nation, undeservedly upon the Parliament, and to proclaim us all Rebels, that adhered to them. For it is past doubt, that the Soveraignty being mixt or distributed into the hands of King, Lords, and Commons, no part had Authority to change the Constitution. 2. On the contrary it was the Preserving of the Fundamentall Constitution that the Parliament Declared for. And particularly for the Person and Authority of the King, and for the Power and Priviledges of Parliaments, of which the Lords were part and Authors of those Declarations. It is therefore an injury of the highest Nature, against the Honour of the Parliament, the English Nation, and the Protestant Religion; if any should affirm that they raised a War to change the Government, and overthrow the Fundamentall Constitution, and that when they swore us to the contrary.

> Prop. 5. The Remonstrance of the state of the Kingdom; the Declaration of the Lords and Commons of Aug. 3. 1642. Setting forth the Grounds and Reasons that necessitate them at this time to take up Defensive Arms for the Preservation of his Majesties Person, the maintenance of the true Religion, the Laws and Liberties of this Kingdom, and the Power and Priviledges of Parliament; also the Propositions and Orders of June 10. 1642, for bringing in Money and Plate, &c. to maintain the Protestant Religion, the Kings Authority, his Person in his Royal dignity, the free Course of Justice, the Laws of the Land, the Peace of the Kingdom, and the Priviledges of Parliament against any force that shall oppose them: I say these Declarations, with two Protestations, and the solemn Vow and Covenant, do fully declare what was the Old Cause.

Though no man have more reason to know it then the Honourable Author of the *Healing Question*, yet no Evidences can so fully Declare it to us, as these Declarations and Protestations which were purposed to that use.

> Prop. 6. It was none of the Old Cause that the People should have Liberty, and the Magistrate should have no Power in all matters of Gods Worship, Faith and Conscience.

The words of the Honourable Author I have recited before, without any exception, restriction, or limitation, that I can find, he expresly extendeth the Case to, 'Matters of Religion, or that concern the

Service and Worship of God', p. 5, and to 'matters of Faith and Conscience', and 'All matters of Gods Worship', p. 6, of which he saith, 'We must give account of our selves unto God and Christ alone', and that 'all Magistrates must fear and forbear intermedling with'. Now that this discharging the Magistrate from his Duty, or this disabling him, or stating of his Power, and this extended Liberty in All matters of Worship, Faith, or Religion, was none of the Old Cause, nor is any Good Cause, I shall prove but briefly (yet sufficiently) here, as intending, if God will, a Treatise of that point alone.

But still remember that it is no Controversie among us, 1. Whether men should have liberty for True Religion, true Faith, and true Worship of God? For these should have more than Liberty. But whether, there should be Liberty for false Religion, false Faith, and false Worship, if the persons do but think them true? And whether the reason of this Liberty be, that the Magistrate hath not here to do? 2. Nor is it any Controversie among us, whether the Magistrate can judg of Inward Faith and Conscience immediately? Or whether he should compell men to Believe? Or yet to professe that they do believe when they do not? It is a work that is beyond his power to compell men to believe: else Charity would require him to do it. And we are far from thinking that he should compell them to lye and dissemble a Faith which they have not. But the Question is, Whether he may restrain them for from publique practising false Worship, and propagating a false Faith or Infidelity, and from drawing others to their mind and way.

(i) The toleration of Popery, by too much connivance, and the increase of Popery thereby, was one of the great offences and grievances that this (and former) Parliaments complained of and Declared against in their Remonstrances, therefore that Popery should be tolerated, or that none but Christ should judg men in all matters of Worship, or of Faith, was none of the Old Cause that was owned by that Parliament, but the clean contrary. It was liberty for Popery, that was their great offence.

(ii) The same Parliament made it the Old Cause, to Defend the Protestant Religion, against those that would undermine it by the foresaid encouragement of Popery: therefore they never made it the (Old Cause,) to disown their power in matters of Religion, and to give liberty for all Religions.

(iii) The said Parliament made it a part of their complaints, that the Masse was so openly permitted at the Queens Chappell, and so many permitted to come to it, therefore they took not liberty for the Masse, to be the Cause they fought for. I marvaile how it would have been interpreted, in the beginning or midst of the first War, if any in the Parliament had said, We fight for Liberty for the Mass, and to maintain that we have no power to hinder it, nor in any matters of Faith and Worship.

(iv) The same Parliament (that are the Judges of the Old Cause,) did put the Articles of Religion (and that not for an Universal Toleration, but for establishing the Protestant Cause) into all their Treaties with the King: and insisted on them above all: therefore they made it not their Cause to give liberty to the Mass, or to disclaim any power about the matters of Faith and Worship.

(v) The same Parliament calling an Assembly of Divines, Authorized them but to Advise them, and that only about such matters as they should propose to them themselves: And they debated all that was propounded to them; and passed what they saw meet: therefore it was none of their Old Cause, that Magistrates have nothing to do in these things.

(vi) The same Parliament setled the Presbyterian Government by many Ordinances: therefore they thought they had power in such matters.

(vii) The same Parliament past an Ordinance against Heresies and Blaspheming; Enumerating divers that are against Faith and Worship: therefore it was none of their Old Cause to assert a liberty in such things, and to disclaim a power to restrain them.

(viii) The same Parliament made Laws against Popery, and put an Oath of Abjuration on them, and executed the Ancient Laws against them: therefore they did not fight for Liberty for the Mass.

(ix) The same Parliament made it their great Argument and Advantage against the King, that he favoured the Papists, and intended them a Toleration or Connivance: And on this supposition they had thousands that came in to fight for their Cause: therefore they made it not their Cause to fight for Liberty of all Religions, or of Popery alone.

(x) The same Parliament solemnly swore themselves, and engaged the Nation in Protestations and a Covenant, 'to defend the Protestant Religion, and to endeavour the Reformation of Religion in Doctrine,

Discipline, Worship, and Government, and to bring the Church in the three Kingdomes to the nearest Conjunction and Uniformity in Religion, Confession of Faith, &c.' With much more that shews, that they made it not the cause of their War to prove that they had no power in these matters.

(xi) The same Parliament displaced many in the Universities, upon the account of matters of Religion, and they cast out abundance of Ministers upon the same account: therefore it was not the cause of their War to prove that they had no power in these things.

(xii) The same Parliament accused and condemned the Arch-Bishop of Canterbury for endeavouring to alter Religion, and introduce Popery by befriending it: And Windebanke and others were accused for befriending Priests and Jesuites:[9] therefore they took it not to be a matter beyond their power or duty to meddle in these things, nor was liberty for Popery the Old Cause.

And as it is not the Old Cause, so it is not a Good Cause.[10]

For 1. It contradicteth the expresse revelation of the will of God, in the holy Scriptures. Moses had to do in matters of Religion as a Magistrate; and so had the Ruling Elders of Israel that assisted him: And so had the Kings of Israel and Juda, as is well known. Insomuch that in Asa's daies they covenanted to put him to death that would not seek the Lord God of Israel. But of this more in due place.

2. It tendeth to the ruine of the Commonwealth: and therefore it is no good Cause. How God was provoked by Aarons Calf, and by his Sons, that offered strange fire which the Lord commanded not, Levit. 10. and what was the effect, and what benefit the Calves at Dan and Bethel brought to Israel and to Jereboams House, and the High places, and other errours about Worship, brought to the Princes and People of Juda, we need not particularly recite. Law and Providence are quite changed, if Toleration of false Worship and other abuses of Religion, tend not to the ruine of the Commonwealth.

[9] Baxter's source for Parliament's case against both Archbishop Laud and Sir Francis Windebank – as in so much other anti-Catholic material – was probably William Prynne. See the latter's *The Popish Royall Favourite* (London, 1643), pp. 18 and 25, on both these figures.

[10] On the history of the phrase, 'the Good Old Cause', see: A.H. Woolrych, 'The Good Old Cause and the Fall of the Protectorate', *Cambridge Historical Journal*, 13 (1957), pp. 133–61; J.G.A. Pocock, 'James Harrington and the Good Old Cause: a study of the ideological context of his writings', *The Journal of British Studies*, 10 (1970), pp. 30–48; Barbara Taft, 'That Lusty Puss, The Good Old Cause', *History of Political Thought*, 5, 3 (1984), pp. 447–68.

3. That is no good Cause that vilifieth the Magistrate, and teacheth the People so to do, and sets up the Ministers of the Gospel above him, more than a Prince in wordly splendor is above a Slave. But such is the Cause that I am now opposing. The matters of Gods Worship, of Faith and Religion, are more above the matters of this world, than that comes to. If Magistrates be once taken to be such terrestriall Creatures, as that their businesse is only about these vile corporeall things, their office will be esteemed of, no better than the Object of it, or the work in which they are imployed.

4. The Decalogue was the Vitall part of the Jews Political Laws, and every Commandement of the first Table was seconded with a Penall Sanction: therefore these things belong to the Magistrate.

5. That is not the Good Cause that tendeth directly to the destruction of Faith and Piety, and the Everlasting damnation of mens souls: But such is this of Libertinism which we oppose: For, Popery, Mahometanism, Infidelity, and Heathenism, are the way to Damnation: But Liberty to preach up and to practice them, is the means to make men Papists, Mahometans, Infidels, and Heathens; therefore this Liberty is the way to mens damnation.

It's well known by experience, how ready the multitude of ignorant, unsetled and proud people are to be led into any damning course, if they be dealt with by men of voluble tongues, and that come with any advantages to deceive them. A man that will deny the life to come, or revile Christ and the Scripture, or teach men to worship Mahomet, or the Sunne and Moon, if he have liberty, and a plausible tongue, may look to have Disciples. The preaching of falsehood hath as true a tendency to damn men, as the preaching of truth hath to save them. None can be wicked against their wills: He that will bring men to damnation, must do it by deceiving them, and enticing them thither: They that most promote mens delusion in the matters of Faith and Holy practice, do most promote their damnation.

And how deadly an enemy contention is to charity and holy living, and how certainly the Liberty in question will kindle continual contentions, is a thing too evident to need proof.

6. That's not a good Cause that gratifieth Satan, and promoteth his Kingdom, and his malicious ends: But so doth the Liberty now in question: For it is his Liberty, to deceive by his Instruments, and so to damn as many as he can. When he is let loose to deceive them that dwell on the Earth, it is saddest with the Church, Satans Liberty

to deceive, is not the Churches Liberty, nor purchased by Christ for us, but is a heavy judgment. As Christ teacheth and saveth by his Ministers and Doctrine, and hath liberty when his Word doth run and hath its liberty; so Satan teacheth and destroyeth by his Instruments and Doctrine, and hath liberty when they have liberty.

7. We must pray for our selves and others, that 'we be not led into temptation': Therefore it is not a good Cause to let loose Tempters by a Law, or to permit men to exercise their wit and eloquence and other faculties, to draw as many as they can to sinne; even to those sinnes that have the strongest tendency to perdition.

8. If Magistrates must give Liberty for all to propogate a false Religion, then so must Parents and Masters also: (For their coercive Power is rather lesse then the Magistrates then more; and they are no more Lords of Faith or Conscience.) But if all Parents and Masters should give such liberty, it would be a crime so horrid in the nature and effects, as I am loath to name with its proper titles.

9. *A Pari*: It tendeth to the destruction of an Army, to give liberty to all men to do their worst to draw them to Mutinies and Rebellion: It tends to the ruine of Families, that all have liberty to do their worst to tempt the Sonnes to theft and drunkennesse, and the Wife and Daughters to whoredome: It tends to the destruction of the Commonwealth, if there be liberty for all to perswade the people to sedition and Rebellion: And therefore it must tend to the destruction of the Church, and of mens Souls, and consequently of the Commonwealth in the chief respects, if all have leave to do their worst to preach up Infidelity, Mahometanisme, Popery, or any false Doctrine or Worship, against the great and necessary Truths.

10. The particular Churches by the Power that Christ hath given them in the Gospel, may judg men for Heresie and false worship; and must not give such liberty. Tit. 3. 10, 11. 'A man that is an Heretick, after the first and second admonition reject: Knowing that he that is such, is subverted, and sinneth, being condemned of himself.' 2 Joh. 10. 'If there come any to you, and bring not this Doctrine, receive him not into your house, neither bid him, God speed: For he that biddeth him God speed, is partaker of his evil deeds.' Rev. 2. 14, 15, 20. 'But I have a few things against thee, because thou hast there them that hold the Doctrine of Balaam — So hast thou also them that hold the Doctrine of the Nicolaitans, which thing I hate — Because thou sufferest that woman Jezabel, which calleth her

self a Prophetesse, to teach and to seduce my Servants, to commit fornication, and to eat things offered to Idols.' Elymas was struck blind for resisting the Gospel; and this (though miraculously) by the Ministry of the Apostle. Ananias and Saphira were slain for thinking to deceive the Holy Ghost. Simon Magus feared such a judgment for such another sinne: Paul wisht them cut off that troubled the Galatians. He delivered Blasphemers up to Satan. All this shews that it is not true, that Christ only is to judge such Errours, or that we are to give account to him alone. (And if Pastors may judge them as to non-communion, Magistrates may judge them as to a necessary restraint.)

Hence also it is apparent, that Pauls words, Rom. 14. 'Who art thou that judgest thy Brother, &c.' are nothing for this Libertinisme, or debasing of the Magistrate: For he speaketh not to them that call'd their Brethren to the Magistrates Barre, but to them that censured them in their own minds, or in the Church by too rigorous uncharitable censures: And yet nothing is more apparent then that Paul did severely censure greater errours in Faith and Worship himself, as the forementioned passages bear witnesse: He calls the Judaizers, dogs, evil workers, of the concision, &c. The whole context shews, that in Rom. 14, and 15, it is about smaller matters, yea things in themselves indifferent, that Paul doth condemn the censuring of our Brethren, either by mental or Church-censure, which is nothing to the subversion of mens Faith, by damning Heresies, or to false Worship in the great substantial Points.

> Object. But he that saith, that we must give account to Christ alone, excludeth not the Church, but only the Magistrate: For Christ judgeth by the Church, and they are subordinate to him.

Answ. 1. It is expressly 'the judgment seats of men' that by the Authour is contradistinguished to the judgment of Christ: And the Church, both Pastours and People are men, as well as the Magistrate. 2. The Magistrate also is the Minister of the Lord, Rom. 13, and what he doth rightly is owned by the Lord, and he is subordinate to Christ in his place, as well as Ministers are in theirs.

11. The honourable Author tells us Pag.21. that 'the desired and expected end of this blessed work in the three Nations, is the bringing in Christ, the desire of Nations as the chief healer

among us'. Yea Pag. 19, 'That the choice of persons bearing his Image into the Magistracy, may produce to the setting up of the Lord himself, and chief Judge and Lawgiver among us.' Now either he meaneth that Christ immediately by himself shall be the Judge, or mediately by his Officers The first cannot be his sense, as I have many reasons to believe. And if it be Christ by his Officers, then either by Civil Officers, or Church-Officers. The first cannot rationally be judged to be his sense: For a Holy Magistrate is supposed to be the Means to bring in Christ as Judge: and the Means and End are not the same. And if it be the Government of Christs by Church-Officers, that is intended, I know not in particular what is intended. For if neither the Government by Bishops, Presbyters, People, or all conjunct, or any that we have had in England, be the Government of Christ, I know not what Government by man we can expect that is truly his: And therefore if we have not the Government of Christ already, I despair of having it (Though I hope we may have it better exercised by his Officers.) For I dare confidently say, that the Government by the Romane Vice-Christ, is none of the Government of Christ that we should hope for, and that I have proved it.

But this is my Argument: If the Legislation and Judgment by Jesus Christ among us be the End that our Government should aim at, then the liberty in all matters of Worship, and of Faith, is not the Good Cause; for this is against, and most inconsistent with this Government of Christ. I appeal to Reason, whether to give men liberty to preach down Christ as a deceiver, to preach up Mahomet, to worship the Sun or Moon, to deny the Resurrection, or perswade men that there is no life but this, no Heaven or Hell, and to cry down Scripture and a holy life, and all actual worship of God, &c. I say, whether liberty for these (yea or the Masse alone) be liker to be the Government of Jesus Christ, or conducing to it, then is the restraint of all this Infidelity and impiety? Doth Christ rule more when all we have leave to spit at his Name, and call him Beelzebub, and to deny his Faith and Worship, then where none are suffered to do this? This will be believed but by few that consider of it. At least when a Christian that's now deluded with the specious name of 'Religious Liberty', should see the practice, and hear his Saviour reviled by the Jews, and the Mahometans, and the wicked heardened in their sinne, by being told that there is no life but this, it would make his heart to turn and tremble, and then he would say, that this Liberty signifieth the Reign of Satan, and not of Christ; and that it is the loosing of the Dragon, and not the liberty of the Saints. It's an unholy Saint that would have liberty to reproach his Lord, or deny the Faith, or any Essential Article of it, or to speak against his holy Worship.

12. Liberty in all matters of Worship and of Faith, is the open and apparent way to set up Popery in the Land: Therefore it is not the Good Cause.

The Antecedent hath such evidence, that it would be injurious to a wise mans understanding, to suppose that he doth not see it (that Popery were thus likely to be set up.) And he that seeth it, and yet would effect it. —

Consider 1. How sutable Popery is to a carnal inclination, (as I have manifested elsewhere.) 2. What plausible Reasons Papists have to delude poor souls, from pretended Universality, Antiquity, &c. 3. And how few of the vulgar are able to defend their Faith, or to answer the two great Sophisticall Questions of the Papist, 'Where hath your Church been Visible in all Ages?' and, 'How prove you the Scripture to be the Word of God?' 4. And how it will take with the People to be told that their Fore-fathers all died in the Romane Faith. 5. And above all, what a multitude of Jesuites, Fryers, and Priests can they prepare for the work, and pour out upon us at their pleasure, from Flanders, France, Rome, and other places. And how these men are purposely trained up for this deceiving work, and have their common Arguments at their fingers ends; which though they are thredbare and transparent fallicies to the wise, yet to the vulgar, yea to our unstudyed Gentry, they are as good as if they had never been confuted, or as the best. 6. And what a world of wealth and secular help is at their becks in France, Flanders, Italy, Spain, Germany, &c. They have Millions of Gold, and Navies and Armies ready to promote their work, which other Sects have none of. 7. And what worldly Motives have their Priests and Fryers to promote their zeal? Their superiours have such variety of Preferments, and ample Treasures to reward them with, and their single life alloweth them so much vacancy from Domestick avocations, and withall, they so much glory in a Pharisaicall zeal in compassing Sea and Land to make Proselytes, that it is an incredible advantage that they get by their industry: the envious man by them being sowing his tares, whilest others sleep, and are not half so industrious in resisting them.

8. What abundance have they lately won in England, notwithstanding they have wanted publique liberty, and have only taken secret opportunities to seduce? Persons of the Nobility, Gentry, and of the Clergy, as well as of the common people, and zealous Professors of Religion of late, as well as the prophane have been seduced by them. Princes in other Countries have been wonne by them; and the Protestant Religion cunningly workt out: And what a lamentable encrease they had made in England before our Warres, by that connivance and favour which through the Queen was procured them, (though incomparably short of this absolute Liberty) is sufficiently known.

9. And it is not the least of our danger, that the most of our Ministers are unable to deal with a cunning Jesuite or Priest: And this is not to be wondered at; considering how manay of them are very young men, put in of late in the necessity of the Churches (which the world knows who have caused) and there must be time, before young men can grow to maturity, and an unfurnished Nation can be provided with able experienced men; And the cessation of Popish assaults of late, hath disused Ministers from those Disputations: The Reformation seemed to have brought down Popery so low, that we grew secure, and thought there was no danger of it: And the Papists of late have forborn much to meddle with us bare-fac'd, and have plaid their game under the vizor of other Sects; and withall young godly Ministers have been so taken up with the greater work of winning souls from common prophanesse, that most have laid by their Defensive Arms, and are grown too much unacquainted with these Controversies. We have so much noted how Controversie in other Countries hath eaten out much of the Power of Godlinesse, that we have fallen by disuse into an unacquaintednesse with the means of our necessary Defence, and while we thought we might lay by our weapons, and build with both hands, we are too much unready to withstand the adversary. Alas, what work would Liberty for Jesuites and Fryers, make in our Congregations in a few Moneths space! I must confess this, though some will think it is our dishonour. It is not from any strength in their Cause (for they argue against common sense it self;) but from their carnal advantages, and our disadvantages

fore-mentioned. It's easier to pull down then build; and to set a Town on fire than to re-edifie one House; and to wound than to heal.

10. And then if Popery should come in, what measure Protestants may look for at their hands, we need not go out of England and Ireland for proof.

I leave it therefore to the Judgment of all men that are not fast asleep in their security, and utterly unacquainted with the advantages of the Papists, Whether this Designe of Engaging the Magistrates by a Fundamental Constitution, not to meddle with Matters of Faith and Worship, but leave them all to Christ alone, be not the present setting up of Popery in England; and the delivering all the fruit of our Labours, Prayers and Victories into the Papists hands?

And I would be resolved, Whether he that is not wise enough to know this? Or, He that knoweth it, and yet would do it? Be either of them desirable Rulers for this Commonwealth?

Obj. But Liberty for Popery and Prelacy is still excepted.

Answ. By whom? Not by the Honourable Answerer of the Healing Question. Clean contrary, it is 'Matters of Religion, or that concerns the Service and Worship of God, yea All matters of Gods Worship, & c.' without any such exceptions at all. And if all Worship be out of the Magistrates reach, than so is the Masse, and the preaching for it. And if all Matters of Faith, then the Papists Faith.

But if there had been an exception against Popery put in, it would have been to little purpose, as long as a general Rule is laid down that condemneth that exception. For if it be the standing Rule, that matters of Religion and Faith, and all matters of Worship are out of the Magistrates power: To say then, that 'Popery shall be excepted from Liberty', is to say, The Magistrate shall 'intrude into the proper Office of Christ' (as the Honourable Author speaks, pag. 6.) to restrain the Papists. The unreasonablenesse of this will quickly procure a repeal. And how can such a Senate deny the Papists Liberty, when they plead their own Principles, yea their Fundamental Constitution for it? It's past doubt this Doctrine delivereth up England to the Pope: I know Infidels, and also many tolerable Sects are all at work as well as Papists: But Infidels go against so much, so clear prevailing light, and make such a horrid motion to mens souls, and the tolerable Sects are broken into so many parts, and with-all would use us tolerably, if they should prevail, and all of them are void of those Magazines of Learned men, and Money, and Arms, and Power at their backs, which the Papists have, that it's easie to see that the Papists (yet smiling on the Infidel) would swallow up all. I am past doubt that I shall offend by these expressions. But if it were my own case, I should hardly yeeld to die, lest my friend would take it unkindly, if I resisted him, that would amicably deprive me of my life. And should I silently see the Nation and Churches here undone, lest I give offence, when the matter is of greater consequence than ten thousand lives?

So much to the Old Cause: now of the Persons.

> Prop. 7. It is not the Party that hath owned, and now owneth the fore-described Cause, that have the Right of being free Citizens, or of Composing the Commonwealth, or of Governing or choosing Governours, any more than those that own it not: Nor is any man to be divested of this Right, for not owning this Cause: And should that Party only take themselves for the free Electors of our Parliament, and divest all others of their freedom, it would be one of the most tyrannical, impious, perfidious acts, that History ever revealed to the world, and would prepare for the perpetual shame of the Agents (to say nothing of the misery of their souls.)

I prove it. 1. Falshood and wickednesse can give none a right to Chuse, or to Govern, nor can the want of it prove men void of that Right: But the Cause here described is false and wicked: The first branch of it 'That the People have the natural proper Soveraignty,' I have proved false in this Book: But yet I insist not so much on this, 1. Because it is but 'Liberty of choice' which we all maintain, that some men miscall by the name of 'Soveraignty'. But for those that mean ill, as well as speak ill, their opinion subverteth the foundations of Government.

And the other part of the Cause 'the Universal Liberty in matters of Faith and Worship, and the nullity of the Duty and Power of the Magistrate herein' I have proved it (and hope to do more fully) to be a wicked Cause. And if none shall have Power or Liberty in the Commonwealth, but those that own such a wicked Cause, let the world judge on what grounds you go, and what kind of Commonwealth we shall have constituted.

2. By this Rule (of confining Power and Liberty to the owners of the fore-described Cause) the Old Parliament must be excluded from all Power and Liberty, and so made slaves: For they fully signified their Judgment to be against it: Not only in all the forementioned waies and acts, but also by Acts or Ordinances against prophane Swearing, and for the holy Observation of the Lords Day, and divers the like about Religion.

3. And all the Parliaments that have been ever since (that which the people chose not, I call not a Parliament:) have all discovered their Judgments against this Cause.

4. So did the old Lord Protector (or General, which you will) in his time.

5. So did all the Parliaments in King James and the beginning of King Charles his time, that made such ado against the connivance at, and encrease of Popery and Arminianism (as you may see in Mr. Rushworths Collections:) And were none of these fit to be exempted from slavery, and to be free men in a Commonwealth?

6. This very Parliament as it was before its dissolution, declared themselves of another mind, and medled with matters of Religion and Worship, as in many instances I can quickly prove.

7. The Army according to this Rule, must be enslaved, and deprived of Liberty and Power. For they have more than once declared themselves against this Universal Liberty in Religion. First in their Agreement of the People, and then in the Instrument of Government, and now in their Proposals to this Parliament, they exclude from Liberty, Popery, and Prelacy, and all that profess not Faith in God by Jesus Christ, or in the Trinity; and that professe not to believe the holy Scriptures. And if the Army also must be denied Liberty, who shall have it? When yet you describe the good Party by their adhering to the Army? Even in this cause, which the Army was against? They were indeed for too much Liberty, but not for such a Liberty as this.

8. The same I may say of all those Judges and Citizens of London, and other persons of quality, that owned the Instrument of Government.

9. Yea, I may boldly say, That it is the farre greatest part of the godly in the Land that must be disfranchized by this Rule: For the far greatest part of them abhorre the thoughts of Liberty for the Masse, and for preaching up Popery, Mahometanism or Infidelity:

Most of them desired the Acts for the Lords Day, which sheweth that they are for no such Liberty.

10. And if it were a just and pious opinion, yet there is nothing in it, that our Liberties should lie upon. If men have a natural Right to their Liberties, as you intimate; how can it be proved that this Right is lost to all that do not thus debase the Magistrate, and are not for such extended Liberty? We may differ much more than this I hope, without forfeiting our Civil Liberties. Good men are as lyable to differ in judgment about a point in Politicks (which is little studied by them) as of Religion: And in Religion it self, if other differences deprive us not of Liberty, why should this only be thought sufficient. If one that believeth not a life to come, may have Liberty, why may not one who thinks that such should not be tolerated to propagate their unbelief? Are those uncapable of Liberty in England, that have Liberty in all other Christian Commonwealths? And are those uncapable of Liberty in England now, under the intended Commonwealth, that have hitherto enjoyed it, and constituted the Commonwealth? We shall then see how Liberty is promoted.

> Prop. 8. Conquest doth give neither the Army, nor the friends of the fore-described Cause, any Soveraignty, or Right to deprive us of our Liberty that disowns that Cause, or any Right to Rule us, or to Resist our Rulers.

I prove it thus: 1. They fought and conquered but in the capacity of Subjects; and therefore could win no more then the Rights of Subjects to themselves. They fought not for Soveraignty to themselves, therefore they won no Soveraignty to themselves. I suppose they will not say, they fought for it; nor for more than the Securing and Improving of the Rights and Liberties which they had before.

2. What Armies win (beside their pay and lawfull prize) they win for their lawfull Governours, under whose Authority they fight, and not for themselves. If Towns and Castles won by Warre be not the Armies, but the Civil Powers under whom they serve, much lesse is Soveraignty theirs by Conquest. If any could win it by Conquest it was the Parliament, to whom the Souldiers did professe subjection.

3. The Parliament that had a part in the Soveraignty were not (justly) conquered by the Army: Therefore the Soveraignty could not be won from them by the Conquest. For the Parliament had no Warre with the Army, or none wherein the Army could have a just Cause and pretence of Conquest.

4. It is the Peoples Right to choose their Governours.

But the People of England (besides the Cavaliers) were not conquered by the Army: Therefore they have not lost their Right by being conquered, nor can be denied the exercise of it, nor can any pretend a Power of Ruling them by Conquest without their choice.

(i) That we are not conquered by the Army is plain, in that we never fought against them, and therefore could not be conquered by them.

(ii) In that many of us fought for our Liberties as well as they.

Obj. But the Army were not Mercenary Souldiers, and therefore are not tied to the Laws of such.

Answ. Either the meaning is, that they never took pay, or else that they made not their pay their ultimate end. The first will not be said or believed. The second is a secret of the Heart: but charity binds us to believe it to be true: For it is a hard Question, Whether such a mercenary Souldier that kills men meerly for eight pence, or two shillings six pence a day (or more) be not as bad as a Cannibal, that killeth them to eat. Sure we are he is unworthy the name of a Christian, if not of a man. And it's no good consequence, that men have acquired Soveraignty, or a Right to Resist the Soveraign, because they were not so inhumane. And yet none can speak such things certainly of any but himself, because we know not the hearts of others.

But still they fought as Subjects, though not as such Mercenary Souldiers; and therefore as Subjects they were bound to continue in Obedience for conscience sake.

5. If Conquest be a Title either to Rule, or risist Rulers, then it is either the General only, or the Army under him that hath won to themselves this Right. If the General only, then the Army are nevertheless Subjects still: If to the Army, then either to the Officers only, or to the common Souldiers. To the Officers only it cannot be; for the same reason that will put by the General from that Soveraign or Right, will put by them. And if it did not, how should we know whether it were All the Officers, or which of them? If it be the common Souldiers that have won the Soveraignty, and so it is in the Major Vote, why then do the Officers presume to command them? Yea then they must be Ruled by them, as their Supream Governours.

6. If Conquest were a Title to Soveraignty it would belong to all that conquered: And I doubt not but there are ten, if not twenty Souldiers in the Countrey that have laid down Arms since the enemy was conquered, for one that is yet remaining in the Army that had a part in that Conquest.

7. If Conquest were such a Title, I have reason to believe that it is but a small part of the Army comparatively that have that Title, as being not in the Army at the Conquest: I believe that most of them are since come in, or very many at least.

8. You say that the Good People not in Arms, owning the same Cause, have the same Right: Therefore it is not meerly by Conquest. For they conquered not so much as we that continued in the Army, till the first Warre was ended.

9. The present Officers at this last Change were not all of a mind, that yet had an equal hand in Conquest. And how comes an Opinion to make one part of the Conquerours to be the Rulers of the rest?

10. If Conquest gave the Army Power to Rule or Resist, then it seems they had just Power to put out this Parliament when they did it, and may do so again, if they think it best: And may they do so by all future Parliaments in their time, or not? If not, how come they to have more Power over that Parliament which they served under, than over others? If they have such Power over all, then why do they not tell us so, and exercise the Government themselves.

In a word, here is no room for any rational plea for a Right of Soveraignty by Conquest. And if there were, it would be in the Majority of the Conquerours, that are not in the Army. And if there be no Right of Soveraignty, there must be Subjection, and no more Right of Resisting than other Subjects have. And if it be confined to the owners of the fore-described Cause, then the Army is excluded, that hath disowned that Cause: Or if they did own it, it seems they would lose their Power, when ever they should change their opinion.

Teach not all Armies (that say they have higher ends than money) to take themselves for the Conquerours of their Soveraigns: And teach not future Parliaments that Doctrine, lest they choose a cheaper slavery from the enemy, rather than the raising of an Army to depose themselves.

In all this, I pretend not that the Honourable Authour is any further against my Propositions, than his plain expressions satisfie the

Reader: For I am not sure in this point of Conquest that I well understand him.

But I may safely conclude, That they that go against 'the Laws and Constitutions of Government' and take 'Successe and Conquest for their Law' and 'their military capacity for their utmost and last reserve, in case all other fail', (as he speaks, pag. 9.) have a lamentable Cause, and setting their wisdome against the Lords, and making their conceits or interest their Law, do fall under the terrible Threatnings of the Word, against the Resisters of Authority.

> Prop. 9. They that pretend 'the inward warrant of Justice and Righteousnesse' (as he speaketh pag. 9.) and 'the inward reason and spirits of Government' for the violation of Laws or Constitutions, or Resisting of Authority, as being above 'the Letter, Form, outward circumstances, and empty shadows' do reject the Government of the Lord, and 'become their own Governours'.

Reason 1. The Rule of Righteousnesse is without us in the Laws; and there can be no such thing as an Inward Righteousnesse, which is contrary to that outward Law, the Rule of Righteousnesse. There can be no such thing as an inward Righteousnesse, that is not conformed to the Rule of Righteousnesse, because that conformity is its essential form.

2. If it be the 'Intention of a good end, that is here meant by the Inward Reason and spirit of Government' it's commonly known that the means must be good as well as the end; and that a Good end will not justifie bad means.

3. Were it the proper sense of the Law that is called 'the reason and spirit of it' that's distinguished from the Letter, we should all acknowledge, that the sense is the Law, and the Letter is but to signifie the sense or matter: So that all would not have failed, to cast them on their military capacity as a last reserve.

4. We all confesse that there are cases in which the Law of God may nullifie contradicting Laws of men, and the end being of Gods appointment, and the means but of mans, or else but of Positive institution, when the means ceaseth to be a means, and is inconsistent with the end, it may cease to be a duty. But 1. That will not allow men to set up means of their own, forbidden by God, and to do evil that good may come by it. 2. And I have proved that it must be a greater necessity than any could be here pretended. As it is dangerous

pretending a Necessity of Violating other Laws as in the Letter; and to murder, commit adultery, steal, bear false witnesse, upon that pretence; so it is dangerous as to dishonour our Natural or Civil Father, or Resist them, much more to depose them, on such a pretence, where there is not indeed a warranting necessity.

I long thought that the too easie pleading the Reason and spirit of Gods Laws and Ordinances of Worship against the Letter and Form, would grow to the like usage of Magistracy and mans Laws. But what God hath joyned, no man should seperate. As the Body may be kept under, and used as a servant to the soul, when yet to separate them is self-murder; and as the outward Ordinances of Worship must be used in a subserviency to the internal graces of the Spirit; but not be cast off on supposition that they are hinderances: So Magistrates and their Laws must be obeyed in a subordination to God and his Laws; but not cast off, resisted, or deposed, without and against the Authority of the Universal Soveraign.

But if all this were otherwise, yet the owners of the fore-described (evil) Cause, have nothing from the Spirit and Reason of Government, against them that have the Wisdom and Honesty to disown it.

Yea, if men should really do good to a Nation by such unwarrantable Resistance, it will not justifie them from the guilt of the sinne.

Prop. 10. For all this the Honourable Author doth assert, (pag. 10.) That 'unto the wisdom of the Laws and Orders of the Soveraign Judicature, the Sword is to become most entirely subject and subservient': Therefore so should your Sword have been to the Parliament that was violated.

They are no small fruits that would be procured by your conviction, if these evident Reasons might prevail for your Repentance.

1. Your souls would be saved from the guilt.

2. Thousands may be saved from making the sinne their own by an after-consent or approbation.

3. You will stop here, and go on no further, and no longer keep out so many faithfull Members, under the name of the corrupt Majority. And when we are set in joynt again, by your Restitution to your Subjection and Integrity, and our Rulers Restitution to their Power and Trust, and the Peoples Restitution to their Rights and Liberties, our Peace and safety will be Restored.

As I was concluding, I received two Writings: One by Mr. Harrington, expressing his just indignation against an Oligarchy, or the setting up of a self-conceited Party, in stead of a true Commonwealth.[11] The other to Mr. Harrington in a Letter (of the same style with the Answer to the *Healing Question*) pleading for the Godly's Interest, and a Senate to have the Proposing and Executive Power.[12] I leave it to the Reader, whether the way I here hold be not the true Mean between the extreams? That All be acknowledged free Citizens, that subject themselves to God in Christ, and to the true Soveraign Power: yet so as that wickednesse forfeit their Liberty.

And we must earnestly crave, that the Godly Party may not be defined by the fore-mentioned points of the ill Cause (Popular Soveraignty, and common Liberty in all matters of Worship, and of Faith, as things without the reach of Magistrates.) The lesse Humility, the lesse Godlinesse: But how little Humility have they that take all to be ungodly through the Land, that agree not with them in this bad opinion? It is 'the whole Party of Honest men' that the Authour of the *Healing Question* would have one civil Incorporation, pag. 11. where he shews the danger to 'the Army and their Governours, that may come by setting and keeping up themselves in a divided interest from the rest of the Body of Honest men'. But he that can confine the whole body of honest men, to so narrow a room as the Owners of the aforesaid Cause, will give away one of his best Arguments (his Charity) by which he should prove himself an Honest man.

And we as earnestly crave, that neither such a Senate, nor any other new form of Government, be imposed on the Nation or set up without their free consent.

And if these just demands should be denied us, and we should be unrighteously enslaved by our Brethren, we Appeal to the Justice of the most righteous God.

The snare is here laid so open to our eyes (even the Design to set up a party over us, that by a Fundamental Constitution shall be engaged to debase the Magistracy, and let in Popery and Impiety upon the Land,) that nothing but force can procure the Body of the Nation to Consent. If ever so vile a thing be done, and the name of Liberty or Commonwealth, be used as a scorn to an enslaved Peace, the Lord be Judge between us and our Oppressours.

[11] J. Harrington, *A Discourse of the Saying* (London, 1659).
[12] Sir Henry Vane, *A Needful Corrective or Ballance in Popular Government* (London, 1659).

Adam Contzen the Jesuites Directions for Preserving and Restoring Popery and Changing Religion in a Nation, before the People are awake: In his Politicks, *Lib.* 2. *cap.* 16,17,18[13]

Cap. XVI

Is to shew that Princes must determine of nothing in Religion, as having Power to defend that which the Pope determineth of, but no power to appoint or change any thing themselves: or judge of Controversies, as pag. 673. The Church must Judge, and the Prince must Execute.

Cap. XVII

Is to shew, That to preserve Religion, that is, Popery where it is, no other Religion should be permitted: and that Riches tend much to strengthen the Clergy and preserve Religion: And [scorning the poverty of Protestant Ministers], saith, That after their first attempts, their Ministry declineth into meer contempt, and that poverty and necessity forceth them to please the people. Lastly, he perswadeth to

---

[13] Cf. *The Plots of the Jesuits, viz. of Adam Contzen, a Moguntine, Thomas Campanella, A Spaniard, and Robert Parsons, an Englishman etc ... How to Bring England to the Roman Religion, Without Tumult* (London, 1658), *The Harleian Miscellany*, I (London, 1808), pp. 29–36. This anonymous tract may have been written by William Prynne: the printer is Michael Sparke, who printed many of Prynne's works. Certainly Contzen, Campanella and Parsons are also Prynne's key figures in his 'Popish Plot'. Prynne had protested at the reprinting of Parsons's works: Prynne, *The Substance of a Speech* (London, 1648), p. 109. He had argued that Parsons and Campanella had master-minded the Jesuit plots in 1659: Prynne, *A Brief Necessary Vindication of the Old and New Secluded Members* (London, 1659), p. 31. Finally Prynne contributed an introduction to a translation of Campanella's writings in 1660: Campanella, *An Italian Friar and Second Machiavel ...* (London, 1660). The translator (Edward Chilmead) was notably less agitated than Prynne about the success of Campanella's projects.

speedy punishing of the erroneous, and cutting them off in the first appearance, and to prohibit their Books, and to take heed of Julian's *device, of destroying Religion by Liberty for all Sects: [Thus they do in Spain, Italy, Austria, Bavaria, &c.].*

Cap. XVIII

The way to bring in Popery, and work out the Protestant Religion, [he thus describeth]:

1. That things be carried on by slow but sure proceedings, as a Musician tunes his Instrument by degrees: Lose no opportunity; but yet do not precipitate the work.

R.2. Let no Prince that is willing despair: for it is an easie thing to change Religion. For when the common people are a while taken with Novelties and diversites of Religion, they will sit down and be aweary, and give up themselves to their Ruler's wills.

R.3. The Doctors and leading Pastors must be put out: but if that may be all at once: but if that cannot be, let it be by slow degrees. When the Leaders are down all will submit.

[Here he pretends the examples of some Princes that expelled Lutheranism, and giveth his advice under the cover of instances:]

1. The purpose of changing Religion, and extirpating Lutheranism, must be concealed: Not but that some of the wiser sort may know it, but the People must not, lest it should move them.

2. Some must be suborned to beg importunately of the Prince for Liberty to exercise their Religion, and that with many and gentle words, that so the People may think the Prince is not enclined to Novelty, but only to Lenity, and to a tendernesse for tender consciences, and that he doth it not as from himself. For the Vulgar use to commend a Prince, that cannot deny the Subjects their desires, though they are such as were fit to be denied.

3. One or two Churches only must be desired at first, as being so small a matter, that the people will not much regard.

4. When the Zeal of Professours begins to rise against the change, they are to be pacified by admitting both parties to conference before the Governours.

5. Let there be a Decree for Pacification, that one party do not rail at the other, nor calumniate them. And so the errours that are to be brought in will have great advantage, when they are covered, and may not be contradicted, or so much as named: And so the Rulers will be thought to be onely Lovers of Peace, and not to intend a change of Religion.

6. Next that let there be some publick Disputation between the Parties, but with some disadvantage to them that are to be outed.

7. Let all this be done but on pretence that the several Parties may be joyned lovingly together in Peace: And when the Ministers refuse this, let them be accused of unpeaceablenesse, and pride, and obstinacy, and disobedience against the Magistrate, and not for their Religion.

8. When it comes to the putting out of some Ministers, and the People begin to Petition for them, let the matter be carried silently; and in the mean time, let the People be told, that it is because those Ministers are heady, obstinate men; that the People may be persuaded that the Ministers are faulty, and have deserved it, and may be put onely to desire Liberty for the more Peaceable men.

9. When thus the people are deluded, and there is no danger of a resistance, then turn the Ministers out of the Churches, and put in those that you would set up in their stead.

10. Then change the Universities, and tell all the Fellows and Scholars, that they shall hold their places if they will turn, else not, &c. Many will change Religion with the Rulers.

11. [Next he instanceth in Aasia where the Prince pretended, that all the] Professors and Ministers places were void at the death of his Predecessor, and he had the disposall of them, by Law.

12. And the change was there made [as he pretends] by slow degrees, one or two Opinions only changed at the first, and not the whole controverted part of the Religion; and so the people will think it but as a small matter to yield in one or two Opinions, and be easily brought to obey.

13. Lastly, They fall to writing against each other; and those that have the Court-favour seem to carry it.

[All this Advice is about the third Direction, that is, how to work out the Ministers safely, which he covers under pretended instances of such as have changed Religion in Germany.]

4. The fourth Rule is, To put out of Honours, Dignities, and publique offices, all those that are most adverse to Popery: It is but just that those that hinder the safety of the Commonwealth, should be deprived of the honours and Riches of the Commonwealth. If men are deposed for heynous Crimes, why not for Blasphemy and Contempt of Truth? [You must believe the Jesuite that this is the Protestant Case.] If those of a contrary Religion be left in honour and power, they will be able to cross the Prince in many things, and encourage the People of their own Religion.

5. The fifth Rule is, That when a Heresie [for so is the Protestant Religion to them] is wholly to be rooted out, and this must be done by degrees, and in a way of reason, and cannot be done by meer Command and Power, then you must first fall on those opinions that the Common People are most against, and which you can quickly make them think absurd: [so he instanceth in some] that would work out Lutheranism, that speak honourably of Luther, and fell on them only under the name of Flaccians: so the Arminians at Utrecht, when they would extirpate Calvinisme, made a Decree, that no man should Preach any thing, that seemed to make God the Author of sinne. Thus a Magistrate that would bring in Popery, must fall upon such heynous opinions, which the impudent themselves are half ashamed of; and bring these into the light that they may be odious, and so the Teachers will lose all their Authority, when the people see that they are taken in a manifest fault.

6. The sixth Rule to bring in Popery, and abolish the Protestants Religion, is, to make use of the Protestants Contentions. How easie is it [saith he] in England to bring the Puritans into Order if they be forced to approve of Bishops? Or to reduce the Puritans in the Low Countries, if the Prince adhere to the Arminians? For the Variety of Opinions makes them doubtfull, that before seemed certain; so that when the Magistrate joyneth with one side, he easily overturns the other, and leaves the whole obnoxious: As Paul did by the dissention between the Pharisees and Saduces, joyning to one side, he escaped. This [saith he] I would principally perswade an Orthodox Magistrate to [that is, a Papist.] For he may with as much advantage make use of the Protestants disagreements, as of the Papists Concord, to extirpate Protestants. As in Warres, it is not only the skill and strength of the Generall, but often also the Carlesnesse of the Enemy, or his Mistake that give very great advantages for successe. When rigid Calvinism

was assaulted by the Lutherans in the heat of the Paroxysm, it was exasperated, and the suddain restraint did much hurt: But now the Arminians have of their own accord let go the hardest part of their rigor, and judg the Calvinists to be impious, and persecute them in the very University, and in other Towns they force them to banishment; and would venture to do more and Crueller things, if they were not afraid of the strength of the adverse Party. Verily if Prince Maurice alone did but stand for the Arminians, the rigor of the contra-remonstrants would flag, or be broken.

7. The seventh Rule is to forbid the Protestants privately or publiquely to Assemble together.

8. The eighth Degree must be to proceed to severity of Laws and punishments: Here he endeavours to prove this violence lawfull, [Fire and fagot, is reserved to the last.] But this violence though it must be for the change of all, need not be exercised on all. Cut off the Leaders, and the multitude will follow the Authority of the Rulers. Shame will retain some, and fear others, but a vain security will prevail with most, when they know not how to help it. Within these few years, [if he say true,] above an hundred thousand have been turned to Popery in France, and more in Germany. Not any of the Princes of Germany that did endeavour to draw ever his People to the Catholicks, did ever find any force or Resistance contrary to his Laws. [Note this all you slanderous Papists that accuse Protestants so much of Rebellion to hide your own: Here's a Jesuites Testimony on Record for our vindication.]

His next Rule is, The good life of the Popish Magistrates and Clergy: [And that let them use as much as they will.]

Chap. 19.   He commendeth many smaller helps: As I. Musick, to entise people by delight. 2. To cause all at their marriage to professe the Popish Religion, and so rather than go without a Wife or Husband they will do it. 3. So also to deny to Protestants Church-Priviledges, at Baptism, Buriall, &c.

Lastly he Concludes, That where the work must be secretly done by degrees, the Magistrate must keep the Institutions, Presentation, Confirmation, and Examination of Ministers in his own hand; and so (if he cannot cast them out at once) he must cast out the most dangerous, [that is, the ablest Protestant Pastours,] and put over the Churches, the Disagreeing, and those that do not mind matters of

Controversie much, and those that are addicted to their own Domestick businesses [worldly men,] and such as are addicted to the Rulers: Let him coole the heat of Heresie, [he means true Religion;] and let him not put out the Unlearned: and so their Religion will grow into contempt.

Let the Magistrate cherish the Dissentions of the erring [he means the Protestant] Teachers: and let him procure them often to debate together and reprove one another. For so when all men see that there is nothing certain among them, they will easily yield to the truth [he means Popery.] And this Discord is profitable to shew the manners of those wicked men. For he that will read the Contentious Writings of Lutherans against Calvinists, or Calvinists against Lutherans, will think he readeth, not the invectives of men against men, but the furies and roaring of Devils against Devils. [A fair warning! But the Jesuite tells you not what is done at home.] From these things the Ruler may take occasion for a change: Let him enquire into the Original of these accusations: And if he find them true, he may punish the Guilty. If false, he may punish, [that is, cast out] the Accusers.

I have given you the summe, (not the literall translation) of this Jesuites Politicks, for the bringing in of Popery into a Nation: It all supposeth that the Rulers seem not to be Papists themselves, that they may do this in the dark.

The summe of Campanella's Counsell, for the promoting of the Spanish interest in England, in Queen Elizabeths daies: was, 1. Above all to breed dissentions and discords among our selves. 2. To have Seminaries in Flanders, that for the changing of our Religion, may first sow the seeds of Division in points of natural Sciences. 3. By suborned forreiners to promise great matters to the great ones here. 4. To promise to King James the help of Spain, so he would set up Popery, or at least not hinder the Indian Fleet. 5. At the same time to perswade the chief Parliament men, to turn England into the form of a Commonwealth; by telling them that the Scots will be cruell when they come to Rule them, &c. 6. To perswade Queen Elizabeth that King James would revenge his Mothers Blood, &c. 7. To exasperate the minds of the Bishops against King James, by perswading them that he was in heart a Papist, and would bring in Popery. And by these means the seeds of an inexplicable War will be sown between England and Scotland, so that no party will have leave to disturbe the Spaniard. Or if King James prevail, he will be a friend to Spain. Or if the Island be divided, or the Kingdom made Elective, we shall neither have mind nor Power to enlarge our Dominions: Or if the Island be turned into the form of a Commonwealth; it may keep continuall War with Scotland, and mannage all its affairs so slowly, as that they can little hurt the Spaniard. 8. The Catholicks here also are to be awaked and stirred up, that the Spaniard may take the first opportunity to enter upon England under pretence of helping them.

9. The Irish are perswaded to Rebellion. These (with the hiring of the Dutch to defend the Spanish plate-Fleets and fall out with us, that we may not hinder it) are the summe of this Fryars design against England . . .

A Holy Commonwealth

My work is not to write a Treatise of Politicks, taking in all thats meet to be understood concerning the Institution, Constitution and Administration of a Common-weal: nor yet to follow the Methode that would be requisite for such an Undertaker: but only to lay down a few Political Aphorismes, containing those things that are denyed or passed over by some of the proud Pretenders to Politicks, that opposing the Politician to the Divine, acquaint us that their Politicks are not Divine, and consequently none, or worse than none: and also to cleare up some of those things that seeme to me to be too darkly delivered in the Writings and Speeches of many good and learned men; and which the Consciences of many are much perplexed about, in these times; to the great loss and hazard of Church and Commonwealth: And I must begin at the Bottom, and touch those *Praecognita* which the Politician doth presuppose, because I have to do with some, that will deny as much, as shame will suffer them to deny.

CHAPTER I

There is a God that is mans Creator

Thes. 1. There are men inhabiting the earth.

He that denyeth this, denyeth himself to be a man, and therefore is not to be disputed with yet proveth it to others, while he denyeth it.

Thes. 2. Man is not Eternal; but had a beginning.

We see it of all the Individuals, that they by Generation receive their Existence; There is no man alive now here in flesh, that was alive a thousand years ago. Generation succeedeth Generation. And as all men that are now on earth had a Beginning, so must there be one first man that also had a Beginning. Or else he must have been a pure Act, without Composition, or imperfection, self-sufficient, and without cause, and so not have been Man but God, and therefore not the supposite that we speak of: And as he had been infinite in Duration on *a part ante*, so must he be *a parte post*: for that which have no cause, can have dissolution or end. But this is not the case of man: therefore man had a Beginning.

Thes. 3. Man did not make himself.

For before he was, he was not: and that which is not, cannot work. Nothing can do nothing: whosoever made him, knew what he did, and how, and why. But neither he that was not, nor his parents knew either what was doing while he was formed in the womb, and how he was fashioned, nor to what end each part and motion was appointed. Therefore neither did we make ourselves. Nor are our Parents the principal cause of our Being. Nor could the first man be made by himself when he was not, or his Parents that had none.

Thes. 4. Therefore man hath a superior Maker.

If he be an effect, he must have a cause. Nothing below can be his principal Cause: Nothing doth lay claim to such an honor; Nothing is sufficient for such a work: All things below are effects themselves, and therefore have their causes.

> Thes. 5. Man being a living Creature, consisting of soul and body, his soul is vegetative, sensitive and rational, (or intellectual) and hath an Intellect to direct, a Will to chuse or refuse, and a Power to execute its Commands.

Sense it selfe is a sufficient Discerner that we are sensible: and Sense and Reason that we are vegetative: And Reason sufficiently discerneth that we are rational: not by an immediate intuition of the Power but by an immediate Intellection of its own Acts. While I reason to prove that man is rationall, and you reason against it, we both prove it.

> Thes. 6. Wisdom is the due qualification of mans Understanding; and Vertue, or moral Goodnesse of his Will, and Ability, and Promptitude for Execution of his executive Power.

Mans soul is capable of these; and some in a less, and some in a more excellent degree are possessed of them: so few men will confess themselves to be wholly void of Wisdom and Goodness, that we need not prove the existence of these Endowments.

> Thes. 7. He that made man, doth excell all men that he ever made in all perfections of understanding, Will and Power.

For no one can give that which he hath not to give, either formaly or eminently: Nothing of it self can make that which is better then it selfe: for then all the superabundant perfection of the effect should be without a cause. He therefore that made man, must needs have more Power, Wisdom and Goodness then all the men that are, or ever were in the world: because they had none but what he gave them.

> Thes. 8. He that is the principal cause of man, is an Eternal, Immense, most perfect Being, an infinite Power, Wisdom and Goodness, that is, he is God.

Either man was made by a Creature, that had himselfe a Maker, or immediately by the uncaused Primitive, Simple, independent being, which is the cause of all things else. If he were made by a Creature, that Creature being but a dependent Being, could be but dependent in its causation, and so could be but the instrument of, or subservient to the principal cause. And as the first cause is not diminished, or loseth not any of his perfection by making the Creatures, and communicating to them, no more is he the less in any effect, because he useth them: But as they have no Being but from him, so they can do nothing but by him; and as his perfections are as glorious, as if there were no Creature in Being; so the effects, which as his instruments, the Creatures perform, are as much his own, as if there had been no Instruments. For if they are Creatures, they can neither have or do any good but wholly from the Creator; so that if it could be proved, (as it cannot) that the first cause did immediately make man, yet would it not alter our case, or conclude him to be ever the less our Maker.

And that he is an eternal Being without Beginning or cause, is clear: For else there should be a time, (as we may call it) when there was Nothing. And if ever there had been a time when there was Nothing, there never would have been anything: For nothing can do nothing, and make nothing: He therefore that thinketh God had a Beginning, thinketh that he was caused by nothing, without a cause: and so that all things were made by nothing.

And as the Eternity of God is thus most clear, and is his Immensity. For he made not that which is greater than himselfe, or that can comprehend him, else he should communicate more then he hath, and the effect to be beyond its total cause, which is impossible: And if he comprehend all things, and be greater then all things, he must be immense. And that he is infinite in Power, Wisdom, and Goodnesse, and so most perfect, is clear, because all the Power, Wisdom and Goodnesse of the Creature is from him; and therefore he hath more himselfe then all the Creatures have: and therefore is infinite in all. If all the Power, Wisdom and Goodness in all the world were contracted into one person, it must be less then his that giveth all. None can make that which is better then itselfe. I pass by all other Arguments, as intending at this time no other demonstrations; but these, from the same effects which we are to treat of. And from these the conclusion is now made plain, that THERE IS A GOD: and that HE CREATED MAN.

CHAPTER 2

God is the Soveraign Ruler of Mankind

Thes. 9. The soul of man is capable of knowing that there is a God, whose everlasting favour is his happiness, and of loving him, desiring him, and seeking to enjoy him: and he may know, that nothing here below can be his proper end and happiness . . .

These. 10. The nature of man is fitted to be here ruled by the hopes and fears of a life to come: and without these the werld cannot be ruled according to the nature of man . . .

Thes. 11. Therefore the soul of man is immortal, and he is made for a life to come, where he shall be for ever happy or miserable . . .

Thes. 12. Were there not a life to come for man, his Knowledge, Desires, Hopes and Fears, would be his torment, and the nobleness of his nature above brutes, would make him so much more miserable than they, and the wisest men, and the best would be most unhappy: which are things not to be believed . . .

Thes. 13. If there were no life for man but this, mens pious performance of their duty to God and man, and their prudent care of their own felicity would be their losse; and mens wickedness and folly would be their gain, and the worst would be least miserable: which are things not once to be imagined . . .

Thes. 14. It is not the essential constitutive parts of man, by which he is proximately capable of his felicity or end, but his moral perfections and acceptablenesse to God . . .

Thes. 15. Man therefore must be fitted for his felicity and conducted to his end, by moral meanes . . .

Thes. 16. Man oweth perfect duty to his Maker, and must have moral means agreeable to his nature to direct him in this duty, and oblige him to it . . .

Thes. 17. Man is a sociable creature, and must be obliged according to his nature, to the duties of relation and society . . .

Thes. 18. These Moral means must be the Revelations of our end, and the prescript of duty necessary to its attainment, and the promises of good, and comminations of punishment necessary to provoke us to performance, with needfull exhortations and dehortations, and such subservient helps: that is, man is made a Creature to be instructed by Doctrine, ruled by the use of Laws . . .

Thes. 19. If man must know his End and Meanes, by Doctrine, and be obliged by Laws, then must there be Judgement and Execution of these Laws . . .

Thes. 20. If man must have Laws, and those Laws be executed, then must there be a King, or Soveraign Governour of man . . .

Thes. 21. The Soveraign Ruler of mankind, must be but one, and one that hath sufficiency or chiefest Aptitude, and highest Title . . .

Thes. 22. Therefore God, and only God is the Soveraign Ruler of mankind, as having alone the sufficiency or Aptitude in his infinite perfections, and the Highest Title by Creation, and a plenary propriety thence resulting . . .

Thes. 23. God having created man, a Rational free Agent, to be Ruled as aforesaid, and conferred on him all the benefits of which he is naturally possessed, doth by a necessary resultancy stand related unto man, in a threefold relation, viz. our Absolute Lord (or Owner) our Soveraign, Ruler, (or King) and our most bountifull Benefactor: and man stands Related unto God as his own, his subject (as to obligation) and his Beneficiary . . .

CHAPTER 3

Of the Constitution of Gods Kingdome

Thes. 24. The World then is a Kingdom whereof God is the King, and the form of the Government is *Monarchia absoluta ex pleno Dominio jure Creationis*, an absolute Monarchy from or with a plenary Dominion or propriety of persons and things, by the Title of Creation ... [But one *Thomas Anglus ex Albiis East-Saxonum*, in English, Thomas White, a Papist, in his book about Purgatory,[14] and his other Writings, would perswade us, that such notions as these are but Metaphorical, and the conceits of vulgar heads, when properly applyed to God, and that indeed they that are wiser, know that God governeth as an Engeneer, that is, by a Physicall Premotion only, as men govern Clocks and Watches, or the Pilate governeth a ship.] ...

Thes. 25. The denial of the Soveraignty of God, and his Moral Government is the denial of Deity, Humanity, Religion, Morality and pollicy, most of which I shall manifest brieffly in these following Instances.

1. I have shewed already that it is a denying God to be God, because to be God, is to be the Governor of the world, at least in Title.

2. If God be not Governour, he is not just: For communicative Justice he cannot exercise on Creatures that are wholly his own. And distributive Justice he can have none, if he have not the Relation

---

[14] Thomas White, *The State of the Future Life and the Present's Order to be Considered* (London, 1654).

56

which Justice doth belong to. He that is not a Ruler, cannot be a just Ruler.

3. If God be not our Governour, he hath no Laws? And so the Law of Nature and Scripture is overthrown.

4. Then man doth owe him no Obedience for where there is no Ruler and Law, there is no obligation to Duty: and so man is not obliged by God to be pious, just, honest or sober; but if God will make him such, he will be such.

5. And then it will follow, that there is no sin: All things that men do, are such as God doth move them to: but there being no Rector and Law, there can be no transgression.

6. Hence also it will follow, that there is no vertue, which is but the Habit or disposition to duty: for if there be no obligation to actual obedience, the habit is in vain, or is no moral good: for all moral good is denyed here at once.

7. And hence also it follows, that the Habits of Vice are not culpable, because the Acts are not sinful against God, there being no Law and Governour against whom they are committed.

8. And Christianity is hereby most evidently subverted: For Christ cannot die for sin, nor redeem us from it, if there be no such thing; Nor can the Spirit mortifie it in us.

9. And hence it will follow, that all the Ministry and Ordinances are vain, and not of Gods appointment. If he have no Laws, there is no need of any to teach them.

10. Hence also it will follow, that Scripture is false that pretendeth to be the Law of God, and tells us of all that's here denyed.

11. And therefore there can be no pardon of sin; for where there is no Governour, there is no Law: and where no Law, there's no sin; and where no sin, the'rs none to pardon.

12. And then there needs no confession of sin, nor prayer for pardon, nor care or means to be used against it.

13. Nor can any man ow God any thanks or praise for the pardon of his sins, if there be none.

14. And it will follow, that there is no punishment, for sin either in this life or in that to come, ecept what is inflicted by Creatures for offences against Creatures.

15. And it will follow, that there is no Reward for the obedient; for if no Governor, Law and Duty, then no Reward.

16. And then there is no Judgement of God to be expected. For their is no possibility of Judgement where there is neither King, nor Subject, nor Law, nor Right, nor Wrong, not Reward, nor Punishment.

17. And it will follow that sin is as good as obedience, and a wicked man as good and happy as an honest man: For nothing that men do is morally evill, and all things Equally, Physically good, according to their Physical Being, and God even as Physicall Governour is the chief cause, and therefore the effect cannot but be good, nor can there be an evill man in the world.

18. It will follow, that there are no Devils: for they could break no Law, nor do any evil, but the good that God, or rather the superior Intelligences made them do.

19. In a word, it hence followeth, that man is but a beast, that is, necessitated by Objects, and not a free agent governed by Laws.

20. And because I would make them twenty, let this be the last: It followeth hence, that (God being not our Rector, and Law-giver, and so their being no sin against him) if the Governors of the Common wealth shall hang or banish those that hold this traiterous opinion against the God of Heaven, and divulge it, or if any man that meets them, cudgel them, it is no sin against God, nor doth he need to fear any punishment for it from God.

By this time you see what those men say, that deny, the Soveraignty of God.

> Thes. 26. God is the end, as well as the beginning of the divine Monarchy of the world . . .
>
> Thes. 27. It is the reasonable Creatures only that are the Subjects of Gods Kingdom . . .
>
> Thes. 28. All men as men are the subjects of Gods Kingdom, as to Obligation and Duty, and God will not ask the consent of any man to be so obliged.

For Gods Kingdom is not constituted primarily by Contract, but his Right resulting immediately from his being our Creator, and so our Owner, our Obligation is founded in our being his Creatures, and his Own. The most absolute slave imaginable, cannot be so much obliged to you antecedently to his consent, as man is unto his Creator, from whom he is, and hath all that he hath.

Thes. 29. He that consenteth not to Gods Soveraignty, and is not a voluntary Subject, shall be nevertheless obliged, both to Subjection (or that consent) and to Obedience, and to punishment in case of disobedience: but he can have no right to the Priviledges or Benefits of a subject, and so doth make himself worse then a slave, by being a Rebel.

He that is born under the most Absolute Lord, cannot by his own will exempt himself from his obligations. If he could make Gods Laws not obligatory, and himself no Debtor to God for his subjection and obedience, then might he depose his Soveraign at his pleasure. And most would take this as a readier way to their sensual content and safety, to repeal the Law, and depose their King, to save them the trouble and labour of obeying him, and be from under his Judgement and punishments. No man can acquire benefits or priviledges by his vice: The Law supposeth that a mans faults may not advantage him. But to deny consent to the Soveraignty of God, and to deny our own Obedience, would be our fault. But Benefits we can claim no right to, if we consent not to them and to the terms on which they are conferred. No man can plead for that which he refused: nor can he plead against another for not doing him good against his Will. Though we may offend God, yet we cannot injure man, by not doing him the good that he refuseth. And the greatest blessings of the Kingdom of God, are such as a Refuser is not capable of; Nor is he capable, while such, of the Duties of a Subject. And therefore though he cannot exempt himself from obligation and punishment by dissent, yet may he deprive himself of the protection of the Soveraign, and forfeit all his hopes of the benefits.

Thes. 30. God therefore doth not beg authority by calling for our consent, nor is it in the power of man by consenting to make him King, or by Dissenting to depose him, as to his Right and his actuall Legislation, Judgment and Execution: But it is in his power to make himself a Rebel, and so fall under the sentence of the Law; and therefore Consent is required to our benefit as a condition, and as the necessary cause of our following Obedience: but as no cause or Conveyer of governing Authority to God.

A man would think the earth should never have bred a man that would contradict this truth that is in his wits. For by so doing God is pulled down, and man set over him, or made a beast, and all morality, (as by the former opinion) overthrown. But Mr. Harrington in his *Oceana*, pag. 16, makes God but the Proposer, and the people the Resolvers or Confirmers of all their Laws, and saith, 'they make him King', Deut. 19, 'They reject or depose him as Civil Magistrate, and Elect Saul', 1 Sam. 8. 7, adding 'The Power therefore which the people had to depose even God himself as he was Civil Magistrate, leaveth little doubt, but that they had power to have rejected any of those Laws confirmed by them throughout the Scripture.'

Answ. They could violate a Law, and deny obedience to it; but they could not nullifie it, or prevent, or destroy its obligation. So they could be Rebels against God, but they could not so reject the duty of voluntary subjection, nor escape the punishment of Rebellion. One single person may thus reject God and his Laws at any time, (to his cost) as well as the Major Vote of the people. Its a lamentable case, that such blind persons that know not such things as these, should so perversely trouble the Common-wealth with their loathsom obtruded fancies. Mans consent doth not make God King, nor his dissent depose him, as to his Power, or the cheif part of his actual Government: He will be K. in spight of his proudest enemies: and he will make his Laws; and those Laws shall actually oblige; and men shall be guilty, that first consent not to be Subjects, and then obey not: and they shall be judged as Rebels, (Luk. 19. 17) and the Judgement executed: Only their consent is, 1. A proper Cause of their own Obedience. 2. And a Condition *sine qua non* of their Interest in the Benefits. A little Power will serve a man to become a Rebel, and be hanged. Will you see the face of this Gentlemans opinion.

1. The world by dissenting may make God no God, that is, no Governor of the world: and so he holdeth his Government on our wills. 2. If his Doctrine be true, the Law of nature is no Law, till men consent to it. 3. At least where the Major Vote can carry it, Atheism, Idolatry, Murder, Theft, Whoredom, & c. are no sins against God. 4. Yea, no man sinneth against God, but he that consenteth to his Laws. 5. The people have greater Authority or Government then God. 6. Rebellion is soveraign power in the multitude. 7. Dissenters need not fear any Judgement or punishment from God. 8. Cannibals and Atheists are free-men, as not consenting to Gods Government. 9. Men owe not any Subjection, Duty, or Obedience to God at all unless they make themselves Debtors by consent. 10.

The troublesome work of self-denying obedience, and all the danger of punishment here, and hereafter may be avoided easily by denying Gods soveraignty and deposing him, and no man need to be damned if he will but deny to be a Subject of God.

These are the apparent Consequences of the Doctrines of Mr. Harrington, if he will be understood according to the open meaning of his words: But if he will tell us that by 'their Power of making God King, of deposing him, and of resolving on, and confirming, or rejecting his Proposals', he meant only a power of voluntary subjecting themselves to their absolute Lord and King, and of obeying his Laws, or else a Power of Rebelling, Disobeying and perishing, he will turn some of our indignation and compassion into laughter, but his language will we not imitate.

> Thes. 31. Mankind being fallen by Rebellion under the heavy Penalty of the Law of God was redeemed by Jesus Christ: and so God hath a second Right of Dominion and Empire, even on the title of Redemption, and is now both our Owner and Ruler and two-fold Right ...

> Thes. 32. The Lord Jesus Christ as Mediator having performed the work of Redemption, hath received from the Father a Derived Supremacy over the redeemed world, and is established the King of the redeemed, and Administrator General ...

> Thes. 33. There are divers Ranks of Subjects in the Kingdom of God: as some are Rebels, and only subjects by Obligation, or strangers that have not yet consented; and others voluntary plenary subjects, that have right to the priviledges of the Kingdom: so those that are free-subjects are of several ranks, as to Office, and Place, and Gift.

Some are Officers, and some only such as must obey: Some Officers are Civil, some Ecclesiastical; Some are rich, some poor: some adult, some Infants: some weak of parts, some strong, & c.

> Thes. 34. All that will be free Subjects of the Kingdome of God, must be engaged to him in solemn Covenant; which regularly is to be solemnized by their Baptism ...

CHAPTER 4

Of the Administration of the Universal Kingdom

Having spoken of the CONSTITUTION of the Kingdom of God, I shall proceed to speak of the ADMINISTRATION thereof.

> Thes. 35. God as the Soveraign Ruler of mankind hath given him the Law of nature, commonly called the Morall Law, to be the Rule of his obedience.

1. The Law of nature in the primary most proper sence, is to be found *in natura rerum*, in the whole Creation that is objected to our Knowledg, as it is a Glass in which we may see the Lord, and much of his Will; and as it is a Signifier of that Will of God concerning our duty. 2. The Law of nature is sometime taken for that Disposition or Aptitude that there is in mans nature to the actual knowledg of these naturally revealed things, especially some clear and greatest Principles, which almost all the world discern. 3. And it is sometime taken for the Actual knowledge of those plain and common Principles. 4. And sometime for the Actual knowledge of all that meer Nature doth reveal. When I say God hath given man this law of nature, I mean, both that he hath made an Impress of his minde upon the Creation, and set us this Glass to see himself, and much of our Duty in, & also that he hath given to the very nature of man a Capacity of perceiving what is thus revealed, and a disposition especially to the Reception of the more obvious Principles; so that by ordinary helps, they will be quickly known; and the rest may be known if we be not wanting to our selves.

> Thes. 36. This Law of Nature commandeth us much duty, to God directly, to our selves, to our Neighbours in their private and publike capacities.

Thes. 37. The sum of the dutie commanded towards God, is to love him with all our hearts: more particularly it is, that we most highly esteem, honour, reverence, believe and trust him, and adhere to him in love, and seek him, depend upon and serve him with all our powers and faculties: worshipping him according to his nature and revealed will, and using honourably his Name, and devoting to his special worship a fit proportion of our time.

Thes. 38. Our duty towards our selves, is an ordinate Love of our selves, and care of our bodies, but especially of our souls, for the great ends of our Creation and Redemption ...

Thes. 39. Our duty towards our Neighbour as such, is to love him as our selves, that is, to love him with an Impartiall Love, not drawing from him to our selves, by an inordinate selfishness: which must be expressed about his Life, Chastity, Estate, Honour, and any thing that is his: Godliness, Soberness, and Righteousness, are the general Titles of all these three.

Thes. 40. Besides these Natural Laws which are promulgate to all, God hath a Law of Grace, and hath many Positive Laws; and both sorts are contained in the holy Scriptures.

Thes. 41. God hath appointed an orderly course by the mission of fit persons as his Messengers to promulgate, preach, and explain these Laws, both of Naturall and Supernatural Revelation to the World; and to command their obedience, and exhort them thereunto: and it is the duty of the hearers to learn, and obey, yea, and the duty of those that have not the Gospel, to enquire after it, and seek it, according to the measure of that light they have, which giveth them intimation of its being.

Thes. 42. God hath appointed both in Nature and Scripture, that the world be divided into Rulers and Ruled, Officers and meere Subjects; and that the Officers Govern under him, by Authority derived from him, and the people obey them as his Officers. And he hath not left it to the choice of the Nations whether they will have Government or not

Those Politicians therefore that say a Commonwealth in its own nature doth not participate of moral good or evil, but is a thing neither commanded nor forbidden, doe fundamentally erre in their Politicks. It is possible for one or few persons in extraordinary cases to be disobliged from living under any Government. (But the Cases are so rare, that it is not one of many millions of persons that is ordinarily in that case.) But to man-kind in common, it is made a duty to live in this order of Government, where it may be had. He therefore that should think he is born a Freeman, and therefore will maintain his liberty, and be Governed by none, (being not a Governour himself) doth sin against God, in violating his Order, as Souldiers should do in an Army that would have no Officers, nor be commanded by any but the General. This is easily proved, for,

1. Nature immediately makes an inequality in our procreation and birth, and subjecteth children to their Parents as their undoubtedly rightful Governours.

2. Nature doth make such inequality of persons in point of sufficiency and endowments, as necessitateth Government, while some are unable or unapt to subsist comfortably without the Government of others: And therefore even in state of marriage Nature subjecteth the weaker sexe to the Government of the stronger. And its natural for persons of weak understandings, and other endowments to have some that are wise and able to Govern them, lest they be destitute of help and left to ruine.

3. Nature hath made man a sociable creature, both by Necessity, and Inclination; and therefore must be in ordered societies.

4. Nature hath made man a lover of man, and so far as he is good, so far to be Communicative: and therefore the wisdom and strength that any doe excell in, is for the good of others; and all things must be so ordered that the whole may be the better for the gifts of the several parts, and the weak for the strong; and therefore there must be Governed societies.

4. Providence keepeth some in such necessitie of others, as requireth their relief and protection, and Government. Some by paucity are insufficient for their own defence: some by the proximity of potent Enemies and Thieves: some by the scituation of their Countries, and some by want.

5. The vitiousness of men hath made Government now of double necessitie, to what it would be if man were innocent, when men are Wolves to one another, and the weaker can keep nothing that the stronger hath a minde to, and no mans life can be safe from cruelty and revenge; when there is so much backwardness to vertue and well doing, and so much vice to be restrained, it is now no more question whether Government be naturally necessary, and subjection a duty; then whether Physitians be necessary in a rageing plague, or food in a famine.

6. Experience tells us that Gods work, or our preservation cannot be well carried on without it; without it the world would be a confused crowd. It would dishonour the Soveraign Ruler, if his Kingdom were turned into a tumultuous rabble, God doth not immediately, that is without sutable means, exercise his Government by himself. He could have easily done it: but it is the beauty and perfection of his Kingdom that there be diversity of Orders. He could lighten the world without the Sun: but he hath chosen rather to communicate so much of his Splendor to a Creature: He will have men like our selves to be his Officers among men, as fittest for our familiar converse. And what would a Nation be without Government, but a company of miserable men, robbing and killing one another, what would an Army be without Commanders? And how would they defend themselves against the enemies.

7. The Law of Nature requireth Justice; that it may goe well with the good, and ill with the evill; and that vertue be encouraged, and wickedness punished: therefore it requireth that there be a course of Government in the world to this end.

8. There is Government among the very Angels and Divels: therefore it is not to be avoided or thought a thing indifferent among men. All places have some Order.

9. The Analogicall Government in the Microcosme, man, doth prove a Natural need and excellency of Government. The Intelect in man is made to guide, and the Will to Commnand, & all the inferiour faculties to obey: shewing us that in societies the Wise should guide, the Good should command, and the Strong and all the rest should execute and obey. An ungoverned man is a mad man, or a bad man.

10. The great disparity that is among all Creatures in the frame of Nature, intimateth the beauty of Orderly Political disparity. Look but to the Sun and Moon, and Stars and see their inequality and Order. Beasts differ in strength, and the very stones of the field are not of equal bigness and shape. The silly Ants have an Order among them, and a Hive of Bees are a Natural Common-wealth.

Thes. 43. As the difference of our faculties, and our personal self Government, so also Domestical, Political, and Ecclesiastical Order of Government and subjection, are the Institutions of God, commanded in his Laws.

1. The well governing of a mans selfe (which is taught by Theological Ethicks) is both necessary to his own felicity, and a principal

requisite to the safety, beauty, and felicity of the societies, that consist of individual persons.

2. Domestical Order is commanded of God, partly in nature directly, as the Rule of Parents, and obedience of Children: partly by the intervention of contracts for the application of the Law to the individual persons, as in the Relations of Husband and Wife, or Master and servant, where note, that in the first, it is one thing for Nature to give the Law, and another thing for Nature to produce the person: Nature as procreative brings forth the Childe? From whence the mutual Relations result: but it is Nature partly as Indicative of Gods will, and partly as endowing us with Principles or Dispositions of Morality (that is, as a Law) that obliged Children to obey, as Parents to Govern: so also the Law of Nature and Scripture is it that imposeth on Wives and Servants the duty of obeying, as on Husbands and Masters the care and duty of Governing; but it is Choice that determineth of the Persons that are to Rule and to obey, that this or that shall be the man or the woman that shall be a Husband or Wife is of choice: and that this or that shall be the Master or Servant, and also (these being free Relations) it is here of choice, whether they will be Married or not, and servants or not. (To the world in general, the Relations are necessary, but not to every individual person.) But whether the Husband shall govern, and the wife obey, and whether the Master shall govern, and the servant obey, this is not of choice: so that if they should by Contract agree, that the wife shall not be subject to the Husband, it were *ipso facto* null, as being contrary to the divine Institution or Law.

3. As many Families cohabiting without Political or Civil Government, would want that which is necessary to their own Wel-fare and the Common good. As an Empire is divided into several Provinces, or Principalities, so God hath made it necessary that the world be distributed into many particular Common-wealths. An Universal humane Monarchy is impossible, it being beyond the Capacity of any one so to govern; (the more to blame the Pope for pretending to it) God only can govern all the world. But men as his Officers have their several Provinces, which in due subordination to him and his Laws, must be governed by them.

4. Because men have immortal souls to save, and an everlasting life of happinesse to attain, or misery to suffer, and God himself hath a final Judgment to pass on all according to his Laws, and because

men are rational free Agents that must by knowledge and choice be brought into a fitness for felicity, and be kept in acceptable obedience to their Soveraign; therefore hath he appointed Pastors to teach and guide the people in the way of life, and to acquaint them with his Laws, and his future Judgement, and in free ordered Churches to lead them in the publick Worship of God, and exercise that spiritual Government by his Word, which shall preserve the honor of his holinesse in the world, and difference between his servants and the rebellious, and lead his people towards perfection.

Thes. 44. As God is the universal King, and hath a universal Kingdom and Law, so doth he in this life exercise himself some part of his executive power; in protecting his faithfull Subjects, encouraging the good, and punishing offenders by himself, and by the Ministry of Angels: But his full Universal Judgement will be after this world, when all shall be finally sentenced by him to everlasting Joy or Misery. So much of Gods UNIVERSAL ADMINISTRATION.

CHAPTER 5

Of a subordinate Commonwealth in General

Having spoken of Gods Universal Kingdom, I am next to speak of the distinct, subordinate Common-wealth which God hath by institution made the parts of it. And here first I shall speak of the NATURE of a Common-wealth in General; and then of those Modal differences which have obtained the name of the divers species of Common-wealths: and that, 1. As the difference is in the number and quality of persons that have the Soveraignty. And, 2. As it is in the gradually or modally diversified Matter, or Object of their power. And having spoken of the Constitutive Causes, I shall speak of the Efficient.

Thes. 45. A Common-wealth is sometime taken for the society Governed, sometime for the Government of that society; sometime it is taken properly in the first signification, and sometime analogically, for that which is a Common-wealth, but of an imperfect kind, or only *secundum quid*.

Thes. 46. A Commonwealth properly so called, is 'A society of Gods Subjects ordered into the Relations of Soveraign and Subjects for the common good, and the pleasing of God their Absolute Soveraign.' Or, 'It is the Government of a society of Gods Subjects by a Soveraign subordinate to God, for the common good, and the Glory, and pleasing of God.' Or it is 'The order of a Civil body, consisting in the Authority of the Magistrate, especially the supream, and the subjection of the people, for the common good, and the pleasing of God.'

Many Definitions you may find in politicks, almost each one having one of his own, though most of them to the same sence. And therefore if I use not any of theirs in all the terms, I am as excusable as they.

> Thes. 47. A Common-Wealth *secundum quid*, or Analogically so called, is 'The order of a Civil body, consisting of Governours and Subjects intended for their corporal Wel-fare, but acknowledging not Gods Soveraignty, nor intending spiritual and everlasting good, nor the pleasing or honour of God.'

As the best actions of Atheists, or any men that have not just Principles or ends, are not simply or properly Morally-good, but only *secundum quid*, and Analogically, so is it with their Politicks and Common-wealths. The absence of any one of these Essential Ingredients, makes their Government another thing. If it want either Moral-dependence upon God as absolute Soveraign, or the acknowledgement of his great Universal Laws which must be the Fundamentals to their own, or if they intend not any spiritual and everlasting good to the societies, or intend not the honour and pleasing of God, but begin and end their Government with their carnal selves, this is not simply or properly a Common-wealth, but *secundum quid*, and Analogically; even no more then an Ideot is a reasonable man. Its agreed on by Politicians, that a Company of Robbers that choose them a King, are no Common-wealth, because they deviate from the Universal fundamental Laws; Much less is a Company of Rebels a Common-wealth that seek both the subversion of King and Kingdom: and so want both the necessary Beginning, Means and End. And a Justice of Peace or Judge may as well have Power, when they have renounced their Dependance on the Soveraign, and Loyalty to him, as a King or any other can have just Power when they have renounced their Allegiance or subjection to God (of which anon).

> Thes. 48. The form of a Common-wealth is the Relation of Soveraign and Subjects to each other; The Subject matter is a civil body, or Community of Gods Subjects: The Relate and Correlate are the Soveraign and the Subjects: The fundamentum being the chief controverted point shall be spoken of by it self. The Terminus is actual order, and the common good, and the pleasing of God thereby attained . . .

> Thes. 49. The Soveraign of one Common-wealth must be One, and but one Civil person, but one natural person may be the Soveraign of many Common-wealths, and many, yea, many thousand may possibly be the Soveraign of one . . .

Thes. 50. Though the Soveraign and subjects are always civilly distinct, yet the same natural persons that are Soveraigns in one respect and degree, may be Subjects in another, and *è contra*.

But this belonging to the species, we shall say more of it in the Differences of Governments.

Thes. 51. The people as people are not the Soveraign Power, neither as natural persons aggregate, nor as having the chief Propriety and strength, nor as any way endowed by God with governing Authority: And therefore the distinction of some Politicians (Papists and Protestants) of *Majestas realis & personalis*, and the Assertion of the Popular, that the People are the real Soveraign, or have the *Majestatem Realem*, (unless the constitution of that individual Common-wealth shall give it them) is false, and not to be endured.

If the people any otherwise then by particular Constitutions, (by fundamental Contracts) be the Soveraigns, or have any Governing civil power, it must be either by nature, by accident, or by divine Institution: But none of these wayes: therefore not at all.

That they have none by nature is plain in that they are not by nature a Community or Aggregate Body. And when they are so, they have naturally no Soveraignty, as I prove.

1. Where there is no Common-wealth, there is no Soveraignty: but in a meer Community or Aggregation of men before any Contracts, or voluntary Constitution, there is no Common-wealth: therefore there is no Soveraignty.

2. If a meer Aggregation of natural men did make a Common-wealth and Soveraignty, then a Fare or Market might be a Common wealth: or a ship laden with Passengers or a Prison full of Captives, or an invading Army of enemies. But the Consequent is confessed a falshood, therefore, &c.

If meer nature make an Aggregate body of men to be a Common-wealth, or to have a real Majesty, (or Soveraignty) then every aggregate Body of men are a Commonwealth, and have that Soveraignty, but the consequent is false: for there are Schools, Colledges, Societies of Merchants, and many other Corporations and Societies that are no Commonwealth; therefore, &c.

3. If nature make a meer Aggregation or Community of men to be a Commonwealth, or to have Real Majesty, then men may be a

Common-wealth, and have such Majesty without, yea, and against their own consent: (For there may be a Community of Men that consent not to be a Common-wealth.) But the Consequent is false, therefore so is the Antecedent.

4. It will follow also, that no End intended by the people is necessary to the being of a Common-wealth; (For men may meet, or cohabit, or associate, and combine for severall ends.) But the Consequent is false against the nature of all such Relations and Associations, therefore, &c.

5. If nature make the people Soveraignes, then either all conjunctly, or a Major Vote: But neither all, nor a Major Vote: therefore none.

(i) Not All: For, 1. Where there is no Subject, there is no Soveraign: But if all conjunctly are feigned to be the Soveraign, there would be no Subject: therefore, &c. The Relate cannot be without its Correlate. 2. If all must be conjunct in the Soveraignty, no one would be punished, nor any righted: for every man would be judge in his own cause, and every Delinquent would have a negative voice in his own sentence, and no Murderer would suffer, till he, and all his friends consent.

(ii) If it be the Major Vote that is affirmed to have the Soveraignty; I answer, 1. Nature giveth no such Power: There is nothing in nature to tell us that 1,001 should have Power of Governing (and so of the lives) of 999. 2. Nature giveth them not so much as an Aptitude, much less Authority and Right. The Aptitude is in a Supereminency of Wisdom, Goodness and Power: but nature giveth none of these, much less all to the Major Vote; therefore it gives not to the Major Vote so much as an Aptitude for Government. 1. The world knows that knowledge followeth not the Major Vote. A few Learned experienced men, may be wiser then a thousand times as many of the Vulgar. 2. And their Vertue will be defective as their Wisdom is. 3. And (though Power be more for execution then for proper Government, yet) it is known that ten strong men may beat twenty weak ones, and that an Army of 30,000 doth often beat an Army of 40,000.

(iii) Yea, Nature usually denyeth the Aptitude for Government to the Major Vote. For, 1. They are ordinarily most imprudent, wanting the natural and acquired parts that others have. 2. They are usually most vicious: The most are seldom the best, in the Best Countreys of the world. 3. They are commonly divided, and hardly kept in Unity among themselves; and therefore are unfit to be the Center of Unity to the rest.

6. If Nature place the Soveraignty in an aggregate body of the people, then either in a certain number, or an uncertain. Not on a Certain Number: for nature limiteth it not to such a number, nor doth any affirm it: Not to an uncertaine number, for then every member that is added to the Common-wealth may possibly alter the bent of the whole Soveraignty. E.G. If it be half Protestants, and half Papists, and one Papist be admitted into the company, he will give the Papists the Major Vote. And thus the enemies may at any time subvert them, and the society will wheel about like the Weather-cock, one party making Laws, and the next Repealing them, as each can get the Major Vote.

7. If Nature do make the people the real Majesty, or give them any Governing power, then it is either because they are the wisest, the best, or the strongest: But it is by none of these: For, 1. It is proved, that ordinarily they are void of the two first and oft of the last. 2. If not, yet they are but an Aptitude, and not a Title. 3. Else if one Nation be wiser or better than the rest, all should be subject to them; or if an enemy stronger then we set footing on our soil, they are naturally our Governors. And 4. Then there can be no Injustice, if strength or wit may carry it: for he that cheats or beats another that hath Right to all he hath, or if any man can prove too hard for the Prince, his strength would be his Title.

8. If Nature had given the chief Governing Power to the people, then God would not have gone contrary to this in the institution mentioned in his word: But he hath gone contrary to it, (as shall be shewn) therefore, &c.

9. Nor would the commonest Governments of the Nations of the earth be contrary to it: for that which is of nature, is most common to naturall men. But no men that I hear of, are Governed by the people as set over them by meer nature: And few take them to have a naturall aptitude: and therefore most places have Monarchy or Aristocracy.

10. (i) The Power of Governing a Common-wealth is not a natural thing, but a Right that must come by Commission from a Superior; therefore it is not directly conveyed by meer nature: therefore the multitude have it not by nature.

(ii) And if they have it not by nature, then either by some supervenient Accident, or by Contract: If by Accident, either by Propriety in Riches, or by acquired Prudence or by Conquest. But none of these ways can it belong to the Community, or Major Vote, as such.

For 1. A few men may be richer then many, and have Dominion of more Lands and Cattle. And this giveth no man Right to be the Governour of others.

2. Acquired Prudence is but an Aptitude, and not a Title; and yet it is such as the multitude are void of.

3. They cannot be said to be Conquerors of themselves, or of the minor part.

(iii) Nothing therefore remaineth to be pleaded for the popular Soveraignty, but Contract, or Divine Institution. And if Contract do the deed, it is either a Contract about this very form and end in question, or about some other. 1. If about another, it cannot give them Power in this. If a society Contract about Merchandize, Physick, Literature, or other subjects and ends, this makes them not a Common-wealth. 2. And if it be a Contract to this special End, then it is not by Nature, and then it belongs not to a Major Vote as such, but followeth the consent of various Republicks as each are constituted by that consent.

(iv) And immediate Divine Institution cannot be pretended for it, as shall be shewn ...

> Thes. 52. Though the people have not any Soveraignty or Governing Authority as people, yet have they a certain Right to that Common good which is the End of Government, and each man hath that propriety in his life and faculties, and Children, and Estate, and Honour, that no Rulers may unjustly take these from him; which Right as it is secured partly by the Law of Nature, partly by other Laws or Institutions of God, and partly by the specifying Fundamental Contracts of the Common-wealth, and commonly called 'The Liberties of the People' and the just security of these Liberties, is it that some Authours have mistaken for a *Majestas Realis* and a popular Authority to Government.

> Thes. 53. Majesty or Soveraignty is the Highest Power of Governing the Common-wealth, and the Fountain of all inferiour Power.

Thes. 54. As Power or Authority is *Jus Regendi*, a Right to Govern, so the Soveraigns power in special consisteth in the Only Right of making the Universal Laws of the Common-wealth, and conveying Authority to inferiour Governours, and having the Highest Power of Judgement from which there is no appeal to any but God . . .

Thes. 55. Soveraignes are some perpetual, that is for life, and some temporary, or for a limited time; And therefore Politicians should not make it Essential to Soveraignty to be perpetual . . .

Thes. 56. The Soveraign is above all the Humane Laws of the Common-wealth; that is, he hath power to make Laws and to repeale them, correct them, adde to them, dispense with them, and pardon the breach of them to particular persons, and as a Soveraign is not bound to keep them by obedience himself, nor to suffer by them . . .

Thes. 57. Yet is not the Soveraign free from the Obligation of the Laws of God, nor from the Obligations of the Fundamental contracts of the Common-wealth, nor of any of his publick promises: nor may he dispense with his own Laws, (much less make Laws) against Gods Laws or the Common-good . . .

Thes. 58. But it is possible (how fit I dispute not) that the same natural person that hath the chief part of the Soveraign Power, may be both Soveraign and, subject in severall respects, and so have several civil capacities, and then he may as subject be obliged by the same Laws which as Soveraign he makes, and may be punished accordingly; that is, If by the Constitution and by his own consent (in receiving a power on such terms) he be thus subjected . . .

Thes. 59. The existence of the Natural Person of the Soveraign is not necessary to the existence of a Common-wealth . . .

Thes. 60. But the natural existence of Subjects is necessary to the existence of a Common-wealth. Because it is not a Body capable of living in a meere constitution, or the mindes of men, nor to be revived presently by mans determinations.

Thes. 61. Subjects are either Imperfect, and only such by Obligation and not consent, (as are Rebels) or plenary by consent. Obligation is for Duty: Consent is the condicion of the benefit, and the necessary cause of Duty it self.

Thes. 62. Consenting Subjects are either such as have only the benefits of Protection and Justice for their Lives, Honours, Estates, &c. or such as also are Burgesses of the Commonwealth, and are capable of bearing Office, and choosing Governours.

The reason of the difference is sometimes from the difference of expressions of consent, but usually from personal differences of Aptitude and Capacity: some being children, Idiots, servants, poor, and so depending upon others, and unfit to have a hand in Government.

Thes. 63. It is not the defect of secret intentions of the Ends of Government, that can nullifie the being of a Common-wealth; but if the Common good be not the professed end, it is null.

Thes. 64. It is no further true Government then it is a means to the Ends of Government, which are better then the means; nor may it be set up against its Ends.

CHAPTER 6

Of the several sorts of Commonwealths

Having spoken of the Universal Kingdom, and next in general of particular subordinate Common-wealths, that God hath by institution made the parts of it; I must First speak of the CONSTITUTION, and next of the ADMINISTRATION of these. And about the Constitution I shall first speak of the MODES (or SPECIES as commonly called) and then of the Individuation.

> Thes. 65. God hath not in his Universal Lawes restrained the Nations of the world to any one Mode or Species of Government, but left it as a variable thing to be determined according to the condition of each people, whether one or many shall have the Soveraignty under him.

There is a twofold diversity of Governments: One is in the Persons Ruling; Another is in the Matter of Government: whether the former do deserve the name of Specification or not, it hath by Custome obtained that name: And so Monarchy; Aristocracie, and Democracie are called the distinct Species of Governments or Common-wealths. In the Matter of Government there is difference, in that some have greater power, and some have less: some Soveraigns are limited to certain things, and degrees of power; and some are unlimited: and some limited more, and some less. And one would think this difference were as great as the former.

I know some pretend to a Divine Institution for Monarchy, but they mean onely that it may from Scripture be proved to be best; but not that no other but it, is Lawfull. Thus Michael Hudson and others assert it to be *Jure Divino*[15]: As for their pretences, that would make Democracie the onely Government that hath the stamp of God, I think them not worth the writing against.

> Thes. 66. The true formal nature of a Common-weal is in every one of the Modes or Species now in question; so that it is absurd to appropriate the Title of a Common-wealth to any one of them alone.

Yet so do the new Popularists among us, calling Democracie only 'a Common-wealth' which they should rather call 'a Common-government' if it imply no contradiction. The Constituting Matter of every Common-wealth is the *Pars Imperans*, and *Pars subdita*: the Governours and Subjects: and the forme is their Mutual Relation as respecting the End: the neerest End is Order, and the next the peoples safety and welfare hereby maintained and promoted; together with the Honour of the Governor: the more principal End is our present pleasing of God and honouring him, and the ultimate end is our more perfect everlasting pleasing him in our fruition of him in glory. It is named *Respublica* a Common-weal, partly from the matter, because it is the publick Affaires that it is exercised about: and partly from the end, because it is the Common good that it is instituted for, and is to be intended. A Vicinity or Community, City or Society may be where there is no Common-wealth. Any Number of men in capacity are the remote subject of it. A City or Community drawn neerer by contract, are usually or oft the more neer subject of it. For usually some Contract disposeth them, and makes them a Community, or City, before they become a Common-wealth, or so it may do at least. Though some call it not a City till it be headed with a Governour, and so it is a Common-wealth. Its not the Attaining but the Intention or Tendencie of the Government to the Common-good that is essential to a Common-wealth. An accidentally unhappy Common-wealth hath yet the forme, and must have the name.

> Thes. 67. The reason why God did not Universally by his Law tye all the World to One forme of Government, is because the difference of persons, times, places, neighbours, &c. may make

---

[15] Michael Hudson, *The Divine Right of Government Natural and Politique, more particularly of Monarchie* (London, 1647).

one forme best to one people, and at one time, and place, that is worst to another. Monarchy is best for some, Aristocracie to others, and Democracie to others . . .

Thes. 68. That is the best form of Government to this or that People, that all things considered, doth most powerfully tend to their spiritual and everlasting welfare, and their Holiness, Obedience, and pleasing of God . . .

Object. But the Common corporal Prosperity is the near and proper end, and therefore that must estimate the meanes.

Answ. Even that nearer end is it self but a means to our ultimate end; nor to be any further valued or regarded by a rational Creature, then it hath a tendency thereto; and therefore that which hath no value itself, but what it hath as a means to the ultimate end, can convey no other to its subordinate means. Nothing more sure then that our ultimate end must turn the scales of our estimation of all means. A horse may be stronger then a man, and a dog sounder, and a Tree live longer here. The Turkish Dominion may have more riches, and Power, and larger Command then the English Commonwealth: But it is not therefore the happier: That which most advanceth the people to salvation, and keeps out sin, and keeps our holiness and pleaseth God, is the best Government. He that beleveth not this, is at the heart an Infidel. A prison with holiness and the favour of God, is better then all the Riches and Glory of the world without it: The common cause of the Damnation of all that perish is the preferring of Riches, Honor, Pleasure, Liberty, and such fleshly accommodation before God and Glory. No men on earth therefore can more promote the Devils work, and the perdition of souls, then these that plead for corporall advantages in the framing of their Common-wealths against Gods interest, and the well-fare of mens souls! They too grosly play over again the game that the Devil playd with Christ that foiled him, Mat. 4., when he offered him all the Kingdoms and glory of the world, if he would worship him. None but those that have forsaken God shall be so far forsaken by him as to follow these impious Principles. We will not contrive our own adversity, nor refuse Prosperity when God affordeth it: But we must estimate all with respect to our ultimate end, and prefer the flames before a Crown when it is against this end.

Thes. 69. That is the best form of Government that most conduceth to the common safety of the interest of God, and the
well-fare of his Universall Kingdom.

The good of the world, and the whole body of Gods faithful Subjects is more to be lookt at, then the good of a particular Common-
wealth. The same Principles that prove it sordid and impious to value
our private personal prosperity before that of the Common-wealth,
do prove it as bad to value the good of one Common-wealth before
the Universal Kingdom of God on earth. If a people could live most
prosperously to themselves in the state of some petty Republicks and
Free Cities, but yet are thereby uncapable of doing much for the
safety or wel-fare of their brethren abroad, it is not the most desirable
Government.

Thes. 70. As that is properly a Domination, or Governing of
servants, which is principally for the Rulers benefit, and that is
a Common-wealth which is principally for the Common-benefit,
so the more any form of Government tendeth to the Common-
weal or Good of all, the more desirable it is; (supposing the two
fore-mentioned conditions.)

This also is plain, because the end still estimates the means. And
as Millions are better then one and Gods interest more concerned
in their wel-fare, so their wel-fare is more the end of the Common-
wealth then his. The Prince in this respect is for the people, more
then they for him.

Thes. 71. Yet is the Honour of the Prince, as he is Gods Officer,
and participateth of Authority derived from him, one part of the
end of a Common-wealth, and not to be separated from the
peoples benefit, in our intentions.

Mr. M. Hudson maintaineth that this Honor of the Soveraign is
the nobler end, and to be preferred before the peoples good. I think
they are so admirably linckt together, that we cannot fairly bring them
into Competition or Dissention. Gods Interest in other respects is
most in the people: though it is only the Rulers that participate of
his Governing Power and Honor. Gods interest in the Magistrates
Honor, is better then the Peoples prosperity as theirs: And Gods
Interest in the Peoples Wel-fare, and the Worship and Obedience
that he hath from them, is better then the Magistrates Honor as

his own: And the peoples Wel-fare as their own, is better then the Magistrates honor as his own: There remains therefore no question to be decided, but this, 'Whether Gods Interest in the Rulers honor, or in the peoples Wel-fare, must be preferred.' Which needs no further decision, because they are never to be separated, but both to be still regarded. Honor is commanded us to our Superiors in the fifth Commandment, and if any sin of theirs do make them uncapable of their own part in the honor, still Gods part must be secured, that is, when they are bad Rulers they must have the Honor of Rulers, though not of good Rulers, and that resulteth unto God: and if they cease to be Rulers, Magistracy ceaseth not, and therefore it must still be honoured, and God in it.

> Thes. 72. That form of Government is not to be judged most for the common good, which giveth the greatest Power to the multitude, but that which provideth them with the greatest advantages to serve and please God, and help their Brethren . . .

> Thes. 73. The great burden and work of the Ruler, is the Principal thing to be lookt at in his office; and the Honor is but for the work sake, and for God that giveth him his Power? The people therefore are more beholden to a faithful Governor, then the Governor is to the people, and receive more from him, then he from them . . .

> Thes. 74. Of all the three ordinary sorts of Government, Democracy is to most people, and usually the worst . . .

> Thes. 75. 1. A Kingdom is a Common-wealth that hath one person only for its Soveraign, the end of whose Constitution and Administration is the common good.

The very Title of *Rex*, a King, is the most modest and convenient that a Soveraign can have: for it signifieth but one that ruleth, directeth or guideth, whereas *Imperator*, an Emperour, signifying a Commander, is fitted to the General of an Army, and of too high importance for him that Ruleth by Laws. And *Dominus* a Lord, in its proper signification, is higher then that, and signifieth one that hath a Propriety and Power of Disposing of, as well as Ruling the persons and things that are under his Government, and ordereth them for himself as his own. A Protector is a name that I may not now descant on; but I may boldly say, that a King, and a Prince, *Rex*, & *Princeps* are lower as to pretension, and have in them the least appearance of Arrogancy, or sound of Arbitrary Power, and are most suited to a moderate Government.

> Thes. 76. The Corruption of Monarchy is commonly called Tyranny which is when the One that is appointed to rule for the Common-good, doth destroy the Common good, or subject it to his private interest ...

> Thes. 77. Aristocracy is a Common-wealth that's Governed by some of the best for the Common-good.

The Corruption of it is called Oligarchie, which is the confusion of the Community, when some of the strongest or richest, but not the best to get possession of the supream Government, and manage it for their private Interests, and not for the common good. If they be chosen by full Suffrage, yet it may be an Oligarchie, as well as by Invasion: the persons and abuse may corrupt the form.

> Thes. 78. Democracy is a Common-wealth where the Soveraign Power is in all, or the Major Vote of the people to be exercised for the Common-good.

Some popular forms admit all the multitude to vote in Government without distinction: Most are wiser, and admit only persons thus and thus qualified, that have such Estates, or of such Ranks and Orders: some give equal power to all that have Votes: some limit the inferior sort, and give more power to those of greater riches, The Corruption of this is called Ochlocratie, which is the confusion of the Community, when the Rabble rout or multitude have the Rule, which they exercise to satisfie their giddy humors, or some private Interest against the Common-well-fare: Scarce any Democracy escapes this.

> Thes. 79. A mixt Common-wealth is that, in which either two, or all three of these forms are so conjunct, that the Supremacy is divided among them, sometime equally, sometime unequally.

It hath been a Controversie, to which of these forms our English Common-wealth was, and is to be reckoned: the uncertainty of this was one cause of our Wars: Many thought it was a pure Kingdom or Monarchy, where the whole Soveraignty is in the King. The Parliaments have affirmed it to be a mixt Common-wealth, yet denominated a Monarchy or Kingdom from some eminent Prerogatives of the King: The Reasons given by them I shall not stand on, save only this One. The Legislative Power is a part, if not the highest part of the Soveraignty; but much of the Legislative Power is, and hath been in the Parliaments hands: therefore much of the Soveraignty is in their hands.

But to put all out of Controversie, the King himself in his Answer to the Nineteen Propositions of the Parliament, averres the same himself. As to them that argue from the Oath of Supremacy, and the Title given to the King, I refer them to Mr. Lawsons Answer to Hobbs Politicks,[16] where he shews that the Title is oft given to the single person for the honour of the Common-wealth and his encouragement, because he hath an eminent interest, but will not prove the whole Soveraignty to be in him: and the Oath excludeth all others from without, and not them whose interest is implyed as conjunct with his. The Laws and Customs of the Nation must expound such Names. The eminent Dignity and Interest of the King above others, allowed the name of a Monarchy or Kingdom to the Common-wealth though indeed the Soveraignty was mixt in the hands of Lords and Commons. If in the mixture the interest of the Prince had been least considerable, it should not have been called a Monarchie or Kingdom, but an Aristocracy or Democracy from the Party that had the most eminent interest.

> Thes. 80. Whether the natural persons that have the Soveraignty be One, or ten, or ten thousand, yet they are all but one Civil person, called the Soveraign ...

> Thes. 81. That Democracy or Popular Government is ordinarily the worst, is proved by all these Arguments; 1. Because it comes nearest to the utter confounding of the Governors and Governed: the Ranks that God hath separated by his Institution ...

> Thes. 82. 2. Nothing more incident to corrupted nature then for self-love: to blind men, and every man to be partial in his own cause: Now it is the people that are to be Governed, judged, punished, &c. and therefore how likely are they by partiality to themselves to make the Government next, to none ...

---

[16] George Lawson, *An Examination of the Political Part of Mr. Hobbs His Leviathan* (London, 1657), p. 41.

Thes. 83. 3. Government requireth natural strength of reason, that the Governors may be prudent men: They are things oft-times of exceeding difficulty, and usually of very great weight that they have to judge of: But the multitude of the people are usually of lamentable understandings, utterly unfit for such weighty things.

Multitudes in England, and more in Wales, Cornwall, Ireland, the High-lands, are scarce able to talk reason about common things! And are these fit to have the Soveraign Power to Rule the Commonwealth? I have been very sensible of this at an Assize, when I have heard the Judge and Counsellers industriously opening the case to the Jury, who stood by them as innocently as if they had heard nothing but Hebrew or Arabick all the while, and go their way, and bring in their Verdict, either as some one cunninger than the rest, perswades them, or else at random or hap hazzard, speaking that which was next the tongues end, so that I thought it much at one, as to throw the dice upon it, who should have the day. But O! If our people came to the work of Law-making, and our Senate must *Rogare & Abrogare, & obrogare & subrogare*, and the people resolve all as having the highest Power, what work should we have? And what a Herd would Govern us.

Thes. 84. 4. The great and weighty work of Government requireth an answerable Education to prepare them for it: But the Major part of our people have no such Education: therefore &c.

If we could possess them with the Holy Ghost, as Christ did his Apostles, we would call them from their fishing and tent-making to be Preachers or Rulers, and from their Plows, and Carts, and Dung-hills to make Laws: But till then, let us have the common Reason to conceive, that as a man that hath studied Physick, Divinity, or any Art, or Science, or Doctrine, is liker to be skilled in it, then he that was never bred up to it: so is it about the Government of Commonwealths also.

Thes. 85. 5. They that are the chief Governors of a Commonwealth, have need to be wholly or mostly vacant from all Aversions for so great a work: But common people must follow their Plows and Trades, and cannot be vacant for it: therefore they are unfit to Govern a Common-wealth.

If any say that their bare Election of Governors may serve turn, I shall shew you anon that that is not Governing, nor any part of it. The wisest men on earth will find that the Government of a Common-wealth will take up the whole man, and that they need no other Trade besides. We find in the Ministry how intolerable another Calling is; and why not here also?

Thes. 86. 6. They that shall Govern a Common-wealth should be good as well as wise, that they may resist temptations to partiality, and not prefer their private interest. But the Major part are not onely likely but certain to be bad, yea Enemies to the very principal ends of Government, in most places of the world: therefore they are utterly unfit for Soveraignty.

It is the badness of men that causeth the corruption of all the forms of Government before mentioned, and subjecteth the publick good to private; and certainly (however some dream that their Laws and Engines can hamper any men) the Devil would never Govern well by any Laws. And Scripture and all experience tells us that the most are selfish, sensual, Worldlings haters of Godlinesse: An enmity being put from the beginning between the seed of the woman and of the Serpent, all this stir of the Republicans is but to make the seed of the Serpent to be the Soveraign Rulers of the earth: when God hath promised that the Kingdoms of the world shall become Christs Kingdoms, these men would have them the Babels of Satan, the seat of confusion, and the enemies of Christ to raign through the earth. When Christ told his Apostles that he sent out them as Lambs among Wolves, these men would have these Wolves to be the Governors of the world: even those that Christ threatneth to slay: because they would not have him to raign over them, must be the men that must every where raign themselves, even those that he threatneth to bruise for their Rebellion with a Rod of Iron, and dash them in pieces as a Potters vessell, Psalm 2, Luke 19. 27. Were not this multitude restrained, they would presently have the blood of the godly. Late experience hath told us somewhat. Their hatred to piety is so wonderfull and unreasonable, that I confess it confirms me in my belief of that Word of God, that doth affirm it of them. And if these men had once the Soveraignty, what a case were the World in.

But Infidels that take evil for good, may flatter these persons, and make them believe that I unjustly reproach them, and may tell them, that they are all honest men, and it is but some self-conceited persons that censure them: But this will not cure their sin, nor prevent their misery, nor make them fit to govern us: Nor can they make us believe that Wolves are sheep in the open day light.

Nor can they pretend that their Laws shall keep them from doing harm. For, 1. The Soveraign Power is the Law-giver, and therefore can change them at his pleasure: Our brutish impious rout may at any time make Laws for the banishing of piety and Christianity: and for the worshipping of Bacchus; and if they but hoot, that 'Great is Diana', it is a Law. They have not the Soveraignty, if they cannot make and abrogate Laws. 2. And were they only inferior Governors, he is a fungus, and not a man that knoweth not by experience how easily bad men can make good Laws to be a nose of wax, and knock down their Adversaries with the very Manicles that we put upon their hands. It was a Proverb at Rome, that Vices had nailed the Laws to the Walls. Living Officers can easily abuse dead Laws. But of this more anon.

> Thes. 87. 7. Though no contrivance of man can ascertain a Nation of a succession of good and righteous Governors, yet that is the best Government that giveth the strongest Probability of it; and that the worst, that maketh it impossible, or next to an impossibility: But that the Major Vote of the people should ordinarily be just and good, is next to an impossibility: therefore, &c.

We have some Hopes of just and honest Governors if we have Monarchy or Aristocracy: but we have so little hopes, as is next to none, if the Popular Vote must have the Soveraignty. For it is the whole humane nature that is corrupted, and is fallen into Rebellion against God the absolute Soveraign; every man is by nature a Rebel against Heaven, and at enmity with God, and the matters of his own and others happiness, which the true common good consisteth in. And Scripture and experience assures us that it is in almost all places, the smaller number that are converted to Loyalty and subjection to God, and by sanctification reconciled to him, and laid down their enmity: so that ordinarily to plead for a Democracy, is to plead that the Soveraignty may be put into the hands of Rebels, and our welfare may be desperate, and the common good may be in the hands of the enemies of it, and that by a certain succession.

> Thes. 88. 8. Democracy is furthest from Unity, and therefore furthest from perfection: and therefore the most imperfect sort of Government.

That Unity is the companion of perfection, and Division departeth from it as it doth from Unity, is commonly acknowledged: which caused the Pythagorans to Curse the number of [Two,] because it was the first that presumed to depart from Unity.[17]

Thes. 89. 9. That is the most imperfect Government which departeth furthest from the Divine Universal form: But so doth popular Government, therefore, &c . . .

Thes. 90. 10. It is ordinarily the most imperfect form of Government which is furthest from the Angelical order: But such is popular Government. therefore, &c . . .

Thes. 91. 11. That Government is the worst which departeth furthest from the frame of nature in the Government of individual men: But so doth Popularity . . .

Thes. 92. 12. That is the worst Government of a Commonwealth that is the worst in all other-Governed societies: But such is Popular Government, therefore it is worst . . .

Thes. 93. 13. The Government that recedeth furthest from that which Christ hath settled in the Church is the most imperfect and the worst. But such is popular Government: therefore, . . .

Thes. 94. 14. A safe Government must have secrecy that the Enemie may not be acquainted with their Counsels unseasonably: But a Popular Government is most uncapable of such secrecy in their designs: therefore, &c . . .

Thes. 95. 15. Thats the worst Government (*cæteris paribus*) that giveth the Enemy the greatest advantage to raise tumults, and mutinies, or get a faction for himself to work his own designs among them: But such is the Popular Government: therefore.

Its a most easie matter for masked Enemies to be members of a Democratical Body, and there in every case to make a party and trouble all things, and at least hinder others and tye their hands, we have no Popular Government in England, and yet it is so easie for masked Papists, and Infidels, &c. to get into our Parliaments and

---

[17] Henry Stubbe drew the logical (heretical) consequence from this formulation: 'Is this not a fine argument for a Theologue: Doth it not overthrow the Trinity, as well as a Common-wealth?': Henry Stubbe, *Malice Rebuked* (London, 1659), p. 18.

there make disturbance that we feel the evill of it, but feare much more, if not prevented.

Thes. 96. 16. A safe and good Government must be able speedily to determine and execute in cases of great weight, that require haste: But the Popular Government is delatory, and will let the Common-wealth be lost, while they are debating . . .

Thes. 97. 17. That is the worst Government (*cæteris paribus*) that is least agreed, or most subject to Division in it selfe, and to factions and tumults in the Common-wealth: But such is Popular Government therefore, &c . . .

Thes. 98. 18. That's the worst Government (*cæteris paribus*) which is exercised by unconstant fickle men: But such is popular Government: therefore it is the worst . . .

Thes. 99. 19. That is the worst Government that will exercise the greatest Cruelties, especially against the best: But such is popular Government, therefore . . .

Thes. 100. 20. That Government where the Rulers have all the foresaid Incapacity, Ignorance, Levity, Naughtiness, &c. and yet have the greatest strength to do evill, and are least restrainable or reformable when they do miscarry, is, *ceteris paribus*, the worst of Governments: But such is the Popular Government: therefore it is the worst . . .

Of the Objective or Material Differences of Government

Thes. 101. Governors are some limited, some *de facto* unlimited: The unlimited are Tyrants, and have no right to that unlimited Government . . .

Thes. 102. Limited Governours are either limited from exercising so much power as God himselfe hath appointed the supreme Magistrate to use, or else limited only in things that God hath left undetermined, as to any universall determination. The former limitation is sinfull in the Limiters, and yet may be submitted to in some cases by the Soveraign innocently: the latter may be lawfull in both . . .

Thes. 103. God himself by enacting his own Universall Laws, and instituting Magistracy for the Execution of them in the subordination to him, doth thereby plainly tell us, that the Soveraign Powers in each Common-wealth are not to be restrained by the people from the Execution of any of his Laws, which belong to them as Magistrates to execute . . .

Thes. 104. If the peoples limitations would frustrate the end of Government, the prince ought not to consent, but rather to be no Governour: But if they only hinder the *melius esse*, or higher perfection of the Common-wealth, he may receive a sinfully limited power . . .

Thes. 105. The people can restraine a Prince *de facto*, because they have the strength, and he cannot govern them without their own consent, either in whole, or in part: and therefore their dissent doth make the exercise of a further Power impossible to the Prince (or other Soveraign) and consequently justifie him . . .

Thes. 106. Yet is this no act of Governing Authority in the people, nor doth it prove them to have the least measure thereof:

but it is only an exercise of their natural Resolution upon the advantage of their strength, and in unlawfull cases; it is only a mutinous disobedience against God, which is far from Authority . . .

Thes. 107. Though the Prince may omit some good by reason of the peoples Dissent and Limitations, yet he may not commit any evil on any such pretence . . .

Thes. 108. Though God have not in his Universall Laws determined of the Degree of Princes Power in all Circumstantials or variable matters, yet he hath given general Laws for regulating of such determinations as there shall be cause . . .

Thes. 109. The Principal fundamental Rules for the Magistrates Government, are 1. That he doe all in a due subordination to God the fountaine of Authority: 2. That he frame all his Laws and execution so as that they may be a means to the ends of Government! viz. both the neerest end, the Order, peace, and happiness, Corporall, and spirituall of the Common-wealth; and the ultimate end, the Pleasing of God in our salvation for ever . . .

Thes. 110. Another Divine limitation of the Soveraign is, that he fit all his Laws to a due subserviency unto Gods universall Laws, and do nothing against any of them.

Thes. 111. Yet as Gods Laws are not all of absolute necessity to the being of a loyal subject of his Kingdom, though all are obligatory, so the Magistrate that in point of Duty is bound to subserve and observe all Gods Lawes, yet nullifieth not his office or power by sinning against those that are not of absolute necessity as aforesaid . . .

Thes. 112. The people ought not to restraine the soveraign Power from a usefull Determination of things in themselves indifferent, according to the Generall Rules of God, for the ends of Government . . .

Thes. 113. But in case that Rulers would. 1. Have a power to trouble the Common-wealth with needless Lawes. 2. Or would determine Circumstances dangerously, so that it may as probably, or more, doe hurt as good: 3. Or would have such a power to do a lesser good which he cannot have without the power of doing much more hurt: 4. Or would actually do hurt to the Common-wealth, the restraint of the people (in the Constitution) is here innocent and prudent . . .

Thes. 114. The People may have a true Propriety in their estates, though they have no Right of Governing: and therefore here they may more Capitulate with the soveraign and restraine him from taking their Moneys, Goods, Lands, &c. Without their consent, or but on contracted termes . . .

Thes. 115. It is not safe or Lawfull for the people to limit or restrain the soveraign Power from disposing so farre of the estates of all, as is necessary to the safety of all, which is the end of Government.

It is not the whole of mens Propriety that is to be subject to the Governour but part. And that Part is subject for the preservation of the whole remainder. Men have the primary Propriety in themselves, and the secondary in their estates: and as no Governor may take away the lives of all the people on pretence of justice or necessity, but only some on just occasions, and that for the good of the rest, so no Governor may take away all the estates of the peoples, but only part to preserve the rest: Nor may he justly take from them the Propriety, leaving the possession. The King of Egypt could not take the peoples Lands and Cattle, as Governor, but as Contracter, by Purchase, when Joseph sold them corn, and they parted with a great part of their propriety to save their lives. But to make Propriety dependent, and limited as a Tenents, may be lawfull, if not by injustice nor unmercifulness accomplished.

If the Ruler have not Power to preserve the Common-wealth, he is not capable of the ends, and so not of the work of Government. It is for the peoples good that part be used to save the whole and themselves. But yet it is just and wisdom for the people in the constitution to limit the Ruler by convenient cautions that he may not under pretence of Preserving them have advantage to oppress them: and therefore it is unfit for the ordinary stated Revenews necessary to his personal or annual-publick use, should depend upon their after-Consent; (for so Princes would be brought into the case as those Ministers that live on the peoples voluntary contribution, and would find both murmuring and mutable Pay-masters) yet in extraordinary Taxes it is fit the people should restrain the Rulers from arbitrary seizures. And yet it is unfit that this restraint should be exercised by the people themselves, but rather by some prudent chosen persons, as it is in our Parliaments. For the multitude are covetous, tenacious, injudicious, and incompetent judges of the necessities or commodity of the Common-wealth: and will make a small matter of their dangers, and publick commodities, and a great matter of their payments, till they are undone, and wise too late: And almost all Contributions will occasion seditions, tumults, or unsettledness in the Commonwealth.

If the people, or any as chosen by them to that end, have only such a limiting self-preserving Power to themselves reserved, or a meer *judicium discretionis* about the necessities of the Common-wealth; this proveth not that they have any power in the Government, but if they have also a deliberating power about the common dangers or diseases, and a directing or disposing Power about the Remedy (whether money arms, &c) as a Remedy, then it is a part in the Government that is reserved to them.

> Thes. 116. The propriety of particular men is subjected to the Governor as a Governor, so far as that he may judge in cases of difference, and administer Justice in giving every man his own, and may deprive men of part, or all that they possess by way of punishment for their crimes ...
>
> Thes. 117. Yet here also it is fit that the Constitution limit the Soveraign *de modo*, as God by his Universal Laws hath limited him in the substantials of Justice.

For if under pretence of Justice every mans Life and Estate should be meerly at the mercy of an Arbitrary unlimited Prince, it were as bad as to have all left to his will, when he will pretend a necessity for the publick safety or commodity directly. They may see in the constitution that vertues be not punished as vices, nor the innocent (by a Law) as if they were guilty: and that none but well chosen able men be Judges, and that they be responsible to the Supream: and that the penalties exceed not the crimes, not the matter of fact judged without sufficient witness; and such like restrictions they may put to escape Injustice; but such disable not the Governor to do Justice ordinarily.

> Thes. 118. If the Soveraign be not limited in the constitution, or by his own consent, but only in general terms entrusted with the Soveraignty, he may by vertue of his Soveraignty dispose of the Estates of the Subjects in order to the ends of Government: But though there be no 'express restraint' upon him in the constitution, yet can he do nothing against the Laws of God, or the ends of Government.

It is implyed in the constitution of every Government, that it cannot be used against its superior Power, or its end. This God hath obliged them to already, and therefore it is firm, though men say nothing. And therefore a Governor as he is a subordinate Officer of God, is restrained from Injustice, and so from seising on the Estates of others, for himself or his Favorites, or without the demand of Justice, or the publick good. But in these cases his office alloweth, yea, and bindeth him to do it, if not restrained notoriously by the constitution. And he would be an enemy to the Common-wealth, if he suffer it to perish in tenderness of mens private good.

Thes. 119. It seems to many a very difficult Question, Whether a Soveraign should save the Common-wealth when the limitations in the constitution disable him? But the Answer is easie. If the danger be not certain or very great, he is to keep his bounds and Covenant: and if mischief fall on the common-wealth, the people by their foolish limitations were guilty, and its they that must bear the main loss. But if the danger be great, and the people express not their dissent, the Soveraign may trangress his limits to save the Common-wealth, because the constitution being for the common safety, it is to be supposed that the Authors of it did intend the end, before they chose the means, and therefore did mean, that if the limitations should fall out to be inconsistent with the end, they should be nul . . .

Thes. 120. But it seems a harder Question what the Soveraign should do in case the people not only limit him by Covenants, but actually desire the way that would destroy them, and dissent from his preserving them, whither may he save the commonwealth against the peoples wills? The Answer is easie, that he may do it, both as he is a Governor, and so an Officer of God for the ends of Government, and therefore cannot lawfully be restrained by the people from preserving them, because they have no Power above God: and also as a private man *ex charitate*, he is bound to save a Nation if he can, though without Authority; as we must save a man from drowning or hanging himself, or quench the fire which he kindleth in his own thatch. And because it is still to be supposed that the people desire their own preservation, and therefore mistakingly resist the means, which else they would consent to . . .

CHAPTER 7

Of the Foundation efficient and conveying causes of Power

Thes. 121. There is no Governing Power but what is from God the Absolute Universal Lord and Soveraign . . .

Thes. 122. Every earthly Soveraign therefore is an Officer of God, receiving his power from him as his highest Soveraign, and being obliged to use it for him, being himself but a subordinate Soveraign of a part of the Universal Kingdom . . .

Thes. 123. The fifth Commandment is therefore placed as between the first and second Table, as being partly a Command of our Duty to God in his Officers, and partly the first Command of our Duty to men, even to the men that are most highly dignified by the Communication of that beam of Authority from God . . .

Thes. 124. Our principal search then must be to find out the line of Derivation, how, and by what means this Power is conveyed from God. And to that end, we must enquire what he hath done himself as part of his Universal standing Law, and what he hath left to be done, with variations according to the difference of times, and places, and persons.

Thes. 125. And first, It is most certain that God hath himself determined in the Law of nature, & of Scripture, that there shall be Governors and subjects, Rule and Obedience in the world; and hath not left the world to liberty, whether they will have Governors or not . . .

Thes. 126. Secondly, God hath been pleased in his Universal Laws of nature and Scripture to determine of the ends of

Government; that his Pleasure, and Honor, and the common-good, and order as necessary thereto, It all be the end: this therefore is not left to the decision of man . . .

Thes. 127. Thirdly, God hath himself made certain Universal stated Laws, which all Princes and States must promote and execute as his Officers; and no man on earth have Power to null them, or dispense with them: It is not therefore left to mans decision whether they will observe these Laws of God, or not . . .

Thes. 128. God hath described in his word (and much in the Law of nature) the Rulers, that shall receive Authority from him as his Officers: so that it is not left to the liberty of any people whom they will choose: but this description containeth some qualifications necessary to the being of an Officer of God, and some that are necessary but to the well-being: therefore if the latter be violated by the Choosers, it is a sin, but not a Nullity; if the former be violated, it is a Nullity as well as a sin . . .

Thes. 129. All these things being determined already by God himself, it is certain that neither Peoples Election, nor conquest can be the fountain or proper cause of any of these: but it must be somewhat lower that they have to do . . .

Thes. 130. That which God hath left undetermined in his Universal Laws, is 1. Whether it shall be one, or two, fewer or more that shall have the Soveraign Power under him in particular Common-wealths. 2. And who shall be the individual persons. And 3. Much of the matter of their Laws, which is to be varied agreeably to times and persons . . .

Thes. 131. The essentiall Qualifications of a Governour, or that *Dispositio materiæ* that is of necessity *ad receptionem & retentionem formæ*, (and not only *ad melius esse*) are those without which the persons are not capable of performing the essential workes of Government . . .

Thes. 132. The end of Government will best determine What is essentiall to Government in exercise. In a proper Common-wealth that is subject to God the Universal soveraign, it is essentially necessary that the Government be so exercised, 1. As that the Being of the Common-wealth may be preserved, 2. And so much of the well being or Common-good as that the estate of the Common-wealth be better then the estate of the people would be if they had no Government, 3. That justice be more prevalent in the bent of Government then injustice, and the Rulers in the maine be not a terror to good works but to evill, 4. And that the Universall Soveraign be acknowledged and honoured . . .

Thes. 133. The three qualifications of necessity to the Being of the power in that subject, are, 1. So much Understanding. 2. And Will or Goodness in himself. 3. And so much strength or executive Power by his Interest in the people, or others, as are necessary to the said ends of Government . . .

Thes. 134. As Gods Universal Law hath instituted, limited and regulated the Office, and described the Officers, so his effective Providence doth qualifie or dispose the particular Subjects and make them capable, and partly make, and partly permit an incapacity in others: and thus it doth fit or unfit men as to the form . . .

Thes. 135. When Providence depriveth a man of his Understanding, and intellectual Capacity, and that statedly, or as to his ordinary temper, it maketh him *materiam indispositam*, and uncapable of Government, though not of the name . . .

Thes. 136. If God permit Princes to turn so wicked as to be incapable of Governing, so as is consistent with the ends of Government, he permits them to depose themselves . . .

Thes. 137. If Providence statedly disable him that was the Soveraign from the executing of Laws, Protecting the just, and other ends of Government, it maketh him an uncapable Subject of the Power, and so disposeth him . . .

Thes. 138. When Providence thus maketh any uncapable or indisposed, it destroyeth the Power as in such: but yet when it disposeth any for the Government, it doth not thereby immediately give him possession or Title to the Government . . .

Thes. 139. It is the work of Providence to give men, 1. An Eminency of Wisdom. 2. And of Goodness. 3. And by Interest in others, sufficient strength for Magistracy . . .

Thes. 140. It is not the giving of either Wisdome, or Goodness, or strength alone that maketh men capable of governing Authority, but it must be All, (in the fore-described measure.)
The subtilest Politician may be uncapable through wickedness, and the wisest and best man may be uncapable (of full Right and

exercise) through weakness: and if a man have all three, (Wisdom, Goodness, and strength) he hath not therefore Authority, but only an Aptitude therto.

Thes. 141. Though it be a duty for a very weak (though tolerable) Governor for the common good to resign his place to one that is every way more fit and liker (*consideratis considerandis*) to attain the ends of Government in a more excellent degree, yet is it not lawfull for any other to depose him, and usurpe the place because he is more wise, or good, or powerfull nor for the people to do it, contrary to the constitution . . .

Thes. 142. Meer Possession of the seat of Power in it self considered, is not a Title, nor will justifie the Possessor, nor warrant the people to consent and submit.

A man may have Possession of the seat and land, and not of the Government: for he Possesseth not that till he exercise it, and he cannot exercise it, but upon a consenting people. The people may choose to live in slavery, or be destroyed in a state of Hostility, if they please, rather then to submit to the Usurper. And in these cases it is meet that they should do so. The first is, if he would force them else to violate their Covenants to God or man, or to commit any sin against God: so that consenting to his Government must contain a consent to sin: The second is, if his Government will do more hurt then our refusing him or perishing would do, to that Nation. Or thirdly, if consenting might be better to that Nation, yet if it be more injurious to the common good of the world, or the common Interest of God, then our dissent.

But I will say no more of this, because Mr. Edward Gee hath in two books said so much, whose Arguments against the meer Possessors claim are thus far good.[18]

Thes. 143. Conquest in it self is no sound Title to the Government of a people.

If the war was unjust, then the conquest is but the success of Robbery and murder, and therefore can give no Title. If the war were just against the Prince only, and not against the people, there is no appearance of a Title to Rule them from the success. If the war was

---

[18] Edward Gee: *A Vindication of the Oath of Allegiance* (London, 1650); *The Divine Right and Originall of the Civil Magistrate from God* (London, 1658).

just against Prince and people, yet as is said, they may in some cases choose to die, or be used as the Conqueror please, and continue their hostility with unconquered minds. And if so, till they yield to be his Subjects, he is not their Soveraign, though Conqueror.

> Thes. 144. If the person dispossest be one that we are by Covenant obliged, not onely to submit to, & obey, but also to defend, & be not made uncapable of the Government, we ought to defend him, and endeavor his restitution according to the tenor of our Covenants, as far as may stand with the common good, the end of Government. Yea, though we make no such Promise, our Relation, and the Law of God obligeth us to defend our Governors . . .

> Thes. 145. But if the person dispossest be justly dispossest, as by a lawfull War, in which he loseth his Right, especially if he violate the Constitution, and enter into a military state against the people themselves, and by them be conquered, they are not obliged to restore him, unless there be some other special obligation upon them, beside their Allegiance.

This shall be anon more fully manifested when we speak of the Dissolution of Government.

> Thes. 146. If the person dispossest, though it were unjustly, do afterward become uncapable of Government, it is not the duty of his Subjects to seek his Restitution.

I have before intimated by what wayes men become incapable: As by loss of Understanding, by becoming an Enemy to the common good, or to God, and by loss of Power for the ends of Government, which they are unable to restore him to. An Incapacity also may be accidental, as if he cannot be restored but by the Arms of the enemies of God, or the Common-wealth, who will afterwards have the Power of disposing of him & the Government so that the Common-wealth hath no securety but the word of enemies: or if a faction of enemies within must needs be (or apparently will be) the Masters of all when he is restored. He that is incapable of promoting of the Common good, is uncapable of Governing, (which way ever it come to pass:) and he that is become uncapable of Governing, ought not to be restored, unless we can restore his capacity.

> Thes. 147. If an Army (of Neighbours, or inhabitants, or whoever) do (though injuriously) expel the Soveraign, and resolve

to ruine the Common-wealth, rather then he shall be restored, and if the Common-wealth may prosper without his restauration, it is the duty of such an injured Prince, for the common good to resign his Government; and if he will not, the people ought to judge him as made uncapable by providence, and not to seek his restitution, to the apparent ruine of the Common-wealth.

The reason is, because it is essential to Government to be for the common good; and he is for the people finally, rather then they for him: And Government ceaseth to be just Government, when it ceaseth to be a means to its end: much more when it is destructive to it. The *jus regendi* is not like meer Dominion (I mean Propriety,) which is but a power or right to use and dispose of things as our own, and for ourselves. But it is like the office of a Physitian, School-master, Pilot, &c. who are principally for the good of others, and but secondarily for their own reward and honour. And therefore no man on earth can pretend propriety in his Kingdom, or Government, against the common good, and ends of that Government. For that is to change the nature of the thing, and then plead an interest in it, as Government, when they have made it no (just) Government at all.

Thes. 148. That Man that will rather see the blood of many thousands spilt, and the Common-wealth hazarded, then he will give up that Government which he received for the common good, when he may know that his resignation would be for the common good, and his war against it, doth thereby declare that he seeks not the common good, but himself.

These five or six last propositions I have taken in on the by, but to prepare for those that follow, by removing objections that stand in the way.

Thes. 149. It is not lawful for a people to chuse, rather to have no Governour, then not to have him that is their rightful Prince: for that there shall be Government and subjection, is the stated Law of God, to which the right choise of persons is but subordinate: if therefore the rightful Governour be so long dispossest that the Common-wealth can no longer be without Government, but to the apparent hazard of its ruine, we ought to judge that providence hath dispossest the former, and presently to consent to another.

1. The right of persons is in subserviency to the Government it self and the ends of it: and therefore if any man will set the means

against the end, or a circumstance of humane determination against a Law of God, and say, Because we cannot have such a man, we will have none, but be ungoverned; this is to break an express commandment, and to cast off the order and ordinance of God, for a persons sake.

2. If people have no Government, vice will reign, and every mans estate and life will be at the mercy of his enemy, or him that hath a mind to it, and is the stronger: And therefore no people can long subsist without Government.

> Thes. 150. When a people are without a Governor, it may be the duty of such as have most strength, *ex charitate*, to protect the rest from injury.

This is a truth known by the light of nature: no man that is assaulted by a robber, but would have his neighbour help him: And he that will pass by him, and not succour him if he can, doth not do a neighbours part: He that seeth his brother in need, danger, or distress, and shutteth up the bowels of his compassions from him, how dwelleth the Love of God in him? Duties of charity, especially to a Nation, are indispensable.

> Thes. 151. Providence by conquest and other means doth use so to qualifie some persons above others for the Government when the place is void, that no other persons shall be capable competitors, and the persons shall be as good as named by Providence, whom the people are bound by God to choose or consent to; so that they are usually brought under a Divine obligation to submit to such or such, and take them for their Governours, before those persons have an actual right to govern.

A people without a particular Soveraign, are still parts of Gods universal Kingdom, and from him they are to receive their officers, if he appoint them; for still they are under the obligation of his Laws. Though the peoples consent (explicite or implicite) be necessary to the Soveraigns actual Government, and consequently to his right of governing them, by which he must himself be warranted and justified; yet are the people usually under a previous obligation from the Lord, whom they shall consent to, and whom not. And Conquest is the most usual means of the determination: not by giving Right to govern, but by making the Conquerour *materiam dispositam*; the only capable subject of that right, and object of the peoples choice. The same may be said of any other possession of such power as the Conquerour hath, Ordinarily did the Roman Emperours (formerly at Rome, and since at Constantinople) die or suffer deposition, by an Usurper; and yet the subjects obeyed the Usurper, and the Christian Bishops took it to be their duty so to do. If his Conquest or Occupation be sinful, yet if he thereby become the only capable person to Govern, the people are to consent (supposing no special impediment to forbid it.) If they be (though through anothers sin) disobliged from their former Governour, (by his death, incapacity, &c.) they are bound by God to consent to such as are most capable.

> Thes. 152. But if men have by Conquest or other means become the strongest, that yet are uncapable, for want of Necessary wisdom, or Goodness, the people may submit to suffering, but not consent that such should govern them.

Because being supposed uncapable of Governing them, their Government would be as hurtful as to be without a Government. And if Gods honour and soveraignty must be traiterously despised, and the common good destroyed, it is better that it be done without the peoples consent, then with it.

> Thes. 153. Anything that is a sufficient sign of the will of God, that this is the person, by whom we must be Governed, is enough (as joyned to Gods Laws) to oblige us to consent, and obey him, as our Governour.

God being the chooser of his own Officers, and the universal King, who bindeth us to obey his choice, doth make known his will to man by signs: For we cannot immediately see his essence, and therefore not his will. All his Laws that oblige us, are but so many signs of his will: and he may choose his sign.

> Thes. 154. It being already signified in the Law of God, that a people that are without a Ruler shall consent to such as are fittest for them, and the qualifications of such being there exprest, the rest of Gods will to be signified to the people, to bring them under the particular obligation, is but for the discovery of the persons thus qualified: so that Law and providence concurring, are Gods nomination of his Officers, whom the people by him are bound first to consent to be subject to, and then to obey.

Here are several acts of Gods Law, and several acts of Providence, necessary in concurrence, to constitute a Soveraign. 1. There is presupposed the general Law, for Government and obedience, distributing the subjects of Gods Kingdom, into particular subordinate Soveraigns, and their Subjects. 2. There is supposed Gods Laws, that cut them out their principal work, and describe the substance of the office, and limit them. 3. The Law of God describeth the persons, in the points necessary to the Being, and the well being of their Government. 4. The same Law obligeth the people to consent to such, (in case they are called to such a work, as choosing or consenting.) Thus far the Law goeth.

And then Providence, 1. Doth qualifie the person, 1. With tolerable wisdom. 2. And Goodness (so far as to be a capable Instrument for the Ends of Government.) 3. And with Power to defend the people and execute Laws. And many acts of Providence may concur to this: especially it is by giving a man such Interest in the Affections of the stronger part, that by them he may be put into a capacity. 2. And when he is qualified, to bring him upon the stage to the peoples observation, that they may observe his Qualifications, is an Act of Providence for the discovery of Gods Will; and so to bring the people under an Obligation to consent. 3. And when they are so obliged, the bringing of their hearts to consent and accept him, is another Act of Providence antecedent to his Possession, and ordinarily to such a Title as will justifie his Government.

So that the peoples Obligation is thus inferred and induced by God.

Whomsoever I thus and thus Qualifie, and declare to be the fittest person, you shall consent to.

But this man (or these men) I have so qualified and declared: therefore to them you shall consent.

The Major is in Gods Law (of Nature and Scripture, most express.) The Minor is the voice of Providence (taking the word for Actual disposal of Events) and both together infer the conclusion, and induce the Obligation, but with the difference following.

Thes. 155. Hence it is plain that this Disposal of Providence, is not instead of a Law, or speaketh not *de debito*, but *de facto*, and therefore doth not it self efficiently oblige: but it only designeth the person and nominateth him, to whom we shall by the Law be obliged to consent . . .

Thes. 156. When the Nomination is referred to a Lot, that Lot determineth but in this way of Providence, nominating the person, leaving the Obligation still to the Law.

What a Lot may do, another Providence may do; but the lot may determine of the persons: therefore so may other Providence. God hath many wayes of signifying his mind to us, and nominating the persons, and hath not tyed himself to any one; nor must we limit him.

Thes. 157. Where God doth not notably declare any person qualified above others, nor one, two, or any certain Number to be most fit for the Soveraignty of that people, so that the case is not Notorious, but Controvertible, there the people must judge as well as they are able, according to Gods General Rules, or else refer it to a Lot.

This is counted the freest Choyce, when people are not plainly pre-obliged: but indeed there is no more desirable freedom, but oft-times less, in this Case then the other. If God do for our good so plainly qualifie and declare our Governours as to leave it out of doubt to us, and so to pre-oblige us, it is a mercy, and not a depriving us of any desirable liberty: And if there be none of such Eminency, but that we are left to a choyce out of many equals, it doth but make us the more work.

Thes. 158. A free people should have a free Consent, as from men, though they may be pre-obliged to consent by God.

Conquerours or men of strength may not obtrude themselves on a free people, how fit soever they are; but must leave them as freemen, to a free consent.

Thes. 159. All people have not right to such freedom; sometime whole Nations, but commonly a part of every Nation, should be denyed the liberty of choosing their Governours, and be compelled to consent: and to make all Choosers is injurious and destructive to the Common wealth.

The first branch (which denyeth freedom of choice to some whole Nations) is all that is lyable to controversie, which yet is so plain, that it needs not many words.

1. Sometimes divers Nations may constitute One Common-wealth. And then there is as much reason why a whole Nation, as a mixed part, should be thought Capable of forfeiting their liberties.

2. Sometimes divers Nations may be under the same Princes Government. And then if he can forfeit his Crown as to them, by any Covenant-breaking on his part, no doubt but part of them may forfeit their Liberty, by Treason and Covenant-breaking on theirs, and he may Rule them by the power of his other Kingdoms; As the Romans did many of the Nations that they Conquered.

3. Sometime the Neighbourhood of unjust, implacable enemies, is not to be tolerated, without the ruine of the Righteous Nations round about them, unless they be kept under by meer force; and so self-preservation may warrant it. Men that choose to live as enemies in war with us, must be used upon military terms. Till they shew themselves worthy of Trust, they are not to be used as free Subjects.

4. Sometimes men may forfeit their Liberties to God and men so notoriously, that the Law of Nature and Nations warranteth Neighbour Princes to subdue them, and govern them by force. As 1. In Case they should turn Atheists, and defie the universal King, and seek to poyson the Neighbour Nations with this Treason against God. 2. In Case they live as Canibals, that eat mans flesh, and are as wild beasts, that hunt for men to devour them, whether it be their fellow-natives, or the Neighbour Nations. 3. In Case they professedly design the Conquest of all others about them, and will live upon no other terms in peace, but as Conquerers or Conquered. 4. Specially in Case they claim a right to the Kingdoms about them, and specially a Divine Right; that all Princes should obey them, and make it their unalterable Religion, as the Pope doth. He that thus claims a Right to dispose of Crowns and Kingdoms, though but *in ordine ad Spiritualia*, proclaimeth war with all the World, and warranteth any Prince that is within his danger to make war against him.

5. The Law of Nature may bind a Christian Nation in Charity to Rule some Nations by force. If a poor barbarous Indian Nation, like the Canibals, would not consent to hear the Gospel, or suffer Preachers to come among them, and speak to a minor part that would hear, I am sure it hath an apparent tendency to their salvation to master them, and force them to admit the Preachers, and to restrain them from murdering the Christians among them that had received the Gospel: And as long as we did them no hurt, but govern them,

and did not deprive them of their Possessions, I know not what should exempt us from the Obligation to this as a work of Charity. Doubtless a meer Neighbour, by the Law of Charity, is bound to hold a mans hands that would kill himself, or pull him out of the water that would drown himself, and to quench his house though against his will, which he sets on fire, and to save his Children, or Neighbours persons or houses from his fury, in case of the like attempts: And why then a work of ten thousand times greater benefit, should not on the same grounds be done, I know not. If the Prince and major part of the people, in a neighbour petty Common-wealth would put to death the minor part, because they are Christians, and a Potent neighbour Prince were easily able to restrain them, I doubt not but he would be guilty of the murder and extirpation of Christianity, if he do not: And if he cannot continue their preservation, without a continued restraint, or subduing the malignant party, the Laws of Neighbour-hood, and Charity, and the Common good of mankind, and the Ends of the Universal Government require him to do it.

If any say that upon such pretences Atheists and Heathens that are the stronger part, may invade a weaker Christian State to force them to deny God, or Christ, or acknowledge Idols, &c. I answer, 1. Confound not the *Jus* and the *factum*: the natural and the legal Power. They may do it *de facto per potentiam Naturalem*, which is nothing to the case, but they may not do so *de iure per potentiam Legalem*, because God hath given them no such Power.

> Object. But you will give them occasion to pretend Authority; and if they are the stronger party, they will be the Judges.

Answ. No duty can be done, from whence the wicked cannot fetch pretences for their sin. If a righteous Judge shall hang Murderers or Thieves, he is not therefore to be blamed, because an unrighteous Judge may take occasion by it to hang the innocent as guilty of their crimes. If our Armies may destroy the plundering Enemies, and rescue the oppressed Countrey men, and the Enemies Armies may thence fetch a pretence to destroy ours as guilty of that crime, though they be innocent, we must not therefore neglect the defence of the oppressed. Malignant enemies will not be reduced to reason, if we should neglect our duty for it; but the wicked will do wickedly: some inconveniences will still attend the imperfections of humane Admin-istrations. But the final Judgement will set all strait. Let us do our

Duty, and stay till God do Justice upon those that by Power are out of the reach of Justice, from the hand of man.

But that which nearlier concerneth us (and as near as any thing in our frame of Government) is the latter part of the Thesis; that all the people in the same Common-wealth should not have the freedom of choosing Governours, which I shall therefore more distinctly handle.

Thes. 160. It is commonly granted that nature and want of competent wealth may deprive the most innocent of a capacity of this freedom. Much more will a mans wilful crimes deprive him of it.

I grant that all these may be Subjects: and further then by course of Justice they are deprived of them, let them enjoy their Possessions as much as any other Subjects, allowing for the securing of them, the same Tributes and Taxes as all others. But it is a Burgeship, or freedom of Governing, or choosing any Governours, Parliament-men, Justices, &c. that we speak of.

Nature maketh Infants and Idiots uncapable: and women choose not members of Parliament.

Servants are commonly judged uncapable, and so are the poor: not only because they have not those faculties necessary to support the Government, but principally because necessity maketh them dependant upon others; and therefore it is supposed that they are not free in their Elections. How far the reason reacheth to Tenants, the Law-givers, though they are Land-Lords, seem not to be insensible, when all that have not Leases for life are excluded from the number of free-holders.

But that multitudes of wicked criminous persons, how rich soever, should much rather be excluded then honest beggars, and that this, this, this, is the great point that the welfare of most Common-wealths doth depend upon, I shall now make manifest.

Argum. 1. If many Vices make persons less fit to govern choose Governours, then poverty doth, conjoyned with honesty, then should such vicious persons, rather be excluded from both: But the Antecedent is most certain: Ergo.

Argum. 2. If men should lose their lives or estates by way of Punishment for some crime, then should they lose their liberty of Governing and choosing Governours by way of punishment for those or other crimes to which such punishment is proportionable (for there is a parity of Reason.) But the Antecedent is practically confest: Ergo, &c.

Argum. 3. If confessedly crimes should deprive men of a capacity to Govern, so also they must do of a capacity of choosing Governours: (for there is a parity of Reason in ordinary cases, though not in all). But the Antecedent is granted by our Parliaments, who sentence some as disabled to be members any more: Ergo, &c.

Argum. 4. That course which equalleth the worst with the best in the Priviledges of freemen, is not just: But so doth the equal admitting the innocent and the criminous to govern and choose Governours: Ergo &c. Vertue is better then wealth, & Vice worse then Poverty.

Argum. 5. That course that tendeth to the dishonour of Princes, Parliaments, or other Magistrates under them that are Elective, is not to be maintained. But such is the liberty of the criminous to Elect them: For nothing more natural then for freemen to choose such as are agreeable to their wills and wayes: and if they be not free, they should not choose. It will therefore raise suspitions on our Parliaments and Magistrates, that they are friends at least to wicked men and wayes, when they are ordinarily and freely chosen by such men: especially if it be by their own Laws and desires, that such shall be the Choosers.

Argum. 6. Those that are known enemies to the common good in the cheifist parts of it, are unmeet to Govern or choose Governours: (else give us up to our enemies, or to Satan:) But such are multitudes of ungodly vicious men. Ergo.

He that thinketh that wealth is the only common good, or a greater part of it then Vertue, Piety, and mens salvation; and that Rulers have nothing to do with the latter, but with mens Bodily prosperity only, is fitter to be a member of a Herd then a Republike, and to be dimitted with Nebuchadnezzar into a company suitable to his judgement: yea and to be used as a Traytor of the highest and most odious strain, that destroyeth and brutifieth the very office of every Prince and Magistrate, and casteth them into the dirt.

And that ungodly vicious men are Enemies to the greatest part of the common good directly, and to the rest indirectly, is known to every wise and sober honest man. 1. They hate Godliness, which is the truest Honesty; and Holiness, without which none shall see God: and therefore if they can, will choose such as hate it. 2. They hate good Laws, which would encourage the Piety and Vertue which they hate, and punish the Vices which they love. 3. They hate Good Magistrates, and therefore are unlike, if they be free, to choose them. 4. And they are all men of Private spirits, and value their private Interests before the Publike Good, and would sell the chief felicity of the Common-wealth for a little money, if they can scape themselves. 5. They are ready to betray the Common-wealth to a forraign enemy, in meer malignity, to have their wills: As the Papists that joyned with Stanley in 88. and the Powder-plotters after, and so in many Countries else. Are the Irish fit to govern or choose Governours? If not, and if experience forceth us to exclude the main body of the Natives there, we have reason to exclude such here as forfeit their Liberties. We do them neither wrong nor hurt, but preserve our selves from ruine, and them from greater guilt. To govern us, does them no good.

> Arg. 7. Such as God commanded to be put to death, or cut off from the Common-wealth of Israel, should not be Governours or Choosers of such, in any Christian Common-wealth (supposing an equality in guilt.) But such are many vicious ungodly persons among us. Therefore —

I speak not of them that broke some ceremonial abrogated Law, further then the Reason of the Law remaining may direct us to judge of crimes among our selves. But I speak of such as for the like facts are now as culpable as they. And in general I may lay this ground, that the more abundant light of the Gospel, and the greater helps and grace, and the greater Holiness now required, do all shew that the same sins (*cæteris paribus*) are much more haynous now then they were then. But because the point is fundamental, and all our peace lyeth much upon, I shall proceed to Instances.

> Thes. 161. A Blasphemer was to be put to death by the Law of God, and therefore should not Govern, or choose any Parliament men or Governours with us . . .

> Thes. 162. If any one, though a Prophet, or a Brother, or Son, or Daughter, or Wife, or dearest friend entised them to go after other Gods, and serve them, they were to be put to death, yea

and a whole City, if they yielded to such seducers: Therefore such should not Govern or choose Governours with us . . .

Thes. 163. He that sacrificed unto any God but the Lord only, was utterly to be destroyed, as is exprest, Exod. 22. 20. Therefore such should be no free men among Christians.

Thes. 164. The worshippers of such Images, as the molten Calf, Baal, &c. were to be put to death, Exod. 32. 26, 27, 28; 1 King. 18. 40; 2 King. 10. 21, 22. to 29; and 23. 15. 19, 20.

Thes. 165. They that would not seek the Lord God of Israel, were put to death, whether great or small, man or woman . . .

Thes. 166. He that smote or cursed his Father or Mother, should be put to death, Exod. 21. 15.

Thes. 167. He that forsaketh God, breaketh his Covenant, and worshippeth Sun, or Moon, or any of the host of Heaven which God hath not commanded, was to be stoned to death, Deut. 17. 2, 3, &c.

Thes. 168. Murderers, Manstealers, Incestuous persons, Sodomites, Adulterers, and in some cases Fornicatours, Wizzards, false Prophets, &c. were to be put to death, Exod. 21, Levit. 20, Deut 13.20. Yea and those that turn after Wizzards, Lev. 20.6. None such therefore should be freemen here.

Thes. 169. If a man had a stubborn and rebellious Son, that was a Glutton, Drunkard, or the like; and would not obey the voyce of his Father, or of his Mother, and that when they have chastened him, would not hearken to them, he was to be put to death. Read Deut. 21. 18, 19, 20, 21. Therefore such should not choose Parliament men, nor be Burgesses with us.

Thes. 170. The man that would do presumtuously, and would not hearken to the Priest, that standeth to Minister there before the Lord, or to the Judge, was to be put to death, Deut. 17. 12. Therefore presumptuous transgressours against the publike warning of Magistrates and Pastours should not be freemen of our Common-wealths. See also Deut. 29. 19, 20.

Thes. 171. Every one that defiled the Sabbath, and doth any work thereon, was to be put to death, and cut off from amongst his people. Exod. 31. 14, 15. Therefore though the Sabbath as Jewish be taken down; yet by parity of Reason, he that despiseth the publick worship of the Gospel, and the Lords Day, should be no Chooser of Rulers for the Common-wealth.

Thes. 172, Whether the utter cutting off the soul that did ought presumptuously, as a reproacher of the Lord, and a despiser of his word, (Numb. 15. 30, 31.) do not import that presumptuous reproachers of the Lord, and despisers of his word, should be no Burgesses with us; and whether the cutting off then threatned for Ceremonial uncleannesses (as Exod. 12. 15, 19, and 31. 14. and 30. 33, 38, Lev. 7. 20, 21, 25, 27, and 17.4 9. and 19 13, Num. 9. 13, and 19. 20.) import not, that notorious ungodly persons should not be freemen, where it can be avoided, I leave to prudent consideration.

In all these Collections I mention so great an inequality of punishment, that no adversary can modestly quarrel with my consequence. Cutting off, and putting to death is another kind of punishment then depriving men of the liberty of governing or choosing Governors, which addeth to their case, and diminisheth not their wealth, but it is a necessary means to the common peace and welfare. Those that Gods Law put to death, should be no Choosers of Maiors, Bayliffs, Parliament, &c. with us, especially when the sin is greater now. Those that would fetch the form of Government from the Israelites, above all men, can have no reason to contradict any of this.

I conclude therefore, that all that are fit to be subjects, are not fit to be Burgesses, and to govern or choose Governours, though they may keep their possessions, and be secured in them.

Thes. 173. If a people consent to his Government that procured his capacity, in point of strength, by wicked means, it followeth not that they consent to those means, or are guilty of his sin . . .

Thes. 174. If the Progenitors Consent to an established form of Government; and the way of succession, whether Hereditary, or by Elections of each Governour, their Consent obligeth their Progeny, so long, till either a mutual Consent of Governours and people again disoblige them, or the Rulers disoblige them by destroying the Form or End of the Government, or God by Providence disoblige them . . .

Thes. 175. Though a forced Consent be usually from the great sin of him that forceth it (yet not alwaies) it nevertheless obligeth the Consenters.

Deny this, and you overthrow all humane converse. For if men may go from their Covenants on this pretence, then on many the like, and the pretence will be common. Man is a free Agent, and his Will cannot properly be compelled: If you threaten him with death, he may suffer it: It is supposed therefore that whatever be promiseth, he freely promiseth. We use to say, a man is forced, when fear moveth him to consent: But this is not a proper force: It taketh not away the Liberty of the Will. He that consenteth, doth it to avoid some greater evil, which he thinks would else have befaln him; and it is his own Good that moveth him to it; 'He that sweareth to his own hart, and changeth not' is the person that is accepted of God, Psalm. 15.4. If every incommodity would warrant men to break Covenants, no man would trust each other, and Covenants would lose their force.

> Object. But Divines determine it, that if a Thief compel me to conceal him, I am not therefore to conceal him; therefore they think a forced Oath bindeth not.

Answ. 1. They truly judge that if you promise a Thief to bring him so much money such a day, to save your life, you are bound to perform it. I add, unless the case be such (which is possible) that to publick use the money is more worth then my life; and then as it was unlawful to promise, so it to perform: But what you may lawfully promise, you may and must perform. 2. If the concealing of the Thief will do more hurt to the Common wealth, and wrong to God, then the yielding up of my life, I may not promise it: and if I promise it, I may not perform it, because it is evil, and not in my power; But if it be otherwise, I may promise or perform it. So that it is not force that disobligeth a man from his Covenants.

> Thes. 176. The commonest way of Constituting forms of Government is by a forced consent, (as it is commonly called); when a Conquerour, or a person of greatest strength doth constrain the weaker to consent, to escape a greater mischief . . .

> Thes. 177. The true Fundamental Laws of every Commonwealth, are the Laws of God the Universal King . . .

> Thes. 178. The Constitution of Common-wealths by man, as to that modal difference of Governments, which is in their Power, is the effect of Contract. Explicite or Implicite, and not of Law.

So that there are no Humane Constitutive, Fundamental Laws . . .

Thes. 179. An Implicit Consent of the people may be obligatory, and prove the power to be such as is to be owned and obeyed.

If they that have the strength, do not resist and cast off their pretender, it is to be supposed to be because they do consent: For being not from disability to reject him, it is to be judged to be from unwillingness. And if there were some hazard of a battle in the way, yet they that consent to scape a danger, do yet consent: But it is not all silence and non-resistance that may be called 'an implicit consent'. A non-resistance forced by a Colonie or forreign Power, is no signification of consent. A non-resistance forced by Mercenary Natives that are souldiers, is no signification of consent. A non-resistance forced by Servants or others that are not Burgesses or Cives in the Common-wealth, is no signification of consent. A non-resistance forced by a Kindred or Faction, inconsiderable comparatively for interest or number, but that's strong by an accidental advantage, is no signification of consent. But yet it is not the consent of the whole people that is necessary; nor alwaies of a major part: Common wealths are not alwaies to follow a Major Popular Vote. Otherwise in most cases there would be much uncertainty, which way the Major Vote inclineth. And when most are worst, and of the weaker sort, the wiser and the better will think there is no Law that subjecteth them to a Vote that's carried by an inconsiderable part. If a people were without a Prince, and a Major Vote choose a person tolerable, but yet so weak and bad as might much hazzard the Common-wealth; and the wiser, stronger, but Minor part, do choose a wiser, better man, there appeareth no reason why the choice of the first only should be valid. (We are speaking all this while of the Constitution of a Common-wealth, where the way of Election is not yet Constituted by Agreement.) 1. The smaller number are oft of greater interest and Possession. An hundred Lords may have more to save or lose then a thousand Peasants. 2. Nature, saith the Philosopher, made the wise to Govern the unwise; that is, They are most apt: But the smaller number are oft the wiser. 3. And the smaller number is oft the better, and true to the common good. 4. And also they are oft the stronger. Ten thousand prudent valiant men, especially that are animated by the greatest interest, are usually too hard for twenty thousand silly

Peasants. And I see no Reason but the Part that is both Wisest, Best, and Strongest, should be accounted the People of that Nation. Nature valueth not parts by bulk or number, but by Worth and Use: One Heart, one Stomake, one Liver, is more to be regarded then ten toes or fingers.

Object. But who shall be Judge which part is Best, if once you forsake a Major Vote, when every part think themselves the best?

Answ. The Question is either of the *Jus* or *Factum*: Who Ought to Judge, or who will Judge? In a company that hath no Legal Judge the Wisest, though the Weakest, ought to Judge: For Natural Aptitude is there instead of Office, and the ignorant are obliged by God to regard his gifts in others, and to hearken to the Wise: And if the people refuse, that proveth not that they justly do refuse. But the strongest usually will Judge, though the wisest should Judge; and therefore Voting oft determineth it, because the most are supposed to be strongest, and to have most wit and Interest among them. But when it is not so, (as oft it is not) the Reason of the Voting Prevalency ceaseth (except in such cases where it is meerly for Unity and Concord) and no such stress is laid upon the Vote, but that the wise for Peace may safely yield to the unwise. When the Best by Prudence and advantage have the greatest strength, and by Valour over-top a greater number of the bad and foolish, I know not why they should give up their welfare to their Elections. In a Ship full of Mariners and Passengers that have lost their Pilot and Commanders, the valiant and skilful will be loth to commit their lives to the major vote of ignorant and cowardly men, that would deliver the Vessel to the enemy, or the Rocks, or Sands.

If in such a case (when there is no preobligation by Law or Contract) a Prince be chosen by the Minor Better part, (not Mercenary Souldiers, not a Faction animated by a private Interest, nor as before excepted) and that Part be strong enough by the advantage of their nobler Education, Prudence and Valour to enable him to Defend the Nation, and execute his Laws, against any opposition that the Rabble or rude Majority can make, I know not, (*cæteris paribus*) but that he hath a better Call, then if he had been called by the rest that were more in number.

When we speak of an Implicit Consent, complying with custom, we use an improper phrase, it being a Less-express Consent that is meant by it: For if it be in no degree expressed, it falls not under humane cognizance.

As we constantly determine against the Separatists, that such an Implicit Consent of the people, as is signified only by actual submission to Ministerial Offices, is all that is necessary (herein) to prove the Being of a Church: So the Reason will do as much and more as to the Common-wealth; the peoples Consent being more necessary in Church matters, then in the other, because Church Government is exercised only on Consenters. And as he may be a Pastor that hath but such an Implicit Consent; so may he be a Prince that hath no more. When the Body of the people submit to the Government in its exercise, seeking for Justice to the Officers of him that is in Possession, and actually obeying his administrations, it importeth *in foro exteriore* a Consent; at least for the avoiding of greater evil; and if this be stated or in the ordinary Current as Governours are obeyed, it sufficeth to satisfie particular persons that they are obliged to obey.

> Thes. 180. But if the Representative Body of a Nation, enabled thereto, shall expresly consent, and covenant with a Soveraign, the real Body submitting to the Government; and not by any common protestation disowning it; it is the fullest, most regular, obliging acknowledgement, to satisfie the particular Subjects of their duty, that ordinarily can be expected . . .

> Thes. 181. If a people that by Oath and Duty are obliged to a Soveraign, shall sinfully dispossess him, and contrary to their Covenants, choose and covenant with another; they may be obliged by their latter covenants, notwithstanding the former; and particular Subjects that consented not with them in the breaking of their former Covenants, may yet be obliged by occasion of their latter choice, to the person whom they choose.

1. As to themselves, if former violated Promises excuse men from latter, then might men by one sin be free from the incommodities of an hundred after; for such a man that hath broke a former promise, might make an hundred inconsistent ones afterward without being obliged by them: But no man is to have benefit by his crimes. The first Covenant and the second may be impossible to be both Performed. But yet its possible they may both oblige. A man by contrary Covenants and Vows may oblige himself to Impossibilities, though

he cannot perform them. He that makes an hundred covenants inconsistent with one another in the performance, sinneth as a Covenantbreaker in not performing all: though he should sin in other respects if he did perform many of them that are possible: Promises oblige whether just or unjust; But if they be unjust, they frequently cast men into a necessity of sinning; e.g. he that promiseth to give away an Orphans Portion committed to his Tutelage, sinneth if he do it, against the Law of fidelity and mercy; and he sinneth if he do it not as a Covenant-breaker. But when men have by contrary Covenants, cast themselves into such a Necessity of sinning, it may be a duty to choose the lesser sin, or rather to avoid the greater: And which that is, the circumstances of the Case must determine.

2. And as to others, it is most evident, that if I be innocent of the violation of a Covenant to a former Governour; then the peoples Engagement to a latter, may make him the just Governour, and so I may be obliged to obey him. Otherwise, 1. Few Princes on earth should be acknowledged, or people obliged to them. For the original of the succession of most or very many, was a consent that was forced from them by Power, when they were engaged to another by a former Consent. And if this obliged not the Consenters to obey the present Prince, it could not oblige their progeny, nor convey any Title to successive Princes. 2. If the latter Covenant bind the guilty, it may draw an obligation on the innocent, that have a necessity of abiding in the same Common-wealth. He that cannot quit the Commonwealth must obey the Powers that are sinfully chosen by others, as well as if they were lawfully chosen, it being not his sin.

That man that will conclude that the Peoples consent is necessary to the Princes Title, and that no consent of a people pre-engaged is valid, shall null the Title of most successive Governours (at least) on earth, and ravel the slate of most Common-wealths to their confusion, contrary to all Reason.

Nero and other Roman Emperours, that the Apostles and other ancient Teachers of the Church obeyed, and commanded others to obey (with that strictness as we find in Rom. 13.) were some of them chosen but after possession by a party, some but implicitly by that party; none of them more fully then such as I have here described; and few of them by a people that were not pre-engaged.

Thes. 182. When the freest people choose a Prince, they do not properly and efficiently give him his Power, as conveying it from them to him, but are only a *causa sine qua non*, and denominate or design the person that shall from God, and not from them receive it.

It is the groundless confounding principle of Levellers in the State, and (as Mr. Cawdrey notes)[19] of the Church-Levellers or Separatists, that Power of Government is originally in the people, and from and by them must be conveyed to the Rulers. An opinion against Nature and Scripture; against the very essence of a Republicke, that distinctly containeth Soveraign and Subjects. I have sufficiently confuted this before by many Arguments; and shewed that the people as such, have no Power of Government. And even now I shewed you, that we discern our Ruler by such a syllogism; That person who is most agreeable to the description, and so to the will of God, must be consented to as Soveraign: But this is that person. Ergo, &c. —

So that the Law leaveth nothing but the determining of the person here undone. And therefore the people certainly doing no more but to determine of the person, do convey no power, but only do that without which it will not be conveyed; some call them Instruments; properly they are not so much, though we need not contend about the Notion; when this Corporation choose their Bayliff, they give him not a jot of Power: They are but the *Causa sine qua non*: the Charter is the Instrumental cause; and the Soveraign is the principal efficient cause (under God.)

The people cannot give what they never received, nor had: But they never received nor had a power of Governing a Common-wealth, therefore they cannot give it. That is not contained in each mans self-governing power, I have before shewed. As when a man is chosen in marriage by a woman, she giveth him not the Power of an Husband, but only chooseth the person who shall from the Law of God receive it; so is it between Prince and people. God hath said in his Law, The Husband shall Rule the Wife; The woman only adds the Minor, This man shall be my Husband. So that she gives him not the Rule, but by choosing him to be the man, is *à Causa sine qua non*. And if she should agree with him not to Rule her, it were *ipso facto* null, as being against the Law that specifieth the Relations: which sheweth that she giveth him not the power; otherwise she might

---

[19] Daniel Cawdrey, *Independencie A Great Schism* (London, 1657), p. 190: 'an *Anabaptisticall Munster* principle, at the bottom'.

restrain it or limit it. Yet here is this difference from our present
case; that a woman may choose whether she will have a Husband or
none: but so cannot a man choose whether he will be a member of
a Common-wealth or not, except in some rare extraordinary case,
that befalleth not a man among many millions.

> Object. But a servant may give his Master power over him, and
> what degree he please; therefore a people may give a Prince
> power over them: And any man may oblige himself, and thereby
> give another power over him.

Answ. 1. The cases are much different. Government is founded in
the Law of Nature. Angels have such Order, that have no sin: But
servitude is a penal fruit of sin: and no man is to choose a punishment
to himself that may well avoid it: He that may be free, should choose
and keep his freedom. So that the Relation of a servant is such, that
a man may avoid if he can and will; and when he is necessitated to
submit to it, he may limit his Master in the governing of him as far
as he can and will in the matter of servitude: And therefore here is
a greater appearance (at least) of mans giving another the power over
him, then in Political Relations constituted by God himself: And yet
indeed, the matter here must more distinctly be considered. A servant
is considered partly as one obliged to Work for another, and partly
as the inferiour or subject in a family to be Governed by another in
order to the ends of Family Government, which is the good order of
the Family, for its own, and specially the Governors welfare, and the
Pleasing of God that hath appointed that Order. These two are oft
separated, and ever distinct: Some servants are but day-labourers
and no members of the Family, and some are members of it. Every
man having a certain Power of himself and his own Labours, may
alienate what he hath to another, and so by Contract sell his labour
to his Master. But as he is a member of a Family subject to a Master
in point of Morality, bound to obey him in points of duty to God and
man, of the first Table and second, and the due circumstantiating of
these duties, so the servants consent is no proper efficient cause or
giver of the Masters power, but only maketh himself the object of it:
So that it comes 'immediately' from God, as 'immediately' excludeth
an intervening second efficient cause, but not 'immediately' as the
word excludeth all kind of Means for determination of the Object,

without which the Power would not be in that person over that other person.

So in point of Political Government, if there be a Domination conjunct, and the subjects submit themselves to a servitude, that indeed may be their own self-resignation, disposal or selling themselves so far to another, which is when the Governours Benefit is the principal end: (For we are not born for him.) And therefore Tyrannie and Domination of Princes are penal to the subjects, and they may escape them if they can. But proper Political Government, that is exercised over meer subjects for the publick order and Good; and the pleasing of God by Governing Justice, is Gods own Ordinance, and the Power wholly flows from him as the universal Soveraign.

So that if it would hold true that from the self-interest and self-governing power that each individual hath by resigning all to one, he may efficiently be made a Prince or Ruler over them (which yet would be false, as I have shewed, if God were not supposed that way to convey the power, which he hath not done; Political Power being *totâ specie* distinct from that of self-interest, and self-Government) yet God hath left no room for this imagination and dispute, because he hath as universal King, himself instituted the Offices that shall be under him, leaving only the modifying and limiting of Circumstantials, and the determination of the persons to the will of man. And as it would be but a foolish or Trayterous arguing for a Corporation to say, 'Every man hath a self-propriety or interest, and a self Governing Power, which resigned to another maketh him a Governour by conveying the Power from us to him: therefore our Major or Bayliff whom we elect, doth thus receive his Authority from our gift or authorizing Act' (they having nothing left to them but the nomination of the man that shall receive the Authority from the Princes Law or Charter;) Even so it would be no better in any that should argue thus in the other case. If no superior Power had gone before them by his Laws, but a City were all free from Soveraignty, then indeed they might make to themselves a Prince, without the offending of any higher. And so if there were no God, (and yet man could be man) and if the world had no universal King, that had instituted offices under him by Law, and distinguished the world into Rulers and Subjects, then indeed the people might pretend to give the power as far as they have it to give, and be the Original of it: But when God hath given it already by a stated Law, to those that shall be lawfully nominated, the peoples claim comes in too late.

Thes. 183. As the Constitution of Common-wealths is only by Gods Laws, and mens fundamental Contracts, and not by any Fundamental Laws of men: So it followeth that it is only God by way of Authority, and the parties contracting by way of Consent, that can alter the Constitution or any part of it; and there is no Authority of man that can alter it.

1. That the Constitution is not by humane Fundamental Laws, but by Contracts between Prince and People (explicit or implicit) I shewed before; and its plain in the nature of the thing. If a meer Conquerour should say, 'I claim the Empire, and Command you as Subjects to acknowledge me' yet this were no Law, because proceeding from no Authority; and the peoples Acknowledgment, though forced by such words, would be but a forced Contract. So on the other side, if a people should make a pretended Law, that such a man or company of men shall Govern them it were indeed no Law, because from no Authority: For before the Constitution there is no Legislative Power, either in Prince or People: Not in the Prince, for he is then no Prince, not in the People, for they are then no Governours, and therefore no Legislators: What have they to do to command any man to command them, or Govern them against his will? He is as free by nature as they, and cannot justly be compelled; (much less by a Law when there are no Law-givers.)

2. It is a known Rule, that Obligations are dissolved as they are Contracted: And therefore from the way of Constitution the Thesis is plain, that nothing but Gods Authority, and mens Consent, can alter it. If it be altered by proper Law, then either by the Soveraign (whether Prince or Senate) or the Subjects: But neither by the Soveraign nor Subjects; therefore by no man. Not by the Soveraign; for 1. He is bound up by Covenant to the Constitution, and cannot by pretended Authority break his Covenants, but must stay till God or the people Contracted with, release him. 2. And his Legislation is a part of his Government, consequential to his Power, and so to the constitution in which he received it; and therefore hath nothing to do with that constitution, to destroy or alter it that is the cause of his power, and gives it life or is the means thereto. Else Princes when by the Constitution they are limited, might remove their bounds at pleasure. And if a Senate do it, it must be either as Rulers, or as

Subjects. As Rulers they cannot alter the Constitution: For if they be Inferiour Rulers, they have no Power but from the Soveraign. If they be the Soveraign, or (as in England) have part of the Soveraignty, then they have as was proved before, no power as such to do it, any more then a Soveraign King. And as subjects they have no Power to do it: For subjects have none such. 1. They had not Power by Law to Constitute the Government, nor by any force, but by Consent of him or them whom they chose to Rule them; therefore they have no other Power to dissolve it. 2. Subjects are bound to obey, and have as such no Legislative Power; therefore much less have they any to alter the Constitution by.

> Thes. 184. If Prince, Senate, or People alone (before God by certain providence have disobliged them, and dissolved the Government) shall of themselves without the Consent of the other part, dissolve or change the Constitution, they perfidiously destroy the Foundation, (if it be in the substantial points) and put themselves into a state of enmity with the other part.

But of this more, when we come to speak of the Dissolution of Common-wealths.

> Thes. 185. Yet may the first Constitution of a Common wealth be in many particulars changed by degrees, when Prince and People do Consent: But if those Consents shall be called by the name of Laws, thus far they are none indeed, but Contracts.

1. That Constitutions may be gradually and annually changed (possibly, but not fitly) is evident: Because as Consent of the chief Governour and people sufficed to the Constitution, so doth it suffice to the alteration. The same cause may produce the like effect; for here is no impediment. And therefore we need not in this Land go to the Original of the Common-wealth to know the Constitution: For wherever it is to be found that Prince and people have thus or thus Consented, so much of the Constitution is there found.

2. In a Law this change of the Constitution may be found: but it is not it self any part of a Law. A Parliament may have a double capacity: To be Soveraign (in whole, or part) and to be the Representatives of the people: They Represent the people, either simply as people, to preserve their Rights according to the Constitution; or else as subjects. A Representative of subjects, as such, have no Power of making Laws, nor by Contract altering the Constitution: A Repres-

entative of People, or a Community, as such, may have power to preserve their Rights, and by Contract to change the Constitution, but none to make Laws: A Parliament as Soveraign, have Power to make Laws, but none by a Law to alter the Constitution. But when the Parliament hath several capacities, their Instrument may accordingly have a various nature and use, and in part it may be a Contract with the Prince, themselves Representing the people, and so it may Gradually alter the Constitution; and in part it may be a Law imposed by the whole Soveraignty. And in the Instrument called a Law, alterations of the Government may be made by Consent of both parties.

> Thes. 186. If by later Consent between Prince and People, the ancient Constitution be changed, or any part of it, it is the last Consent alone that bindeth the Prince and Subjects as nulling the contrary former Contract; and it is perfidiousness to violate the last Consent, upon pretence of recurring to the first constitution.

If Lycurgus by the peoples consent shall settle a form of Government; and say in it, that it shall be unchangeable, this will not disable successive Princes and people by Consent to change it; seeing they have as much power to change it, as he and the people then had to establish it. But if the next age change it, it will be Treason in them that will go about to violate the new establisht Government, under pretence of sticking to the old.

> Thes. 187. The Constitution gives life to the Species of Government, when the individual Prince is dead, till that Constitution it self be altered.

Else there must be a new Common-wealth at the death of every Prince: and posterity should not be obliged by ancestors for their good.

> Thes. 188. Every man that is obliged to obey, is not obliged by his Obedience to Justifie the Title of the Ruler against all others, as the best; not alwaies to defend it by arms.

For there are many (if not most Princes on earth) that seeking Crowns by unjust means, or receiving them as so acquired, or being themselves unfit, &c. do want such a Title as may justifie them before

God; and yet have such a Title as is valid among men, and will require obedience from all the subjects.

Thes. 189. In doubtful cases, or where the subjects are not called to Judge, the possessor is to be obeyed . . .

CHAPTER 8

Of the best form of Government, and Happyest Common-wealth

At his first Creation man was subjected to none but God: though it was provided in Nature, that there should have been Government and Subjection though man had continued innocent: but that would have been only a Paternal assisting Government for our good, having nothing in it that is penal, or any way evil. When God immediately Ruled, and man obeyed, all went right: Had this continued, the world had not felt those fractures and wounds, nor been troubled with rapine, wars or confusion, as it is. God being most perfectly Wise and Just, could not err in Commanding: Man was innocent and able to obey, but free and mutable: and so was tempted from his Obedience. Satan by disobedience having overthrown himself, did know it was the way to overthrow man. God could not be corrupted, nor tempted to unwise or unrighteous Government: And if neither King nor subject were corrupted, the Kingdom could not have decayed. But Satan knew which was the weakest link in the chain: Man was frail, though holy; and not confirmed yet, though upright: and therefore defectable. The attempt of breaking his rank, and forsaking his due subjection, was the Devils fall: and by the same way he assaulted man, inciting in him a desire to be as God, and then provoking him to seek it by disobeying God: A foolish means to an impossible or impious end. The breach being thus made between man and his universal King, the joynts of holy order were loosed; and a breach was made also between man and himself, and man and the inferiour creatures, and enmity and confusion took possession in the world. The creatures Rebell against their Master turned Rebell: His own passions and appetite Rebell against his Reason: and the seeds of all the Confusions that have followed in the world, were sown within us. As the enmity between the womans and the Serpents seed being propagated to posterity, is the great quarrel of the world; so all those vices in which the Malignant enmity doth consist, are propagated and by custom receive an increase. The Root of them all is Selfishness, which much consisteth in Pride, still man would be as God. Every man would be Highest, and have the eyes of others set upon him, and be the Idol of the world. The sin that broak Order, is still at work to widen the breach. He that is a subject, would fain be in Authority; and he that is of a lower rank, is ambitious to be higher: and he that is in Soveraign Power with just limitations, doth hate restraint, and take it for imprisonment or subjection; and striveth till he hath broak all bonds, and hath no guide but his own understanding, and nothing to moderate his impotent will. So that in all Ages and Nations Subjects are still disposed to murmurings and rebellions, and Princes to transcend their bounds by Tyrannie: and all because we are all the aspiring brood of Adam, that was made little lower then the Angels, but fell to be too near the Devils, by desiring to become as God. If the advantage of Greatness, the gate of Temptation, or the warmth of Prosperity, do but heighten this ambition, and hatch it to maturity, men will be then the sons of the Coal, and as so many Granado's thrown by Satan among the people where they live, to enflame, and trouble, and confound the world: The worm of Ambition will restlesly crawl within their stomachs, and make them by a troublous stir to seek for honour as food to quiet it, and keep it from gnawing on their hearts: But this greedy worm is unsatiable, crying as the Hors-leech, Give, Give.

The cure of this mischief hath long busied the people and Politicians of the world: and yet it is uncured. Princes that have strength, do make some shift with much ado, by severity to restrain the Subject from Rebellion. But how to restrain the Prince from Tyrannie without disabling him from necessary Government, is much yet undiscovered, or the discoveries unpractised. The world hath had more Dionysius's and Nero's, then Davids, Solomons or Constantines. Rehoboam is no warning to them, but hath most Imitators, though with bad success. In most of the world, their doleful case doth tell us what their Government is; we see among them Tyrannie is Hereditary: and Princes live among their Subjects as the Pike among the smaller fishes; as if the people were made for them. They divide their Interest from their

Peoples; and live as if their peoples welfare were not theirs; but rather all that is taken from the Subject, is added unto them. The soul and body of most Common-wealths fall out; and the Head and Heart have such diseased obstructions and oppositions, as are their mutual torment, and the Prognosticks of their hastening dissolution: when the Ivie hath kill'd the tree that bore it, it must perish with it. And if they are first themselves dismounted, they seldom ever get into the saddle, and sit fast after it.

Some Nations have thought that the way to prevent this, was to be free; that is, to be Self-governours; and so when All governed, they found that none Governed, but Tyrannie and all Vice did raign in popular confusions: and there was neither peace nor safety to the whole or parts; No waves being greater then the Seas, nor any Tyrant so cruel as the many-headed Tyrant: and it being the surest way to be always miserable, to be Governed by them that are always naught, that is, by the multitude, in most parts of the world.

The sence of the mischief of Democracie hath made others think that the best way is to leave Kings to their wills, and let them use their Power arbitrarily: They think it costeth the world more to limit Princes then its worth: and that if they are absolute, their Interest will lead them to cherish their people: Or if they should grow cruel, God will protect us, and turn it to the best: 'A hundred sheep will flye from a little curre; and yet the Shepherd takes care that few of them are destroyed.' I could the easier digest this Doctrine, were it not for these Reasons. 1. The Heart of man is deceitful and desperately wicked; and what will it not do, if it may do what it will? 2. When men know that they are lyable to no Restraint, it will let loose their lusts, and make them worse. 3. We may not tempt them thus into a life of sin, to their own destruction. 4. Nor must we tempt God by pretending to trust him in a neglect of means. 5. It is against the light of Nature that one mans will should ruine a Nation. 6. If we may give away our Bodily welfare, yet not our souls. The Princes interest may lead him to have some regard to the Bodily welfare of the people, but he will not regard their souls. Greatness will have great temptations; And when there is no restraint, this will make the Greatest to be the worst. And the worst men are enclined to the worst opinions, and to be the greatest enemies to Piety and Honesty; and so would banish Christianity into corners, or from the earth. 7. If we might give away our own Interest, we may not so give away

Gods; nor encourage or suffer every deceived wicked Prince to do as the Infidel Princes do, and persecute Christianity out of their Dominions. 8. At least we may not be guilty of Treason against God, by consenting to an Idol, or Usurper that claimeth his prerogative, and pretendeth to an absolute unlimited Power, as if he were from under the Laws and Government of the Almighty: we must know no Power but whats from God; and therefore none against his undoubted Interest and Laws. As it is unlawful to submit to the Pope that thus usurpeth in the Church, so as unlawful to consent to any Anti-Gods usurpation in the Common-wealth. 9. And the experience of the world hath taught them to abhor unlimited Government, even as intolerable to the people: For though they should not destroy the whole people, yet at their pleasure their particular Subjects must be the fuel of their rage & lust. Every mans Estate, Wife or Daughter that they have a mind to, must be theirs; and their word must command the Heads of the best deserving Nobility to the block: And however the distant vulgar speed, those that are nearest them will be as Lambs before the Wolf. 10. And experience hath told the world, that there is many, and very many bad Kings for one good one throughout the world; and the wicked will do wickedly when they have no restraint. And therefore this were to deliver up the Kingdoms of the earth to Satan, who Ruleth by the wicked; when we have a promise that they shall be the Kingdoms of the Lord and of his Christ, that Ruleth especially by the holy and the just.

Others have thought it a hopeful way of Cure, to have the Government elective, and either *quam diu bene se gesserint*, or for a short continuance by Rotation. But these have found that the Remedy was insufficient. The Nations of the earth have but few men that are wise and good: and if those must Rule but a little while, the bad will succeed them: And if it must run through many, and so there be many bad Rulers for one good one, the bad ones will do more hurt then the good ones can do good. And it will be next impossible so to temper the Government, as that bad Rulers may have power to preserve the Common-wealth, and yet not have power to perpetuate themselves, and invade a perpetual Dictatorship with Cesar; For Armies they must have; and those that can get sufficient interest in them, may use them to their own ends. Some think that the wealthier peoples bearing Arms would prevent all this: for they would never serve a Tyrant against their Liberties. Much should be done I confess more then is, this way, to preserve the peoples Liberties: but yet the Remedy is inconsiderable. For 1. We must have our Armies abroad, and those will be the poor, and those will be mercenary, and return to serve their Commanders minds. 2. Flattering words will mislead them that are not mercenary. 3. Prosperity and Wealth doth effiminate men and make them cowardly. 4. Experience told us in our late Wars, that the trayn'd Bands were as ready, at least in most places, to follow the stronger side that was in place, as the poorer Volunteers were: For they thought they had somewhat more to lose then their younger sons or servants had; and therefore they would not venture to disobey the strongest.

Some think a Lot being a Divine decision, to be the only way to choose the Prince: which hath its place, but solveth not the difficulty without more ado. To use Lots among a company of bad or unjust men to find one good one, is a tempting God; and but like the casting a Net among Frogs to catch Fish. The materials must be first prepared, and the main secured.

In a word, many models have been devised, and most of them have their excellencies, and defects: Some of them secure the peoples wealth and liberty from a Tyrant, and lay them open to an invading enemy: Some of them free the people from oppression by a Prince, and leave them under a multitude of Oppressors: Some so secure Liberty as to introduce injustice and confusion: and certainly cast away the means of spiritual everlasting good, in order to preserve their temporal good. And most of them tread under foot the Government and Interest of the Universal King, and pretend the means against the end. They that can do most to mend the people, and secure us of good Rulers, and so to secure us in the main matters of Religion and Peace, are the best Politicians, though they leave us many inconveniences. And to that end he that could cull out the best of every Mode, and leave the worst, woold shew his Wisdom. Because I pretend not to such skil, nor intend any accurate Tract of Politicks, nor the discovery of an Utopia, or City of the Sun, nor intend to bestow that time and labour which is necessary to improve that little knowledge that I have, to any such ends; but only to urge upon the world the great Divine neglected Principles, that we may be secured of the main; I shall readily give place to any of their new devised Models that are consistent with these Principles; and leave them to beautifie the Common-wealth in their own wayes, if the Life of it may be secured by Gods way.

And yet I must say that for ought I see, the Government of this Common-wealth is already ballanced with as much prudence, caution, and equality, (though with less ado) as the curiousest of the Models that self-conceited men would obtrude with so much ostentation. Might we but see the Foundation of Parliaments Reformed, by an exclusion of truly Unworthy persons from the Elections (from choosing or being chosen) that so we were out of danger of having Impious Parliaments chosen by an impious Majority of the people, we should then build all the Fabrick of our Government on a Rock, that else will have a foundation of Sand: And a multitude of errours would be thus corrected at once, and more done for our Happiness then a thousand of the new Fantastical devices will accomplish. Of this having spoken before, I shall yet add somewhat more, to shew you how the Kingdoms of the world may be made the Kingdoms of the Lord, and of his Christ.

Thes. 190. The Happyest Common-wealth is that which most attaineth the Ends of Government and Society, which are the publick Good, especially in matters of everlasting concernment, and the pleasing of God the Absolute Lord and King of all . . .

Thes. 191. That Common-wealth is likely to be most Happy, which in the Constitution and Administration is fullyest suited to this Heavenly End; and therefore that is the best form of Government . . .

Thes. 192. The more Theocratical, or truly Divine any Government is, the better it is . . .

Thes. 193. A Government may be Theocratical (or Divine) 1. In the Constitution. 2. And the Administration, 1. In the Constitution, 1° As to the subjects; 2° The Relations and their Foundations; 3° And the Ends. 2. In the Administration; 1° As to the Officers; 2° Laws; 3° Judgement and Execution . . .

Thes. 194. 1. In a Divine Commonwealth, God the Universal King is the Soveraign; and none that Rule pretend to a Power that is not from him and subservient to him, nor do any else claim the honour of being the Original of Power . . .

Thes. 195. 2. In a Divine Common-wealth it is supposed that the subjects are all Gods subjects, not only by obligation (as every man is) but also by Consent . . .

Thes. 196. 3. In a Divine Common-wealth a Covenant between God and the people is the Foundation or necessary Condition: And all the free subjects are engaged first to God . . .

Thes. 197. 4. In a Divine-Common-wealth, the Prince or other humane Soveraign doth hold his Power as from God, and under him, and the people consent and subject themselves to him principally as Gods Officer . . .

Thes. 198. 5. In a Divine Common-wealth the Honour and Pleasing of God, and the salvation of the people are the Principal Ends, and their corporal welfare but subordinate to these . . .

Thes. 199. 6. Where the Gospel is published, Jesus Christ, our Lord and King, by the Title of Redemption, is also to be acknowledged by Prince and people, and taken in as the Beginning and End of the Common-wealth . . .

The Kingdom of Christ is proved before. If any man will but read the Scripture, he need no other confutation of Hobbs that from Scripture would prove that the Kingdom of Christ is only at his second coming, and not at present.

Thes. 200. In the Administration of a Divine Common-wealth, the Officers should be such as God will own; that is, men fearing God and working righteousness; men sober, righteous and godly, that by Faith & Love are subjected themselves to God their Creator and Redeemer . . .

Thes. 201. In the Administration of a Divine Common wealth, God must be allowed all that Causality in the choice of Individual Magistrates, which he condescendeth to; that is, 1. All the descriptions and Precepts of his Law must be observed. 2. Those that by his Gifts and Providence do answer his Law must be elected. 3. And to that end, those that he hath made capable only, should be Electors. 4. And that which cannot by these gifts be well discerned, if it be of moment, should be referred to a Lot . . .

Thes. 202. In a Divine Common-wealth the Laws of God, in Nature and Scripture, must be taken for the principal Laws,

which no Rulers can dispence with; and all their Laws must
be as by-law, subordinate to them for the promoting of their
execution . . .

Thes. 203. In a Divine Common-wealth, the sins against God
must be accounted the most hainous crimes; The denying or
blaspheming God, or his Essential Attributes or Soveraignty, is
to be judged the highest Treason; and the drawing men to other
Gods, and seeking the ruine of the Common wealth in spirituals,
is to be accounted the chiefest enmity to it . . .

Thes. 204. In a Divine Common-wealth, Holiness must have the
principal honour and encouragement, and a great difference be
made between the precious and the vile . . .

Thes. 205. By this it appeareth that in a true Theocracy, or
Divine Common wealth, the Matter of the Church and
Common-wealth should be altogether or almost the same,
though the form of them and administrations are different.

1. That the materials or subjects should be the same, appeareth
from what is said: They must all be such as enter the Covenant with
God, which in a Christian Common-wealth can be no other then the
Baptismal Covenant which entereth them into the Church; Circum-
cision entered them by the holy Covenant into Church and Common-
wealth, which among the Jews were materially the same. He that is
by the Covenant given up to God in Christ, is a member of Gods
Universal Church and Kingdom. Yea indeed the Universal Church,
and the Universal Kingdom in the strict sense, are both materially
and formally all one; though the particulars are not so. There are
three senses of Gods Universal Kingdom. 1. As the word signifieth
all that are obliged as subjects to obey him; and so all men, even
Rebels are members of his kingdom. 2. As it signifieth those that
obey him *secundum quid*, or analogically, but not simply and accept-
ably, (nor profess so much.) And so Turks and many Infidels that
worship God, but not by Christ, are in his Kingdom. 3. As it compre-
hendeth only faithful accepted subjects, and those that by profession
seem to be such: And thus his Kingdom, and his Church Universal
are all one formally.

2. But the reason why particular Churches and Commonwealths
are not formally the same, but distinct Politics, is because though the
Universal being United in One undivided Head is but One, as being

denominated from that Head, yet from unity proceedeth multiplicity: God doth not communicate all that Power in kind which is Eminently and Transcendently in himself to any one man, or sort of Officers; but distributeth to each their part; Civil Power to Civil Rulers, and Ecclesiastical to Church-Rulers. When we are once come down below God the fountain in our observation, we find a present Division of that Communicable Power into many hands, which floweth from the incommunicable Power that is in God alone. For man hath not Gods sufficiency to be all. The Popes flatterers may extol him as an Universal Vice-God, or Vice-Christ; but as Scripture tells us that he wants the Form, that is, the Authority: So Nature tells us that he wants the Aptitude and Capacity of matter. And therefore though the Universal Kingdom (in the strict sense) and the Universal Church are One, in One God, yet particular Kingdoms and Churches are diversified *in specie*, as shall anon be shewed.

When I say that the matter (ordinarily) should be the same, I mean not to tye the Governours of Church or State, to a necessary conformity of their administrations as to the matter, in taking in or casting out of members (save only in point of advantage and conveniency, to be mentioned in the next chapter.) For each sort of Governours have the charge of their own distinct administrations. It is not only possible, but too common, that one sort is much more careless and unfaithful to God and men then the other. If a good Magistrate have bad Pastours over the same people, and the Pastors will not difference between the precious and the vile, but will keep the impious and filthy in the Church, the Magistrate is not therefore bound to keep such as Free men in the Commonwealth, but must make it (as containing Free men) narrower then the Church. And if faithful Pastours live under a careless Prince that takes the filthyest and most impious as Cives, the Pastours must not do so in the Church; for they must be accountable to God for the discharge of their own trust.

But that which I mean, is, that the same Qualification maketh a man capable of being a member both of a Christian Church and Common-wealth, which is, his Covenant with God in Christ, or his Membership of the Universal Church, supposing the other circumstantials or accidental capacities which are indeed distinct.

Lastly, Note that I exclude not some just exceptions of ordinary or extraordinary Cases, in which the Members of one sort of Society may be excluded from the other. Persons that are through scruples (innocent or sinful) kept from joyning with a particular Church for a time, being yet capable of their Communion, may be yet members of the Common-wealth. Want of Riches may do more also to keep men out of Freedom in the Common-wealth, then out of the Church. And yet I think that in a Theocracie care should be taken to keep some members from swelling to excess, and others from extremity of want, as among the Israelites there was; yet so as no mans industry be discouraged, nor propriety invaded, nor idleness in any cherished. And Riches and Poverty should not make altogether so great a difference as they do in Prophane societies. If mens Poverty be not so great as to make them the servants of others, and deprive them of ingenuous Freedom, it should not deprive them of Civil Freedom: especially where Criminal and Civil cases have different Judges, they may have more Freedom about Criminals then Civils. Where wealth is concerned, men of wealth should have the power: but where Vertue or Vice, Honesty or Dishonesty is the matter of debate, the Honest though poor, should have more power than the Impious that are rich.

I conclude therefore that though variety of outward States, and the neglects of either Magistrate or Pastours, may be an exception to the Rule, yet as to inward qualifications, ordinarily the same persons are fit to be Members of Church and Common-wealth.

But as the Church hath only the members within, and yet the *Competentes*, and *Catechumens*, and in a more distant sort, the excommunicate, and the Neighbour Infidels, under her care, as owing them some help; so a Christian Common-wealth, though it own none as *Cives*, (or free subjects, commonly called Burgesses, or enfranchised persons) but such as are fit to be Church-members, yet hath it many that are meer subjects, and are to have the protection of the Laws for their lives and possessions, that are of a lower form.

And yet that Church and Common-wealth are not formally (nor *de facto* always, nor usually materially in a great part) the same societies, appeareth. 1. From the difference of Governours. Magistrates Rule the Common-wealth, and the Church as in the Common-wealth, but not the Church with that peculiar Government proper to it as a Church. And Ministers may Teach in the Common wealth, but as Pastours they Govern only the Church as such. 2. From the manner of Government and administrations. The Magistrate Ruleth imperiously, and by force, having power upon mens estates and persons:

But the Pastours have none such, but govern only by the Word of God explained and applyed to the Conscience. 3. From the nearest Foundation. The Common-wealth is constituted by a (virtual or actual) contract between the civil Soveraign and the People: But the Church (particular) is constituted, by a consent between the Pastours and the Flock. 4. From the extent. The Common-wealth containeth all the people in a whole Nation or more, as united in one Soveraign. But particular Churches (distinct from the universal united in Christ) have no general Ecclesiastical Officers in whom a Nation must unite as one Church; but as Corporations in one Kingdom; or as so many Schools, that have a peculiar form and Government; but such only as is under the Magistrates Government in its kind: or as several Colledges in one University. 5. From the accidental incapacities of men to be members of each. A Servant or Beggar is to be a free member of the Church, that is to be limited much more in his freedom in the Common-wealth. And a man that lives as a Carryer or Messenger, in constant travail from place to place, (specially if he have no home) is scarce capable of being a member of a particular Church, who yet may be a member of the Common-wealth. 6. From the Nearest end. Civil Order is the Nearest end of civil Polity: but Church Order, for holy Communion in Gods worship, is the Nearest end of Church Policy. So that formally they are divers, though materially, if Princes and Pastours would do their duties, in reformation and righteous Government, they would be if not altogether, yet for the most part the same, as consisting of the same persons.

> Thes. 206. It is this Theocratical Policy or Divine Common-wealth, which is the unquestionable reign of Christ on earth, which all Christians are agreed may be justly sought; and that temporal dignity of Saints, which undoubtedly would much bless the world.

Whether there be any other reign of Christ on earth to be expected, that is, by his visible personal abode (which I perceive some Papists of late very busy, under their several maskes, to indigitate, partly in order to perswade men that the Church is a Body that hath an Universal visible Head, which must be Christs Vicar, but in the interspace betwixt his first and second coming,) this controversie I do not now determine. For my own part, I reverence the Ancients that were of that mind, and many later that have followed them. I am myself as meerly Neutral in it as in almost any point of so great moment so often propounded to my consideration[20]: I oppose them not in the least, nor am I for them: Not from a carelessness or unwillingness to know the truth, but the difficulty of the case, and the weakness of my understanding. I live in hope of the coming and appearance of our Lord Jesus Christ, and pray that he may come quickly: But that he will after his coming raign Visibly on earth, and if so, in what manner, are things that I have read much of, but am uncertain after all, and scarce can perceive which way my judgement most inclineth.

But in the mean time, why should we not all conspire in our longings after that Raign of Christ, and Dignity of the Saints, and Reformation of the world, which is undoubtedly our duty, and which all agree about that have the fear of God?

If there be such a thing as a visible Raign of Christ here to be expected, he will surely elevate his servants in their Capacities of Soul and Body, as well as in their Dignity of Rule: And therefore we have little now to do but study, and wait, and pray for that Kingdom that is to come. For till we have the Capacity, we can have no exercise of that Dignity.

But in our present Capacity, I would fain know of them that talk of the Ruling of the world by the Saints, what more they can desire or expect in Reason than I here propound. 1. They cannot without factious uncharitableness and immodestly say, that it must be only the Saints of this or that party or Opinion, that shall subdue and Rule the rest: nor only the stronger sort that shall be dignified, excluding them that are babes and weak in the Faith. 2. Nor can they rationally dream that the most uncharitable (that is, in Christs sense, the most graceless sort) that can censure and condemn all others as no Saints, and appropriate holiness causlesly to themselves, should therefore have the Rule of others. If Charity Rules not, Christ Rules not. 3. Nor can they expect sure that all and only Saints shall be Princes, Judges, or other Magistrates: For then the World were worse an hundred fold then now. For now we have thousands of Saints that are Subjects; and then all the Subjects must be supposed wicked, and no Saints, and we must have no more Saints but enow to Rule: And if we had materially such wicked Common-wealths, it would

---

[20] On which see: William Lamont, *Puritanism and the English Revolution* (Gregg Revivals, London, 1991), vol. III, *Richard Baxter and the Millennium*, especially pp. 27–75.

bring the plagues of God upon us: And if Government of Saints do no more Good in the World but to leave all the Subjects wicked, it were liker Satans Government then Christs. It is certain therefore that it is not all, but some of the Saints that must be Governours; and so it is already; and that it may be much Better, and that secured to our Posterity, should be now our joint desire. And let us wait for the coming of Christ in his own way.

> Thes. 207. As there seldom ariseth any turbulent Opinion or party in the Church, but by the occasion of some neglect of Truth or Duty, which by their extremities God calleth us to reform: so I think the Promoting of this Holy Theocratical Government is the point of Reformation that we are called to desire, by them that now plead for the Raign of Christ and the Saints.

It is a special part of our wisdom to know what is our Health by our Diseases, and to learn Truth from the erroneous, and Duty from them that swerve into extreams. The Antinomians have called us to preach more the Dominion of Love, and the Riches of Grace, and divers other things: The Arminians have called us to take heed of a causeless narrowing of Grace in its extent, or of fathering our sins directly or indirectly upon God. The Anabaptists have called us to restore and practice Confirmation, and not take all into the number of Adult members that were baptized in Infancy, and never knew Christ nor a godly life. I could say the like of other Parties that have lately risen up. One sort runneth to them, and another part raileth at them; but he is the wise man that knoweth how to receive from them so much as is good, and leave the rest; could we duly improve them, we might have cause to thank God (though not them) that ever he permitted such occasions of our Reformation. So may I say in particular of the Millenaries: If we could by them be awakened to promote the unquestionable Raign of Christ, what a mercy would ensue?

> Thes. 208. It is no meer frame or mode of Government, whether Monarchy, Aristocraty, Democraty, or mixt, whether the Roman, Spartan, Venetian, or any other Mode, that will make happy a Common-wealth in the hands of imprudent, impious men, so much as one of the other forms; supposed worse, will do in the hands of men of prudence, and the fear of God.

A great stir is made by Mr. Harrington and other self-conceited Politicians for their several forms.[21] No contrivances are of much moment to our happiness, but those that secure us of a succession of good Governours. These particulars I shall here briefly manifest. 1. That their contrivances tend not to secure us of such a succession, nor a present faithful Government. 2. That imprudent and bad men in their contrived form will undo the people. 3. That prudent faithful men in other forms, are likely to be a blessing to the people.

1. That Hobbs his Leviathan, or way of absolute Impious Monarchy, making us, our Religion, &c. tendeth not to secure us of a Righteous Government, is a point that needeth no proof with any reasonable man; were it but because the irreligious Author pretendeth not to any such thing as the securing a succession of the Christian Religion, without which a Righteous Government is not to be expected.[22]

That Mr. Harringtons *Oceana*, and *Venetian Ballot*, have no such tendency, is plain. 1. In that it is such a Government as Heathens have been our Examples in, and in which he thinks they have excelled us, that he propoundeth. And therefore doubtless he intendeth not that his frame shall secure us the Christian Religion, without which we can have no happy Government.

2. And he professeth himself that his Common-wealth is most inconsistent with a Clergy: without which the Christian Religion never was maintained in any Nation upon earth. And Christ saith to his Ministers, whom he promised to be with to the end of the world, that he that despiseth them, despiseth him, Luke 10. 16. And as Christ never Ruled since his Ascension by his Officers, Word and Spirit; so he that purposely designeth the extirpation of his Officers, intendeth not his Raign, or at least promoteth it not. And he that is an enemy to the Raign of Christ, as he is the heir of wrath himself, Luke 19. 27, so would he make others, and therefore murder the Common-wealth.

---

[21] Here begins the *critique* of James Harrington's *Oceana* (London, 1656), the best modern text of which is to be found in: *The Political Works of James Harrington*, ed. J.G.A. Pocock (Cambridge, 1977), pp. 155–360.

[22] Baxter, ironically in the light of what would happen to his own work in 1683, agreed with the Master of Trinity College, Cambridge, in March 1652 that book-burning was the best response to Hobbes's *Leviathan* (London, 1651): (Doctor Williams's Library) *Baxter Correspondence*, vol. III, fol. 272v–273.

3. He thinketh Venice, where Popery Ruleth, and whoredom abounds, is the perfectest Pattern of Government for us, now existent: therefore he intendeth not sure that his Model should keep us from the Raign of Popery (or whoredom.) I doubt not but the same Model among better men, might do much against them: which doth but shew that it is not the Model, but the better men that must do most.

4. The whole scope of the design is by the Ballot and Rotation to secure us from the danger of a probability of being Ruled by Wise or Honest men, and put the business out of doubt, that strangers to Prudence, and enemies to Piety shall be our ordinary Rulers, and consequently Christianity be expelled. Can you doubt of this? 1. He knoweth not what Prudence and Piety are, or knoweth not England or mankind, that knoweth not that the Major part of the vulgar are scarcely Prudent and Pious men. 2. He knoweth not what Piety is, that knoweth not that Impious men abhor it; and he is not a Christian, that neither believeth the Prologue to the first Covenant of Grace; that saith, 'God will put enmity between the Womans and the Serpents seed', which the first born man shewed in killing his brother, because his own works were evil, and his brothers Righteous. 1 John 3.12. Nor yet believeth the words of Christ, that his 'servants will be hated of all men for his sake, because they are not of the world', & c. 3. And he knoweth not *Oceana* (Mr. Harringtons Common-wealth) that knoweth not that the ignorant and ungodly rabble are made the Lords and Rulers of all.

Go to the Foundation, and follow it up to the Head, and Judge. In his first Order, pag.58. in the distribution into freemen and servants, all are freemen that can live of themselves. 2. In his second Order, the younger sort are made the marching Army, and the Elder the Garrisons. 3. In the third, by their estates they are distributed into the Equestrian Order and the foot; only those that have prodigally spent their estates are excluded Suffrages and Government. 4. His fourth Order settleth the Parishes, Hundreds and Tribes. 5. His fifth Order begins with the Parish Ballot; where all above thirty years of age are to choose their Deputies by suffrage: when in most Parishes its too well known that the Major part are Ignorant men, and too many enemies to Piety, and many to common sobriety and Civility. In some Parishes you may go to five, if not ten families, before you meet with one that can so much as read (though I hope that is not the common case). And in abundance of them, the multitude are so educated, that beyond the matters of their Ploughs, and Carts, and Trades, they are scarce men, and can scarce speak sense. And of all men, the rabble hate both Magistrates and Ministers that would bring them up to Piety, and restrain them from a licentious sensual life. And of all their Neighbours, they most hate them that live an holy Heavenly life, and condemn them by their difference.

And *operari sequitur esse*; such as men are, so they will act; and such if they are freemen, they will choose: will they choose wise and Godly men that partly hate them, and partly know not the worth of Wisdom? Would they choose those Magistrates that they know would punish them, and whom they abhor for strictness, and for punishing Vice?

6. In his sixth Order, two parts in three in every Parish must be for the Minister: And how many Parishes be they where a bad man that will suit their humours, shall sooner have two parts, then a godly faithful Pastor? And pag. 65, He provideth that there be no excommunication to make a difference, but Heaven and Hell must be confounded; forsooth because that excommunication is not clearly proved out of Scripture to such capacities as his.

7. His seventh Order gives us Justices of Peace, Jury-men, Captains, &c. by these suffrages. And the choosers may tell us what kind of Justices and Captains they will be. 8. His eighth Order giveth us Horse and Foot-Captains by a Ballot, that its ten to one, know as well how to perform their trust as I know how to guide a ship that was never in one. And as wisely might our Parishes and their Deputies by the Major Vote elect us Pilots and Captains of ships out of stables, and barns, and Cow-houses, as thence elect us Land-Captains and Magistrates. So his ninth and tenth Orders carry on the same work, by giving us Magistrates out of Shops and Threshing-floores. They must elect us the Philarch, the Lord Lieutenant (perhaps my Lord Ale-seller, or my Lord Plow-jogger) the *Custos Rotulorum*, &c. The Philarch must keep the Quarter-Sessions, and hear causes in order to the protection of Liberty of Conscience, who partly know not what Conscience is, and partly hate nothing more then Conscience, though they love nothing more then Liberty. No Tribe may Petition a Parliament, unless the Philarch at the Councel frame the Petition, and propose it by clauses, unto the Ballot of the whole Tribe, &c. We are like then to have good Petitions, and comfortable relief from

Parliamants: When a pack of the rabble are got together, that lately had got the name of 'Damn-me's' that took him for a Puritane that spoak a sentence without 'God damn me' in it; and no man shall put up a Petition to the Parliament, but by their Counsel and proposal and Consent; then we have a perfect Common-wealth! Were it not for fear of abusing the name of God and Holiness, I would here by prediction, draw you up one of their Petitions; but I dare not so far defile my Paper, and the Readers eyes. I am ashamed and a weary to follow this gang any further, and shew you what Parliaments we must have, that being fetched from the Dung-cart to make us Laws, and from the Alehouse and the May-pole to dispose of our Religion, Lives and Estates, can scarce tell whether the Language of a rational Law be humane and intelligible; and if they read such a Law, they scarce know whether it be English, but better understand them that bleat and bellow, then they do these Law-terms. Or if there be a cunning Knave among them, its he that shall be the Prince and lead the rest. When I lately heard a description of the Irish, I was thinking how gallantly they would Rule or choose us Rulers by Vote, especially in Religion; when they know so much of Christ as to tell us that he is a better man then Saint Patrick; and so much of the Devil, as to call him Knave, and thats a great part of their Religion. And yet this is not all; but Mr. Harrington will give the people the supremacy and last resolution. Thats better of the two, then to give it to the Devil, or to worship the old Egyptian gods, an Ox or an Onion: Get all the Nobility and Gentry first to put it to the Countreys Vote, who shall be possessors of their Lands and Lordships: Or get all the learned and Wise men in Philosophy, Physick, Law, Theology, to put it to the Vote how these shall be regulated and used! The best use that we have in England for popular power of judging, is by Juries, that we think preserve our Liberties: And yet (I shall say again) I have thought of the excellency of a Democracie, when I have sat and heard a Learned Judge opening a hard case of Titles to the Jury, and they have stood by him all the while as if he had been talking Greek and Hebrew to them, and gone their way and brought in a Verdict for Plaintiff or Defendant at a venture, as it first came to their Tongues-ends, before they understood the cause any more then the man in the Moon; unless there were a crafty fellow among them, and then he ruled all the rest, and he had the day that had his voyce. Which when I saw, I thought it in such difficult cases almost as good to throw the Dice to decide the Controversie.

But Mr. Harrington doubts not but the people will be wise enough to choose the wise, and good enough to choose the good. As if we knew not what hard, and scornful, and censorious thoughts the vulgar have of Nobility, Learning, and all that is above them. What reproaches do we daily hear from them, not only against Divines, but against Lawyers, Physitians, Princes, and all whose waies they are unacquainted with? Many a time have I heard them say, 'It will never be a good world, while Knights and Gentlemen make us Laws, that are chosen for fear, and do but oppress us, and do not know the peoples sores: It will never be well with us till we have Parliaments of Country-men like our selves, that know our wants.' Nothing more natural, then that the propagation should be of the kind: and that sensual and ungodly men should choose such as themselves, and as will fit their ends: Especially being now exasperated by a war and some attempts of Reformation, they will be more virulent then heretofore, and nothing will satisfie them but the extirpation of those that have crost them, and would have reformed them.

It is easie to bring such on the stage in a dreaming Model, and put a golden Oration into their mouthes, and feign a fool more eloquent then Demosthenes: but when it comes to the execution (if the Nation be so distracted as to try) it will not be found so easie a matter to teach the Elected to speak sense: but the Senate and the Prerogative tribe must presently be put upon wielding the great affairs of Government, Civil and Religions, of Peace and War, which they are utterly ignorant of, as never being exercised in before. If these Polititians will scorn to be equalled in the reputation of their Learning with unstudied men that never took any pains to get it; (yea or to be matcht in point of Prudence by Divines that study its likely much more then themselves, if so be they have but read more of some parts of History or Politicks, though they are ignorant of the principal parts of solid learning;) why then should we equalize unskilful Rusticks that never studied Politicks a day, but are suddenly chosen from the Plough or Alehouse by the vulgar vote, with men that have studied and been trayned up to the skill of Governing, and been exercised in it? Surely if Mr. Harrington be so much a wiser man as he proclaims himself then the Clergy, as may warrant him to give it us as the suffrage of the Nations (pag. 223.) that 'An ounce of Wisdom is worth a pound of Clergie' and that 'Ministers of all others least understand Political Principles'; if all the Clergy, though they are men of the same Country and complexion with himself, and have studied many hours for his one, cannot yet come near the eminence of his wisdom, no nor attain to so much knowledge of Political Principles as all others have (in his account;) we must then expect to be Governed by a constant Miracle, or by constant folly, when men that never studied such things are made our Governours. Are Divines all such fools for all their studies? and will the Plough-mens Vote immediately give us a Senate and Prerogative tribe of wise men! wise in matters of highest moment, that they never heard of or medled with before.

And lest we should have any hope they should grow wiser by experience, the Rotation must turn them out before they well know where they are, and what it is they were Called to do; and from the Academy of the Shop or Alehouse, we must have freshmen in their rooms that are as wise as they were. What Ship was well Governed that was thus used in choice of Pilots? What Army was prosperous that was thus used in choice of Commanders? What School was well taught that was thus used in choice of School-masters? To have the ignorant and unexercised introduced, and then turned out before they can grow wise, to secure us against all possibility of remedy.

But though the National Religion and Conscience must be thus disposed of; yet Mr. Harrington and his Brethren (they know why) do haply secure us of liberty of conscience, and that of a sufficient latitude that 'No gathered Congregations be molested or interrupted in their way of worship, being neither Jewish nor Idolatrous, but vigilantly and vigorously protected, &c.' pag. 130. Popery had been before excepted, but that found place for repentance; and now Mr. H. and his fraternity have Liberty, either never to worship God at all (for that's supposed to be free) or to set up Deism, and worship God without a Saviour, or to set up Mahometanism, or cry down Christ and Christianity, or to make a worship of preaching up impiety and vice, and crying down the Scriptures and all true Worship. I will not talk of such low things as Liberty to preach down the Godhead or manhood of Christ, the Creation, the Resurrection and Life to come, and other Articles of the faith, by parts. But if he felt not some extream necessity of such Liberty, there need not this excessive care to secure it. What need all this ado for liberty of such Consciences, when the major Vote of the impious Rule, who will not only grant you Liberty, but extirpate those that for the defence of Christianity would deprive you of it?

> Argu. To exclude the heavenly treasures of vertue, piety and prudence, is an evil, which Government must be secured against, or it cannot be good.
>
> But Mr. H's government is not secured against it, (but certainly bindeth it upon us:)
>
> Therefore Mr. H's government cannot be good.

The Major is his own, page 10, saith he 'Sad complaints, that the Principles of Power and Authority, the goods of the mind and of fortune do not meet, and twine in the wreath or Crown of Empire! Wherefore if we have any thing of Piety or of Prudence, let us raise our selves out of the mire of private Interest, unto the contemplation of Vertue, and put an hand to the removal of this evil from under the Sun; this evil against which no Government that is not secured, can be good; this evil from which the Government that is secure must be perfect: Solomon tells us, that the cause of it is from the Ruler, from those principles of Power, which ballanced upon earthly trash, exclude the heavenly Treasures of Vertue, and that influence of it upon government, which is Authority. We have wandred the earth, to find out the balance of power; but to find out that of Authority, we must ascend nearer Heaven, or to the Image of God, or the soul of man.' Thus Mr. H.

Out of his own mouth are men invited to oppose his Policy, as they would do the Devil, or at least, the most destructive plague of a Common-wealth. It is not more certain that the earth doth bear us, then that the rabble vulgar multitude are for the greater part not only void of solid Piety and Prudence, and this Heavenly Treasure, but enemies to it: and that all men are byassed and Ruled by a private selfish spirit, till saving grace make God their Center, or common help do elevate one of many to prefer the common good before their own. Is his Common-wealth secure, yea perfect (as he saith it must be, if secure) from this selfish evil? Must we be Ruled by the rabble that (as I before said from the words of Augustine) had rather there were two Stars fewer in the Firmament, then one Cow less in their pastures, or one tree less in their hedges, and this to secure us from Private interest, and the exclusion of the heavenly Treasure? Let us then go to a Brothel-house for a pattern of Chastity, or to Mr. H. for a pattern of Humility.

> Argu. 2. That Government is next to Hell, that ascertaineth us of a constant succession of impious enemies of heavenly vertue in chief Power. But such is Mr. H's Government, that giveth the Major Vote the power, and calleth ignorant men to places of highest trust, and greatest work; and is inconsistent with a Clergy; therefore, &c.

> Argu. 3. A people, saith Machiavel, that is corrupt, is not capable of a Common-wealth. (They are Mr. Harringtons words, pag. 45) But the Major Vote of almost all Nations are corrupt; therefore they are uncapable of a Common wealth.

> I know Mr. Harrington is here involved (as he speaks) by Machiavel. No wonder. But if Machiavel be become a Puritan to him, what is Mr. Harrington to us?

> But perhaps some will say, 'Was not David a Shepherd, and yet a person meet to be a King?'

Answ. 1. It seems then there is an Instance of a worthy King that was taken from a Sheepfold: But to have many hundred persons so prepared for Government, is not ordinarily to be expected. Amos a Prophet, was called from the herd: but argue not thence if you love the reputation of your reason; that the major Vote of our Herdsmen should judge the spirits of the Prophets, or be accounted Prophets as well as he.

2. God can fetch a Ruler from a Sheepfold: but the vulgar Rabble are not so good choosers as God is: At least not so much better then God, as to choose five hundred good ones for one that God did choose.

3. But its well known that in those dayes, when Countries lay open, and mens treasure lay in Cattle rather then in Gold, that Herdsmen and Shepherds were the greatest men, and fittest for Riches to be Princes.

> Object. But do not our common people choose good Parliaments by a Major Vote, &c.

Answ. 1. Mr. Harringtons Model hath not yet made them Independants; and therefore they ordinarily choose such as their Landlords do desire them to choose; and therefore it will go according to the quality of the Landlords, and not according to the quality of the people. 2. Formerly when the peoples Liberties were encroacht on, and no divisions made in the Land among the Gentry, they were all ready to joyn for the common liberty, with some more unanimity then now. But now by the late wars they are divided, and one part think themselves oppressed, and the attempts of Reformation have irritated the sensual gang; there wants nothing but Liberty, to tread these Reformers in the dirt. Let Mr. H. and his party get down the Army, and take off all the late restraints, and let Parliaments be chosen by unrestrained Votes, and that party that hath most tenants, and that is most against Puritans, that will carry it. 3. And even before the divisions and exasperations, the divided Parliament and the war ensuing, and Major part of the Nobility and Gentry adhering to the King, (who by a minor part were conquered) did shew us what a Vote would have done. So much to Mr. H.

2. Having shewed that these new Models secure us not of a Righteous Government, (though there is much good interwoven, which by righteous Governors might be made good use of,) I should next shew that the Imprudent and Evil will not be hindred by these Forms, from undoing the Common-wealth. And for that, what need I more, then, 1. That men at liberty will rule according to their dispositions? An evil tree bringeth not forth good fruit. Men gather not grapes of thorns, nor figgs of thistles. Folly will not do the works of Wisdom, nor Impiety cherish Godliness which it hateth. Why else do not Heathens, Turks and all Infidels set up Christianity, but because they are against it? And as much are ungodly sensual men, though called Christians, against true Piety. 2. What is there to hinder them? Is it Laws, who made them? It is they themselves that are the Law-givers. Whether it be a Monarchie, Aristocracie, or Democracie, the Soveraign is the Law-giver. They are also the Judges of the Law, having none above them: So that in making, repealing and executing Laws, what mischief may they not do, especially which the sensual multitude can but bear?

Name us that Common-wealth on earth that is piously Ruled by impious Rulers, and Prudently Ruled by fools, whatever the Model of Government may be.

And to what use are all their Models, if not to secure us of good and righteous Governours? Is it any better to be impiously and unrighteously Governed by a thousand then by one? If therefore it secure not this, but rather certainly destroy it, their Model is poor relief or comfort to an oppressed undone people.

3. The next part of my task here is to shew you, that in every Form, whether Monarchy, Aristocracie, or Democratie, wise and pious righteous Governors will make the Government a blessing to the people. For, 1. They will act according to their Principles: But the Principles of all wise and pious men, do lead them to prefer God and the Common Good, before any private interest of their own; therefore, &c. 2. They will act according to their Dispositions: But honesty and wisdom disposes them to prefer God and the common good, &c. 3. Governors will Rule according to the attraction of their Ultimate End. But every wise and honest man doth make God his Ultimate End, (and the nearer End the Common Good.)

Holiness is a new Nature: and therefore a constant Monitor and mover unto Good. They that Love God and Vertue, and hate all evil, will Rule accordingly.

Its true, they are imperfect, and have their faults: but that which is predominant in their hearts, will be predominant in their Government.

Thes. 209. From hence the common Question may be resolved, Whether it be better to be Ruled by good Laws and bad Governors, or by good Governors and bad Laws? Answ. It is as if you should ask, Is it better be warmed by cold snow, or cooled by the fire? Laws are nothing but acts of Government; effects and significations of the Governours will concerning what shall be the subjects Duty. Laws antecedent to the Soveraigns will, are affects before the cause. Good Rulers will make & continue good Laws, and bad ones the contrary. All the world have good Laws already made them by God: But if you will needs suppose a separation, I say, that Good Laws with bad Rulers will do little good, but restrain a little of their evil: But if the inferior Magistrates only be bad, the Good Rulers and Laws that are over them may force them to do good ...

CHAPTER 9

How a Commonwealth may be reduced to this Theocratical temper, if it have advantages, and the Rulers and People are willing

Thes. 210. As it should be the desire of all good men, that the Common-wealth might be happy in the enjoyment of the Gospel and Peace, and this secured to posterity, so the open way to attain these ends, consisteth in these following Rules of practice.

R. I. That the Ministers of Christ that are to teach and guide the people by the Word of God, be generally able, judicious, godly, faithful, diligent men.

We cannot expect the people to be good, if the Teachers be bad, unable, or negligent. It is Gods Word that's managed by them, that must reform the people, and work out their vice. As mens Laws suppose the Laws of God, and mens Government presupposeth Gods Government; so the true methodical obedience to mens Laws, presupposeth obedience to Gods Laws, and consequently some understanding of them; and a right subjection to man presupposeth subjection to God. The first work therefore being the Ministers, the true reformation of the Ministry, making them indeed Divine, is the first thing to the making a Common wealth Divine.

Much hath been done already to this of late in this Nation, through the blessing of God: (although much is yet to be done, especially for ripening the Ministry in Judgement and Charity, & bringing them to neerest Unity, which time must do.) And the principal hopes that we have in this Land of a faithful successive Election of Parliaments, from any thing that is yet before us, is the happy success of the Ministry upon the Souls of many, by which the people being much reformed (though yet too little) are more enclined to prudent pious men to be their Governours in Parliament, then they have been heretofore. So that this hath made a hopeful beginning, and if it be carryed on, will do much more.

This is not unknown to the Enemies of Christianity, or to the Papists, that all conspire against the Ministry, as knowing that to make them odious, and their labours vain, or get them down, is the likelyest way to attain their ends.

Let these enemies note, that I am not here pleading for Lordly greatness, nor Riches to the Ministry, nor an aliene Power in State affairs, or any coercive Power at all: (and would they have a Clergie lower?) but only that they may be Learned, Judicious, Godly, Able, faithful men, provided with their daily bread, or food and rayment: And can they for shame oppose this?

> Thes. 211. Rul. II. Above all let there be a fixed Law for the due Regulation of the Electours and Elections of Parliaments.

The true Reformation must here begin; and if the Foundation be well laid in the people, the building will be firm and safe.

And here let me presume to speak a few words of the Necessity, and of the Utility of this course, and then, How it should be done.

1. It is known that Parliaments *qua tales*, are not Divine, Religious, Protestant or just. The six Articles by which the Martyrs were burnt, were made by a Parliament. All the Laws for the Papal interest in the dayes of Popery have been made by them. They have often followed the wills of Princes to and fro. And therefore they are not indefectible, nor immutable as such.

2. It is known that there are Members of various minds in them all, and sometime the miscarrying party is so strong, that by a few more voices they might bring misery on the Common-wealth.

3. It is well known that in most parts, the Major Vote of the Vulgar that are Choosers are Ignorant, selfish, of private Spirits, ruled by mony; and therefore by their Land-lords, and other great and powerful men; and withal they are bitterly distasted against the serious diligent practice of Religion, according to the Rules of Christ.

4. It is therefore apparent that if they had their Liberty, they would choose such as are of their minds; and it was by providence and accident that heretofore they did not so.

5. And it is certain, that the wars, the change of Church government and forms of worship, the differences of Religious men, and the many Sects that have lately risen up among us, and the strict

Laws of Parliament about the Lords day, &c. and specially their Taxes, have deeply discontented them and exasperated them against such as they think have caused these, so that many would now purposely design their ruin.

6. It is known that in the late Elections, the exclusion of Delinquents, and the Countenance of the times made terrible by many late successes against all sorts of enemies, and the present existence of the Army that hath so prevailed, hath been their restraint, so that they durst not go according to their inclinations.

7. It is known that the restrained Gentry, with those that are enemies to serious holy living according to the Christian Rules, are in most places strongest in popular Interest; having most Tenants, and most of the affections of the vulgar: And that they can this day, were they but as free from fear of sufferings as others, bring more voyces into the field in most places then any others can: And that even many well meaning honest men are of cowardly Spirits, and dare not displease their Landlords or great Neighbours, but will vote with the stronger side.

8. And its known that the Leaders never less wanted will upon the grounds fore-mentioned.

And what followeth upon all this, but either still to keep an Army over them (which should not be) or to Regulate the Election, is necessary to save us from ruine by a Parliament? For what probability is there but the next that is chosen by such a Majority of Votes with absolute freedom, will undo all that hath been done, and be revenged to the full on all that were so odious to them, and settle our calamity by Law? The effect lyeth so obvious to a discerning eye, (and almost to all) in the Moral Causes, that we may reckon it as done already, if not prevented.

But could a Prudent course be taken now for the Regulating of future Elections, we should have a moral security of good Parliaments to all Generations, who would make good Laws, and see to the execution, and be under God, the sum of Blessings for the Common-good; We should have Parliaments of the wisest and most pious men; and such as are least for private Interest, but would devote themselves to God and to their Countrey; The Parliament would be the Princes Interest; so that he neither would nor could divide from them. And they would be the peoples Interest, so that they could not disown them, but would lift them up in their esteem, and set them with the first in their daily prayers and praises unto God. And Parliaments would be more Honourable, when they were more Divine, and chosen only by vertuous men, and not by prophane debauched persons. In a word, Piety and Peace were more likely to be secured to Posterity, certainly, easily, and honestly this way then any way.

And then the effecting of it will be an Actual most excellent Reformation of the Common-wealth it self; and the Regulating Laws, excluding the vicious, would engage the people against Vice, and so conduce to their salvation.

> Thes. 212. The Regulating Law must contain 1. the description of the Electors by their necessary Qualifications; and 2. a course for Legal discerning the Qualified from the Unqualified; and 3. a Regulation of the Manner of Elections . . .

> Thes. 213. 1. For the due Qualification of Members, let so much of Gods own Laws be owned, as is still undoubtedly in force . . .

> Thes. 214. The Moral Qualifications of Electors must be this, that no man choose but those that have publikely owned the Baptismal Covenant, personally, deliberately and seriously, taking the Lord for their only God, even the Father, Son and Holy Ghost, the Creator, Redeemer and Sanctifier; and that lyeth not under the guilt of any of those sins for which God would have men put to death, or cut off from his people . . .

> Thes. 215. For what crimes God would have men cut off, I have shewed before, cap. 7. viz. For Blasphemy, Idolatry, perswading to Idolatry, Murder, Manstealing, Incest, Sodomy, Adultery, presumptuous sinning, and obstinate refusing to obey Magistrate, Priest, or Parent, in case of Gluttony, Drunkenness, and the like: and all such as would not seek the Lord: all wizzards, and that turn after wizzards, and more such like, which may easily be collected.

> Thes. 216. It will be a fair and expeditious course, that all these crimes enumerated by the Parliament, for which they allow Pastors to excommunicate men, shall also disable any person from choosing any Parliament-man or Magistrate . . .

> Thes. 217. At least it cannot be denied us, but that those crimes enumerated in the late Humble Petition and Advice, disabling men to sit in Parliament, should also disable the people to Elect . . .

Thes. 218. As no man was to live a member of the Common-
wealth of Israel that entered not into the Covenant of God, and
submitted not to his worship, under the Ministration of the
Priests (though they might have faults) but he that would not
seek the Lord God of Israel was to be put to death, be he great
or small, 2 Chron. 15.11, 12, 13. So no man should be so free
in our Common-wealth as to be choosers of our Parliament-men
or Magistrates, that live not in Christian Order and communion,
for the ordinary worshipping of God, and under the Discipline
or Guidance of some faithful Pastors, (where such are) either
Approved or Tolerated by the Magistrate.

To be an ordinary despiser of Gods publike worship, or a neglecter
of it, and of the Guidance of Gods Ministers, was Death or cutting
off in the Jewish times: And no man can tell us why it should not be
at least a cause of disfranchizing now. A man by disfranchizing is not
a penny the poorer, but only kept from hurting the Common-wealth.
And its a hard case, if we must commit our lives and Religion to the
Votes or Government of them that God would have had then cut off,
and put to Death! Let men have liberty freely in all lesser doubtful
things that good and sober Christians differ about: and if they be
Impious or Infidels, (unless by particular crimes they incur any
penalty) I urge not the Magistrate now to deprive them of their
Estates or personal Liberties: But let them have nothing to do with
Governing us. A man would think this should be a fair and moderate
motion: It is not an Anabaptist, nor an Independent, nor any upon
such kind of differences that I am motioning an exclusion of: But
those that are Members of no Approved nor Tolerated Church. And
there is great Reason. For 1. They Live like Atheists and Infidels,
and therefore they may be numbred, if not with such, yet with them
that are near them. Faith is practical, and tendeth to holy living and
obeying. He that refuseth to give God his publike Worship, and so
denyeth him the chief part of his homage, is an Atheist in life. 2.
There were no Christians in the Apostles dayes that had a fixed
abode, that were not members of the Christian Churches in the
places where they lived: and those that were unruly and walked disor-
derly, were to be avoided and cast out. 3. If they believe not that
God is to be worshipped publikely by his servants, and would perswade others against all publike worship, they are not fit to live among
men; therefore if they themselves forsake it, they are unfit for to

149

meddle with onr Government. 4 He is not ordinarily fit to choose a Governour, that as to his Morals is not capable of Governing (allowing a gradual difference.) But the neglecters of all Church-order, and Communion, and Discipline, are unfit to Govern: for they would destroy Christs Interest in the world: therefore they are unfit to choose. 5. If it be because they know not of a true Church to joyn with, its a sign they doubt of the Head when they doubt of the body, and know not that Christ indeed is King, that know not his Kingdom: Or else are justly to be suspected for Romish Juglers, whose design is to take down all, that they may set up themselves. 6. However it be, they that excommunicate themselves from Christian Churches, can blame none but themselves for it, and have no reason to expect to be taken for Rulers or choosers in a Christian Common-wealth. 7. He that refused all publike Worship under the Priests, would not have been judged to seek the Lord, nor be one of their Common-wealth. 8. God hath no ordinary publike worship but by his Ministers; and therefore to live under the Guidance of no Pastor, is to reject the stated way of worship; nor can he (ordinarily) be numbred with the flock of Christ, that is under no particular Shepherd. Every one therefore should be a member of some Church.

Thes. 219. For the execution of this Law, there should be careful provision, which being a Modal thing, I shall not presume to say so much of, but leave to the wisdom of Governours: only I see before us 1. An imperfect uneffectual way, which is by convincing men for these crimes before some Justice. 2. An effectual Regular more excellent way, which is this: Let all Pastors in England that are approved have an Instrument of Approbation, and all that are Tolerated an Instrument of Toleration; and let no man be a chooser or a Ruler that holdeth not communion with an Approved or Tolerated Church, and is not signified under the Pastors hand to be a member thereof: or that shall be cast out of the Church for any of those crimes that the Parliament shall enumerate: And that there may be no jealousie of Ministers usurpations or abuses herein, let every Parish have one or two of the wisest men by the superiour Rulers made Church-Justices, or Censors to meet with the Church Officers, and to take cognizence of the cause: And let all that the Pastors and Church take in or cast out according to Gods Word, be used by them as members or no members of the Church; But let no man be disfranchised in the Common-wealth, or lose his Vote in Elections, unless the Censor or Church-Justice Ruled by the Parliaments Laws, consent to the censure. And let all that are cast out by his consent and the Churches both, be registred, and disabled to Vote, unless by the consent of both upon Repentance they be restored.

This course is equal: For it is not meet that Ministers should be the disposers of the Liberties of the Common-wealth, nor will it help but hinder their Ministry that they should mix it with any secular Power; and though the penalty were but consequential, it would be inconvenient for them to use that Power. And yet on the other side, it is not Parliament Orders any further then as they are subordinate to Gods Laws, that they must Guide the Church by. Now in this way the disfranchized person hath no more trouble through the Minister then if he had nothing to do in it, but some more ease and benefit: For if the Censors alone should judge him criminous, he would have no benefit by the Churches more favourable Judgement, in case the Censors should be too rigid: Or if they should bear any man a Grudge, it is unmeet they should disable him alone: And therefore when the Judgement of the Church and of the Censors must concur to any mans Conviction, he will be further from the danger of any injury: The Church shall have no power to convict him with Relation to his civil Liberty; but only the Censors shall not do it without their consent, that his Liberty may be the better secured.

If you think that this power of Church and Censors is too great to be exercised over Justices of Peace, or persons of greater place: I answer, 1. Where ever there are Justices of Peace, it is supposed that they be themselves the Censors; and therefore that fear is vain: And for Riches, they should priviledge no man in impiety. 2. You may leave your Greater men (if you will be partial) to some higher Judgement, or leave them the Liberty of an Appeal.

Of the Office of these Censors I shall speak more under the last Rule.

Quest. But what shall be done in the Tolerated Churches? Answ. As you please, either let them also cast out none from his Common wealths Priviledges without the consent of the Censors of that Parish; or rather let them alone to do with their own members as they list in this respect; Because 1. They will be so eager to keep their strength and number, that they will dispriviledge none of their own, with-out great cause. 2. And if they do, it is usually best of all; for it will drive them to the approved Churches.

Quest. But what if Ministers will not admit of worthy persons into their Churches? Shall they therefore want their civil Priviledges? Answ. 1. If Ministers grosly miscarry in their Office, the Magistrate hath power to punish them, or cast them out; and what would you have more? 2. If one Church will not receive them, another will, either Approved or Tolerated. 3. If all this will not serve, let your Censors in this also have the Judgement, or a Negative voyce. Let the Qualifications already given by the Parliament concerning those that are to be debarred from the Lord's Supper for Ignorance or scandal, be the Censors Rule (with what else they think meet to add) and if any man publikely offer himself to be a member of the Approved Church of that Parish where he liveth, and be refused, if the Censor Judge the Refusal injurious (according to the Parliaments Rules) let it not injure him in his civil Liberties, but let him be Registred *inter Cives*; Though I think this caution should be unnecessary, because the Ministers themselves are under your Power. But it is only men that are utterly uncapable of Church communion, or that wilfully refuse it, that we desire may be no Choosers or *Cives* (though Subjects still.)

Quest. But what if your Pastors will neglect Discipline, and let in the most scandalous men; will not the Common-wealth be polluted and hazarded by their negligence? Answ. 1. It can be no worse for that, then it is; and therefore thats no reason against the thing. 2. I confess there lyeth the greatest danger; And therefore Parliaments should not by any causeless jealousies of Ministers doing overmuch, restrain, disable or discourage them from that duty which flesh and blood is most against of all their work; But let the wilful neglect of Discipline (and if you will, excessive rigour too) be punishable according to the quality of the offence. And let there be a Court of Commissioners in every County (those that are for ejecting scandalous Ministers) empowred thereunto; For Ejection should not be the punishment of smaller faults, especially before obstinacy; nor yet should such faults be unpunished; But of this more anon. But that here the Censor should have power alone to deprive him of his civil Liberty (as we grant him alone to preserve it) will be injurious to mens Rights.

Thes. 220. The third part of the Law for Regulating Elections, concerneth the Manner of Electing, where variety of tolerable Modes occurring, I shall not presume to extol any one above the rest, there being no such necessity of any one Mode as the self-conceited Modellers imagine. 1. The *Cives* that are in the Censors Register may meet in every Parish Church, and before the Censors, Ministers, Constables, Church-Wardens, and Overseers of the poor (sworn all to fidelity) may give their Votes for Parliament-men, which these Officers may carry in at a General meeting to the High Sheriffe. 2. Or these *Cives* in the same place and manner, may choose their Deputies (proportioned to the number of the people in all Parishes) which Deputies may at the General meeting (to avoid confusion) choose the Parliament men (being themselves first sworn to a faithful choyce). And these Elections in the Parishes, and the County meeetings may be either by Vote or Ballot.

The confusion that is now at Elections, is very great; and without abundance of cost to the Countrey or the Elected Gentlemen, so great a multitude cannot be brought to the Pole; which if they be not the uncapable rout may intrude and carry it. And therefore for every Parish or Hundred, either to send in their written Votes by Officers, or rather to send their sworn Deputies with power to Vote in their stead, will more orderly dispatch the work, and with much less charge and trouble. Every Deputy may bring in a list of the names which he representeth; and so he that representeth a Parish of an hundred men, shall have the voices of an hundred; and he or they that represent a Parish of a thousand men, shall have the voices of as many.

Where there is danger lest the Greatness of any over-awe the people from their liberties, the Ballot is somewhat the safer way then the open Vote; and yet not much; both because Juglers by slight of hand might convey in five for one; and specially because those great men will beforehand be engaging the people to Promise them their suffrages, and they dare not deny the Promise, if they are such as dare not deny them their Vote; And yet in all these things indifferent, we would not stick to gratifie Mr. Harrington, or any rational Modeller that can get the Parliaments consent. But 1. We must have our *Cives*, the matter of our Republick first reformed. 2. And we would have no more change then needs must, but things done with as little stir as may be, about circumstantials; and not have the Venetian painted dress and toyish gawds, to cover a defiled people; nor with a great deal of cost, and labour, and pomp, to set up an adorned Image . . .

> Thes. 221. Though solicitations cannot be prevented, yet that liberty of Votes may be preserved, let the Regulating Law deprive all men of their Votes in that Election, that are proved to have Promised them to any man before the meeting . . .

> Thes. 222. Rul. III. To make the Common-wealth more Divine, our Parliaments themselves must be more Divine: which must be effected by Description, and by Oath; which are both so happily Ordered already in the Humble Petition and Advice, that, if execution be added, may conduce much to our happiness.

The said Petition and Advice determineth, that under the Penalty of a thousand pound, and imprisonment till it be paid, no person be elected and sit in Parliament but 'such as are persons of known Integrity, fearing God, and of Good conversation — Not such as are guilty of any of the Offences mentioned in an Act of Parliament of Aug. 1650. instituted, An Act against several Atheistical, Blasphemous and execrable opinions, derogatory to the honour of God, and destructive to humane Society. No common scoffer nor reviler of Religion, or of any person or persons for professing thereof: No person that hath married or shall marry a wife of the Popish Religion, or hath trained or shall train up his child or children, or any other child or children under his tuition or Government, in the Popish Religion; or that shall permit or suffer such child or children to be trained up in the said Religion, or that hath given or shall give his consent that his Son or Daughter shall marry any of that Religion: No person that shall deny the Scriptures to be the Word of God; or the Sacraments, Prayer, Magistracy and Ministry to be the Ordinances of God: No common prophaner of the Lords day; nor prophane swearer or curser; no drunkard, or common haunter of Taverns or Ale-houses.'

They are sworn also for the true Protestant Christian Religion in the purity of it, as contained in the Holy Scriptures, and for fidelity to the Protector, and for the Peoples Rights and Liberties. A more excellent Act hath not been made for the Happiness of England, concerning Parliaments, at least since the Reformation. O that it may be but effectually put in execution.

Thes. 223. Rul. IV. The Prudence, Piety and fidelity of the Princes standing Council conduceth much to the felicity of the Common-wealth: and is to be procured, 1. By Description. 2. And by Oath ...

Thes. 224. Rul. V. The Prudence and Piety of the Prince is of high concernment to the Happiness of the People; which is to be secured in Countries where he is Elective, by a duly Regulated Election; and where he is Hereditary, by a duly Regulated Education; and by due Limitations, and by Oath ...

Thes. 225. The safe way for Election, is, that a Parliament choosing or approving the Council, swear them to choose four of the best Qualified persons, and that a well-regulated Lot take one of the four; the people of the chief City, or adjoining parts, seeking God by solemn fasting and prayer, for merciful determination by that Lot.

In elective Principalities, it must be supposed that a Council of State have a sufficient power to keep the Peace till a due Election: and yet that they be sufficiently disabled from perpetuating their Supremacy, or delaying the Election.

The Persons to be Elected may be either left to themselves as to their Rank, or they may be limited, either to take four of the Council (as men first approved by the Parliament, and acquainted best with State affairs); or else the General of the Army (if he be not of the Council) and one of the Nobility, and two of the Council. But however let them at their admission into Council, be strictly sworn to choose the fittest according to the described Qualifications, if they shall be called to a choice.

Here are divers things expressed as necessary, or much conducible to the propounded end. (Supposing still that we speak of those Nations that are setting up, or have already an Elective Prince, that is not absolute, nor hath the whole Soveraignty, but in conjunction with a Parliament or Senate) (i) That the Senate choose the Council, or at least approve of them. And so themselves being first composed as aforesaid, there will be great hopes of a Prudent Pious Council. (ii) That the Council (or the Parliament, if then sitting) choose four, being swore to a faithful choice aforehand.

And here let it be observed, that Election is to be preferred to a Lot, where it may be performed upon grounds of Judgement and

Freedom, and that a Lot is not to be brought into use, but in cases of Necessity, where judgement faileth. For, 1. Else men shall neglect the Law of God, which is propounded to them as the Rule of Judging. 2. And they shall neglect their Reason and Gods gifts, by which they are qualified for Judging. 3. And they will tempt God, and therefore provoke him to afflict them by the Lot, while they take his name in vain. 4. And if they elect not fit persons in preparation to the Lot, but turn loose a Lot among a number that are most unfit; they betray the Common-wealth to ruine. If our new Modellers should carry their Lotteries among the vulgar rowt, where there's one or two wise men among a multitude, and expect that their Lot should find out those few, they might be convinced by experience, that God made them no promise of such success, nor appointed Lots to spare men the use of their Reason. Till I have Gods command or promise to shew for our encouragement, I must believe, that he that casts a Lot to find out one wise and godly man among an hundred simpletons or ungodly men, is likely an hundred to one to be deceived. The Apostles chose two of the meetest men, to be Judas his successor, before they made use of the Lot: and then the Lot did choose Matthias one of the two.

(iii) It is here taken for a matter of great necessity, that yet a Lot should finally determine. (In an extraordinary case indeed, as after a Conquest, usually One only is capable: but we are not giving Rules for extraordinaries.) And the need of this Lot is thus apparent. 1. It will prevent Confederacies and making parties and friends for the succession, which else will hardly ever be prevented. 2. It will avoid the *odium* that else will lie upon the Council, from the rejected party: Men will easier take a rejection from God then from man. 3. It will prevent the dis-satisfaction and consequent rebellious contrivances of the rejected. For it seemeth a dishonour to be rejected by choosers, but its no dishonour to miss it upon a Lot. 4. It is a most rational suitable course, that he that stands next God, should be chosen by God, and God should have the principal hand in the choice. The Apostles gave God the choice of Matthias an Apostle by Lot, because no power under God was fit to convey (or choose a man to) the highest Ecclesiastick power: But they chose not inferiour Officers by Lot. 5. It will more comfortably satisfie the Prince, to do or suffer in his office, when God calls him to it. 6. It will very much satisfie the people in their submission and obedience, and prevent rebellions, and hinder suspitions of the Princes ambitious aspiring to the power. As his choice was Divine, their estimation and obedience will be towards him as towards an Officer of God.

(iv) It is here taken also as necessary, that the Lot be carefully regulated by a Law, e.g. as to be done before many, in the publickest Church of the City, in such and such order, which is easily contrived; that so they that would creep in by unrighteous means may have no hope.

(v) That the chief City or all that are near, that can so speedily meet, may by fasting and prayer seek Gods merciful determination, is a thing of apparent need, by reason of the great weight of the case, and that the Government may be more purely Divine, and the people the fullyer satisfied in the person, and the blessing, of God procured thereby.

> Thes. 226. Where the Prince is Hereditary, and hath a Parliament either to participate in the Soveraignty, or to secure the peoples Rights the education of his children should be secured by a standing Rule, strictly describing the Tutors, both Divines and Politicians, and carefully securing the execution ...

> Thes. 227. The second means of a peoples security as from their Prince, is that in the Fundamental contracts he be limited to Rule them by wholsom Laws to be made by the proposal and consent of his Parliament ...

> Thes. 228. The third means of Security, is, the Princes Oath, which is to contain the summe of the Fundamental contracts which lay the ground of his future Government ...

> Thes. 229. Ru. VI. The security of a Nation, as to their successive Safety, Piety and Peace, requireth that the Militia be in Honest, faithful, obedient and valiant hands which will be accomplished, 1. By the forementioned securing a faithful Prince and Parliament that must Rule them. 2. By arming all the faithful of the Nation that are fit for arms, and suffering none but freemen, to be of the standing force within the Land. 3. By causing all Souldiers to be sworn to the Soveraign and the Constitution. 4. By keeping the Forces that are under pay, in necessary dependance upon the Soveraign power for their pay. 5. By keeping the power of placing and displacing the greater Officers out of the hands of any General Officer in pay. 6. By keeping them by distance, and other means, from uniting in any as a sufficient

Head, but the Soveraign power. 7. By vigilancy against intruding masked Papists and enemies that sow the seeds of sedition among them. 8. By supplying every vacant place with Godly valiant men, and weeding out the ungodly and seditious. 9. By a sufficient encouraging of the faithful in their due pay. 10. By making them strict Laws against Impiety and sedition, and keeping up true Discipline among them.

1. Mr. Harrington truly tels you the necessity of Arming the freemen: men of best Education and Interest, will be most valiant and most trusty; and if Reformed as I forementioned, they will be truest to their Country, in matters of everlasting consequence: It is reason that men of greatest Interest and sufficiency should be trusted with the defence of themselves and their own. The cowardliness of Freeholders is the undoing of their Country: To save their own skin they arm their servants, and so make them their Lords. Especially when it comes to fighting indeed, and they dare not venture their lives: Or else in forraign Wars, where they use to employ their servants only, except in command, and then they return upon them as their Conquerers. Many that are servants may be sent abroad, but not so many as may be able to master their Commanders, and the junior sort of Freemen, that should still be mixt in competent numbers. The most servile and base are usually through the disadvantage of their education the most impious. And so much wickedness as usually dwelleth in such Armies, is worse then the enemy to them. None of the Forces in pay, that intend the common good, and deserve the name of Christians, or Common-wealths-men, will be unwilling to have the faithful people of the Land to be possessed of a strength sufficient to ballance them for their necessary preservation.

The rest also are so plainly rational, necessary and conscionable, that I shall think it needless to give Reasons for them distinctly, there being nothing but ignorance, ungodliness, or a treacherous selfish design to master the Common-wealth, that can have any thing considerable to say against them.

Two things more I add, 1. Let the old tryed faithful Souldiers of the Army be the chief Commanders of part of the Militia of the Countries; yet none but the faithful, and men of Interest, that have somewhat to lose by the ruine of the Common-wealth: nor yet so as to strengthen any to a dangerous redundancy of Power. 2. That every Regiment of Foot have one faithful Minister to teach them, and every

Regiment of Horse two at least (because quartering very distant, one man can be but with few at once). Seducers are the seditious disturbers and destroyers, who will creep in and prevail, if there be none to gain-say them.

Thes. 230. R. VII. It is necessary to the true Happiness of the Common-wealth, that the Inferiour Magistrates (Judges, Justices, &c.) be prudent, Godly faithful men; which is secured to us, 1. By the forementioned Piety of the Soveraign Powers that must choose them; and 2. By good Laws that binde them to their Duty . . .

Thes. 231. R. VIII. The Christian excellency and felicity of a Commonwealth, dependeth exceeding much on the Purity and Unity of the Churches that are there: And therefore it must be the Rulers special care 1. That holy Doctrine, Worship and Order and Discipline be maintained in the Churches; and 2. That they be brought to as much Charity, Agreement and Communion as can be agreed.

Thes. 232. This purity of the Church will be procured, 1. By the (forementioned) care that godly, able faithful Pastors be provided; and the ungodly, insufficient and negligent kept or cast out. 2. By the faithful ordering of the Churches, and exercise of holy Discipline, supposing the previous requisites forementioned.

Thes. 233. For the setling of a sound and holy Ministry, 1. There must be Laws describing such as shall be publikely Approved and encouraged, and such as shall be only Tolerated. 2. The People and Patrons, the Ordainers and Approvers, must each have their due Interest preserved and allowed them. 3. No man must publikely Teach, nor hold private Assemblies, beside such as stand in due subordination to the Churches, but such as have from the Approvers an Instrument of Approbation or of Toleration. 4. Blasphemy and subverting the Essentials of Christianity, or of Christian communion and worship are to be severely restrained, not Tolerated in any way of Teaching or propagation whatsoever . . .

Thes. 234. To the holy order and Discipline of the Churches, besides the Ministers duty (of which I have spoken in other Writings) it is needful, 1. That the Magistrate drive on all that are Pastors and administer Sacraments, to exercise Discipline, by distinguishing the clean from the unclean. 2. And to secure the

Interest of the Magistrate and the Common-wealth, that there be duly joyned some Officer of the Magistrates in all the Assemblies for Worship and Discipline; and Magistracy and Ministry so twisted together, that they may concur and co-operate, without any invasion of each others Offices, but for mutual help.

God hath in wonderful Holy Wisdom so nearly joyned the Church and Commonwealth, and the Magistracy and Ministry, that both are of necessity to the welfare of each Nation; and it hath occasioned many ignorant men to contend about their pre-eminence, as if it were a controversie among sober Christians, which of them were the chief: when it is no controversie, nor is there any room for the comparison, they being *qua tales* of distinct co-ordinate kinds, and each is chief in his proper Office. The Magistrate is as truly the Governour of Ministers by the Sword or coercive power, as he is of any other of his Subjects: And the Minister is as truly the Magistrates Church-guide by the Word of God, as he is of any other of his Flock: yet indirectly he may frequently be bound from exercising any such disgraceful acts of Discipline on them, as may tend to diminish their Authority, or disable them to their proper work. Government is a divine Act, which imitateth Nature. Aristotle and Galen could not agree whether the Head or Heart was the Principal member and first seat of Life. And why may they not be conjunct and co-ordinate, each being the principal in its kind; the Head of the animal spirits and operations, and the Heart of the Vital? Philosophers have troubled themselves with disputing, whether the Intellect or Will be the first Principle of the souls operations? But by this time they are for the most part agreed, that the Intellect is the first *quoad specificationem actus*, and the Will *quoad exercitium*. But if any will make a tough dispute of it, whether Specification or Exercise be first, he will do it to no profit. It is a dead Commonwealth (and that is none, but a meer carkass) that is without the Magistrate: And it is a mad Commonwealth (which is little better then none) that is without a Church and Ministry. I think they that would separate the Intellect from the Will, the Brain from the Heart, the Directive power from the Imperial, are no better friends to the Common-wealth, then he that would deliver a man from the presumption of his phantasie by cutting off his Head, or from the passions of his Heart by pulling it out of his Body. Some Diseases may warrant me to cut off my finger; but none will warrant me to cut off my Head, or to pull out my Heart. Some say the Intellect so participateth of inclination, and is so near kin to the Will, that we may properly say, *Intellectus vult verum*; and that the Will hath so much participation of Intelligence that we may well say, that *Voluntas intelligit bonum*; whether that be so or not, I am sure that it is no humane Body that hath not both Heart and Brain; nor a humane soul that wants either Will or Intellect. The Priests sat with the Civil Judges in Moses time, and had Judicial Power, much further then we now desire. The Ministers sat with the Magistrates in England before the dayes of William the Conqueror. If any would exempt the Ministry from being under the civil Governours Jurisdiction, or would put into their hand the civil Power, or Sword; even any degree of a proper coercive forcing Power, I would Petition with the first against it: But if any Parliament would have some chosen Ministers sit in both Houses without any Votes or Power at all, but only a Liberty to speak when the cause of Religion and Conscience is on the Stage; or if they would have them sit with Judges on the Bench, and Justices at their Sessions, without any power, only with a Liberty of speaking to a case of Conscience, as I would never Petition for it, so I would not think that Commonwealth the less Wise, or Pious, or Happy, or safe that did admit it. But we are all for extreams. Some must have a Pope to carry both swords, and trample upon Kings and Common-wealths; or at least they must have Lord Bishops to set and Vote among the Lords: And others must think them unworthy to speak in the Cause of Christ, which sometime is tost up and down by men that little understand it; and some think them not worthy to stand in their presence, but make them as the scum and scorn of mankind: And what have they but their holy Relation to Christ and his service, to make them so contemptible? They are of the same Nation, blood and parentage as other men: For their lives, though they are imperfect, if any one relation and rank of men be more upright and blameless and holy, let us be banished or die the death. For their studies, unless it be Divine things that make men fools, or much learning and studie that make them less wise then other men, and unless the way to wisdom be to lay asleep our Reason, and cast off study, or at least to study nothing higher then the Moon, undoubtedly they have the advantage by far of any one rank of men. If Divinity be True and Good, then certainly the Students of it are likely to be the wisest and the best of men: For the object ennobleth, and the employment perfecteth the faculties.

Kings themselves were commanded by God of old, to study Divinity continually, and so were other Commanders, yea and all. Deut. 17.18, 19, 20; Josh. 1.8, Deut. 11.19, 20. & 6. 6, 7, 8. Psalm. 1.2, 3. If it debase the Teachers, it cannot honour Princes nor any of the Learners.

The Nation therefore that vilifieth and despiseth the Ministry, despiseth Christ. And the Magistrates that grow jealous of their interest, and set against the work that Christ hath set them to do, do but pluck out their own eyes, and destroy themselves, and unchristen their Common-wealth. Magistrates and Ministers therefore must joyn together in the work of God: yet so that we will not meddle at all with their work; much less desire their Riches and honour: Let them take the Pomp, and Rule, and wealth of the world: We desire them so much splendor as may countenance them in their work. For our selves, we would have nothing but leave to labour, and the Devil chained up from hindering mens salvation, as far as by the Magistrate can be procured.

> Thes. 235. To free the Magistrate from all jealousie of our usurpations, and to further us in our work, by an holy Concord, Let every Parish have one or more Censors, or Civil Officers, enabled to these following works. 1. To keep peace in the Congregations, if any make disturbance, or if any by force intrude to the Sacrament (for the Pastors or people have no power of violence.) 2. To joyn with the Minister and Church-Wardens in disposing of Seats in the Church, to avoid Contentions. 3. To meet once a moneth with the Church-Officers (or others) to hear the Causes that are brought before them: Where, 1. He may force those to appear as Magistrate, (when he sees cause) whom we can but intreat. 2. And he may (when he sees cause) have power to administer an oath. 3. And his Power and Vote concurring or dissenting, may determine how far the Magistrate shall second them; And also, 4. That none be taken to be disfranchised for crimes, by any excommunication, without the Censors conviction and consent (as we said before.)

In every Corporation that hath a Maior or Bayliff, and other Justices, let them also be the Censors. And in small Countrey Parishes where no Justice of Peace abideth, let the sufficientest person or persons be enabled by the Magistrate to this Office: And let him have no further Power. If the Church may propound the fittest persons, and the Rulers accept or reject them as they see cause, and so authorize such as they accept, it may fully satisfie their interest. If they refuse this, we are well content that they choose them as they see meet. This will further the Ministry, and stop the Erastians mouthes, and take away the jealousies that are usually by Magistrates kept up against the Pastors: Their Censors shall be present, and see whether we meddle with State matters, or go beyond our line. But still let this introduce no confusion of the Offices by the conjunction. Let the Churches acts be valid to meet Church respects (as Absolution or Excommunication) whether the Censors shall consent or not: but let them be of no influence upon Civil Rights, if he consent not. As Magistrates are Civil Rulers of Pastors and Churches, and must help them with their power against obstinate untractable ones, so there is no reason that we should desire them to be meerly the Executioners of our Sentence; but they must take cognizance of the cause, and Judge where they must execute: If therefore their Officers be with us, and have notice of the whole proceeding, they may be satisfied how far to own our acts.

Thes. 236. Though Magistrates cannot force men to Believe, Love God, and so to be saved, yet they must force them to submit to holy Doctrine, and learn the Word of God, and to walk orderly and quietly in that condition, till they are brought to a voluntary personal profession of Christianity, and subjection to Christ and his holy Ordinance; and so being voluntarily Baptized, (if they are new converted Heathens, that never were before baptized) or Confirmed (if they were baptized before) they may live in holy Communion with the Church . . .

Thes. 237. The Unity also of the Church is very needful to the safety and peace of the Common-wealth, that Parties be not hatched and animated against each other, who will be disturbing the Common peace to promote their ends . . .

Thes. 238. The means which the Magistrate must use for the Churches unity, are these. 1. He must neither himself impose, nor suffer the Pastors to impose any uncertain or unnecessary points of doctrine, discipline or worship, as necessary to the Union or Communion of Churches, but restore the primitive simplicity, by takeing the Holy Scriptures in general as the sufficient Rule and Law of faith and worship, and the antient Creeds of the Church in particular, as the universal Symbole: or if any more copious be drawn up, let it meddle with no Controversies that may be forborn, and let it be as much as may be in Scripture words . . .

Thes. 239. 2. It is necessary both to the purity and peace of the Churches, that the publishing or propagating of the Certain intolerable Errours be restrained, both by the Magistrate and the Churches: and also the practice of such Errours that are practicable . . .

Thes. 240. 3. It is necessary to the Churches Peace, that no private Congregations be gathered, or Anti-churches erected by any but such as have an Approbation or Toleration for it from the Magistrate: supposing still that such private Assemblies are Allowed of course as are kept by the Approbation of Approved Ministers, in a due subordination to the Church-Assemblies . . .

Thes. 241. 4. It is necessary to the Churches Peace, that no Pastors or Christians be suffered in Print or Speech to rail at one another, and use contentious opprobrious speeches: but that the Magistrate moderate them in their Disputes, and that the Tolerated Churches be not suffered to cast scorn upon the Approved Churches, nor to be over-busie or publike in drawing away others to their mind, supposing them to have leave to worship God themselves in their Tolerated way, and modestly to defend themselves under the Magistrates moderation . . .

Thes. 242. 5. The Magistrate in order to the Churches peace must moderate Controversies, especially as managed by Writings and Disputes: and when he seeth that they are not used to Edification, but to Division, and that they cannot be further suffered without the great danger of the Church, he must either command them silence, or prescribe them necessary bounds . . .

Thes. 243. 6. Fraternal Associations of Churches, and Assemblies of their Officers and Messengers must be encouraged, in order to the needful correspondency and communion of the Churches; and that Gods work may be carried on in concord, the Censor or other Magistrate being present, when he seeth it meet to restrain them from usurpations, and contentions . . .

Thes. 244. 7. The Magistrate must not commit any of his proper coercive power into the Pastors hands, nor trust them with his Sword, either to depose each other, or any way Govern each other by force: But the rejecting others from their communion, and perswading men to avoid them, is all that the highest pretenders can call an Ecclesiastical Jurisdiction over their Brethren, in which also they are to be moderated by the Magistrate for peace.

It would long ago have quieted the Churches, if the Magistrates had kept their Power to themselves, and also had not made themselves the Prelates Executioners. If the Pope had not got the Sword into his hand, nor into the hands of his Prelates, and Magistrates made not themselves his Lictors, he could not so much disturb the peace. If his Excommunications were not seconded by violence, and he could not meddle with mens bodies or estates, he would be at last aweary of thundering against them that care not for it. And no Prelate hath any face of a Title to a forcing Power: who made them Magistrates! What they can do, must be by the Word upon the Conscience; by spiritual, and not by carnal Weapons. And for a Magistrate to punish or destroy a man *eo nomine*, because he is excommunicate, before he knows whether it be just or unjust, is but to make himself the Prelates Hangman, and renounce his Reason with his Authority, and to do he knows not what or why, at the command of another; who yet cannot save him from the wrath of God if he prove a persecutor. As scolds in the street endanger not the Peace of the Land, because they are unarmed, and go to it but with Tongues, or Nails and Fists: so if Divines be kept unarmed, and have no power to persecute one another, they will at last be weary of contending, and when the fray is over, they will be as they were: Or if they passionately excommunicate each other, experience will convince them of their folly, and drive them to return to Unity, when they have felt awhile that they are but weakened by it, and hindred in their work, and made the contempt and scorn of their enemies. But if a Prelate, or a Synod, or any of them have power to displace and cast out, or fine, or imprison, or banish others when they are angry with them, there will be no peace.

Be awakened then, ye Christian Magistrates, to keep your Sword in your own hand, and use it for God, according to his Law, discerned by your own understandings (though taught by Ministers) and put an end to the quarrels of Popes, and Prelates, and Councils, that are partly contending for your power to be in them; and partly disturbing and destroying our peace by your Sword which they have got into their hands, or at their Commands.

So much for the Rules by which a Common-wealth may be made a Theocrasie, or truly Divine, and the Kingdom of Christ may come among us, and his Will be done to the Glory of God and happiness of the people: Which I have, though not wholly, yet chiefly fitted to this Common-wealth, out of a desire of its felicity.

Blessed are the people that are in such a case, yea blessed are they that have the Lord for their King and God. Grant us but these Substantials, and secure us these great things which our happiness consisteth in, and we will not contend either for or against such jingles as Mr. Harrington and others do lay so great a stress upon. Monarchy, Aristocracy, or Democracy will secure us (though a mixt Government, or limited Monarchy we judge best; and Democracy worst, in most places;) so we may be secured in the main. Let us pray, and in our places peaceably endeavour, that we may see the day when the great Voice in Heaven shall say, 'THE KINGDOMS OF THIS WORLD ARE BECOME the Kingdoms OF OUR LORD, AND OF HIS CHRIST', Rev. 11. 15.

And then if all these Christian Common-wealths were but by Association conjoyned for their mutual defence, and promoting the Interest of their common King, the earth would be in its nearest resemblance of Heaven.

CHAPTER 10

Of the Soveraigns Power over the Pastors of the Church, and of the difference of their Offices

Thes. 245. The Office of Magistrates and Ministers (or Pastors of the Church) are *totâ specie* distinct . . .

Thes. 246. The Civil power is Essential to a Common-wealth (or Civil Policy) and the Pastors only necessary to its well-being; and the Pastors are essential to the Church (as a Political Society) and the Magistrate necessary but to its well being . . .

Thes. 247. Magistracy and Ministry are each of them Immediately and co-ordinately from Christ, and neither of them from each other. Though respectively one may be under the other in exercise, as the Object to the Agent, yet neither of them flow essentially from the other, as the effect from its proper cause . . .

Thes. 248. Because the Power that is One and Perfect in Christ, who is perfectly capable of it, cannot in the derived measure, be all received and exercised by one man; therefore he hath divided it, giving part to Magistrate, and part to the Pastors, to be respectively exercised under him . . .

Thes. 249. Magistrates and Pastors having different kinds of Power, must exercise their several Powers on one another: So that the Magistrate is the Pastors Ruler by the sword, and the Pastor is the Magistrates Pastor and Ruler by the Word.

This is unquestioned among all sober Christians: save that the Papists put in some exceptions for the exemption of their Clergy. There is no prudent Christian Magistrate that dare or will deny, that Pastors Authoritatively exercise their Office towards him, as well as towards other men. To exempt them from the Pastoral Power, is but to except them from their care and charge, and so from the benefits of their work: which is no greater a favour then to be exempted from all other helps from God by man: Was it Alexanders servitude to be taught by Aristotle? Would not that flatterer be kickt out of doors by a Prince, that should perswade him not to Obey his Physitians for his bodily health and life, as if it were a debasement of his Majesty? Or that should perswade him not to let his Son be Guided by Schoolmasters and Tutors?

The Government of Pastors is much like a Physitians Government of his Patients, especially in Hospitals, or Cities where Physitians know their charge: Though a man be authorized by the Prince to be a Physitian, it is but unto voluntary Patients: every man may choose whether he will take their medicines or not. If the greatest Prince or the poorest man account it his Liberty, to die or be sick, rather than to submit to the Rule of a Physitian, they may use that Liberty. If they refuse to obey the Physitian, his Punishment is to deny them his help, and let them take their course. If God have intrusted Pastors as his Officers, with a pardon to be by them delivered to the Penitent, and sealed by Baptism or the Lords Supper, or published by Absolution from particular sins, it is not in the power of any Prince here to interpose and force the Pastors to deliver this pardon or the seals to whom he please; or to the Impenitent, contrary to the will of Christ. We must be faithful dispensers of the Messages, Pardon, Seals, and all Ordinances committed to our trust. Nor will I at the command of a Prince, be the Pastor of a Church that will have Church priviledges, and refuse Church-Discipline. If the Prince himself will have me to be his Physitian, and yet will Rule himself, and refuse my directions, and command me to give him my Medicine that he may take it how and when he list himself, I will disobey him, (if the Medicine misused be dangerous) lest I send him poyson instead of Physick; that may be poyson in his ungoverned way, that may be health in mine. And as long as he is free, whether he will use me as his Physitian or not, it is no injury to his Dignity, that I require him to submit to my direction, upon the penalty of being without my help. I need not tell you of Ambrose his usage of Theodosius, or Chrysostoms freedom with Eudoxia, and his resolution rather to lose his hand, then give the Sacrament to the proud contemners of God and discipline:[23] the

---

[23] On the significance of this approving reference to St Ambrose's defiance of the Emperor Theodosius, see: Patrick Collinson, 'If Constantine, then also Theodosius:

nature of the office may satisfie any; he that hath said 'A man that is an Heretick, after the first and second admonition reject' and 'put away from among you that wicked person' and 'with such, no not to eat' hath not said, 'except the Magistrate command you otherwise' or 'except he be a Magistrate.' Though accidentally (as I shall shew anon) he may be excepted.

> Thes. 250. The nature of Pastoral Government, whether over Magistrates or the meanest men, is not Imperial, Magisterial, Coercive by any force on body or estate, but like that of a Tutor over his Pupils, or a Physitian over his Patients, but that it is of a more especial Institution of Christ, and exercised by his Commission, and in his name . . .

> Thes. 251. The Magistrate hath power over the person of the Pastor, but not over his office; and the Pastor hath a spiritual ministerial Authority even over Magistrates, but not over their office: that is, they can make no alteration in it, nor do anything against it . . .

> Thes. 252. The several Powers of Magistrates and Ministers toward the persons of each other are limited, and neither of them are left to their absolute wills . . .

> Thes. 253. A faithfull Minister must be no flatterer, but reprove a Prince as closely as another man: yet so that he be sufficiently tender of his honour, which is necessary to the ends of Magistracy . . .

> Thes. 254. Whether it be in case of Heresie or other crimes, both Magistrates and Pastors are Judges; but differently, as to different ends: The Magistrate is Judge who is to be corporally punished for Heresie or any crime, and this no Pastor must usurp: The Pastors are Judges Directive, who is to be excommunicated for Heresie or other crimes, or Absolved upon Repentance: and this no Magistrate may usurp . . .

> Thes. 255. Though a Magistrate may be an object capable of Excommunication; yet as it is not rashly to be done on the lowest. So it rarely fals out that the Soveraign may lawfully be excommunicate; because by Accident it becomes unmeet . . .

St Ambrose and the Integrity of the Elizabethan *Ecclesia Anglicana*', *Godly People* (London, 1983), pp. 109–34.

Thes. 256. If a Magistrate of higher or lower rank be excommunicate, he must for all that be Honoured and obeyed, and no man is warranted thereby to contemn him . . .

Thes. 257. To deny Magistrates to be the Objects of Pastoral Power, is but to deprive them of the Excellent mercies of the Gospel and Sacraments, and Church-communion, and order, and Absolution, &c. which Christ hath committed into his Ministers hands, and which Princes need as much as others, and have as much right to . . .

Thes. 258 Magistrates may not usurp the Pastoral office, nor do the works that are proper to it . . .

Thes. 259. Ministers as well as other men must be subject to Magistrates, and pay them Honour, obedience and tribute: and are to be punished by them if they disobey . . .

Only one thing I crave the Magistrates of England to see, that the masked Papists are now pleading the same cause by the Libertines, which where they have better opportunity they do in their own names. He is too blind that seeth not who is the Spirit and life of all our common Paradoxes, 'That the Magistrate governeth us but as men, and not as Christians: That he hath nothing to do with matters of Religion: nor may punish men for their consciences' that is, for sinning and defending it as just. The meaning of it is Originally and Finally, that all these things belong only to the Church, that is, to the Pope and Prelates . . .

Thes. 260. Magistrates must not only Govern Ministers as men, but as Ministers; nor Christians only as men, but as Christians, and as Churches; nor only in secular affairs, but in the matter of Gods worship . . .

Thes. 261. Though Magistrates cannot usurp the Ministers office, nor any part of his proper work; yet may they punish him for male-administration, and in case of unfitness, cast him out from the Liberty of exercising his office in their dominions . . .

Thes. 262. If Magistrates punish Ministers unjustly, that is, persecute them, they must not resist, nor dishonour the Magistrate, but patiently suffer the wrong . . .

Thes. 263. If Magistrates forbid Ministers to preach or exercise the rest of their office in their dominions, they are to be obeyed, in case that other competent persons are provided for the work, that the Church receive no dangerous detriment by it, but otherwise they are not to be obeyed, but we must do Christs work till they disable us . . .

Thes. 264. If a Magistrate command us to do evil in Gods worship, or elsewhere, we may not obey him . . .

Thes. 265. Magistrates may determine of some necessary circumstances in the worship of God, which God hath left undetermined in his Word; but yet they must take heed of unnecessary Laws, and of invading the office of the Pastors . . .

Thes. 266. The Magistrate may appoint no new Officers for Gods worship it self, but he may make new Officers for these circumstances of his Worship . . .

Thes. 267. Magistrates have the chief Power of the Temples and Church-maintenance; yet so as that they are bound by God, to dispose of it for his Churches greatest benefit . . .

Thes. 268. Though Magistrates may not lawfully take from the People the Power of choosing or consenting, nor from the Pastors the Power of Ordaining, yet must they oversee both People and Pastors, and not suffer them to choose or order such as are intolerably unfit, but by moderate corrections bring them to a righter choice and Ordination . . .

Thes. 269. The principal work of Magistrates about Religion, is to preserve it, and further the Obedience of Gods Laws, which is a great part of his work; but not to alter it . . .

Thes. 270. It being so high a part of the Magistrates work and honour to promote Gods service and mens salvation, yea an higher end of his Magistracy then meer corporal common good, their doctrine is trayterous and intolerable who affirm 1. That Magistrates have nothing to do with matters of Religion, but are to leave all men to their consciences, and govern us as men, and not as Christians, Churches or Ministers. 2. That the Clergy are exempt from the Magistrates judgement, and so would set up the Pope as a civil Prince in every Common-wealth . . .

CHAPTER II

Of the Soveraigns Prerogatives, and Power of Governing by Laws and Judgement

The Reader need not tell me here, either that the whole should have been handled before the parts, and the Genus before the Species, or that Laws and Judgement are parts of Administration, and not of the Constitution of a Common-wealth: For I intend not exactness of Method, and I purposely past over the *Jura Regalia* generally before, and resolve to say nothing (here at least) of the Administration, but what falls in upon the by in the description of the Power and therefore shall somewhat the fullyer here describe the Power with respect to its acts, which I avoid the fuller handling of, and say no more of the *Jura Regalia* then is necessary hereunto.

> Thes. 271. The Rights of the Soveraign are, 1. His Power of Governing, which is his Office itself. 2. That safety, strength and Honour, as far as the people can afford it, which is sufficient or necessary thereunto . . .

> Thes. 272. 1. It is a Prerogative of Majesty, that the Soveraigns life have a special Guard; and that the crimes that tend to his destruction be Treason, and have the severest punishment . . .

> Thes. 273. 2. Another Prerogative is, to have power to bind all the subjects in an Oath of fidelity . . .

> Thes. 274. 3. Another Prerogative is, to declare enemies to the State, and to have the power of war and peace . . .

> Thes. 275. 4. Another Prerogative is, to have the power of the Arms and Forces of the Nation, for defensive and offensive wars . . .

Thes. 276. 5. Another Prerogative is, by Crown-lands, Tributes, Customs, and other incomes to receive sufficient Revenues to defray the charges of the Government ...

Thes. 277. 6. Another Prerogative is, to have that Eminency of Honour which is needful to maintain Authority, and to have a power of securing it by special Laws ...

Thes. 278. 2. The highest prerogative of Majesty is its constituted form; that is, to be the *summa Potestas*, to have the Supreme Government. This consisteth, 1. In having the supream Legislative power. 2. And the Supream power of Judgement, and execution of that Judgement ...

Thes. 279. A Law is an ambiguous term, and is taken, 1. Sometimes for the internal mind of the Law-giver. 2. Sometime for the external products. In the former sence Gods mind and will is called *Lex æterna*; which properly is but the Fountain of Law, unless you take it as the *Significatum*. In the latter sence, 1. Sometime it is taken for a means of effecting; and sometime for the thing effected on the Subject. In the former sense, sometime it is taken Metaphorically for a connexion of Physical causes; and sometime for meer moral potestative Rules: And sometime it is taken Metaphorically for the orderly disposal of inanimates and brutes; and sometime only for Rules to the rational free Agent.

Thes. 280. I take the mind of the Law-giver, the settled order of Nature among inanimates or brutes, or man as a Natural agent, and also the impress on the soul, as such, to be improperly called Laws: and therefore take not the word in any of these senses.

Thes. 281. The Law of Nature and of Grace, are sometime taken for the imprinting signs, and sometime for the Impressed Image: In the latter sense I take them improperly to be called Laws ...

Thes. 282. The word 'Law' is also sometime taken so largely as to comprehend meer Directions or precepts of such as have no Governing power and also contracts: But I take it not thus improperly.

Thes. 283. By some also it is taken so narrowly, as to exclude verbal Precepts, Commissions, Priviledges, temporary Constitutions, premiant Laws, and all such as meerly constitute the *Jus Possidendi*, or *debitum habendi*, as such: and is made only to signifie those Laws that are by eminency so called; and to comprehend no acts but *obligare aut ad obedientiam aut ad pœnam.* But I follow not that too strict acceptation . . .

Thes. 284. A Law is a signification of the Rulers will constituting the Subjects due: Or, *Potestativa constitutio debiti subditorum* . . .

Thes. 285. Though to be an Aptitudinal sign, be all that is of the Generical Essence; yet to be Promulgate and thereby made an Actual sign, or to be so far revealed, that the subjects may be informed by it that are not culpably negligent is a condition necessary to the Obligation or Constitution of duty . . .

Thes. 286. When I say a Law is a sign of the Law-givers Will, I imply his understanding signified also: As Right, it proceedeth from the Legislators Intellect, and as Imposed, it proceedeth from his Will, and so is to be received by the Intellect and will of the subject for Regulation and Obligation or Obedience . . .

Thes. 287. In the essence of the sign there is a three-fold Respect of the matter of the sign. 1. To the thing signified. 2. To the will of the Law-giver. 3. To the subjects, to whom his will is signified. The thing signified consisteth, 1. Of the matter. 2. The form; that is, Right or Dueness . . .

Thes. 288. All Laws being nothing else but the expressions of anothers Reason and Will, it is certain that subjects are not to esteem themselves self-sufficient or Independent, not enslaved by being Ruled by the Reason and will of others . . .

Thes. 289. It is no Law that is not the effect of Governing Power, or the sign of the Rulers will . . .

Thes. 290. Hence ariseth a double distribution of Laws. 1. Some Laws are but Oeconomical, and some are Political . . .

Thes. 291. 2. Laws are either *Universal* for the whole Commonwealth, or Local and particular; and made either by the Soveraign Immediately, or by a subordinate power Immediately, and only mediately by the Soveraign . . .

Thes. 292. Laws may consist in writings, words, customs or actions, or whatever may truly be called a sign of the Rulers will; and they are not confined to any one sign only . . .

Thes. 293. A Commission or Precept to a single person or more, is truly a Law, having all that is essential to it; but it is the least of Laws, and not a Law as the word is confined to such as are eminently called Laws ...

Thes. 294. Laws may be either permanent or temporary: Even that which is but for an hour or a day, may have all essential to a Law, though of the Lowest kind ...

Thes. 295. The specifick form of this sign which we call a Law, consisteth in Constitution of Due: so that a Law essentially is an Instrument of the Soveraigns will; which the word 'Constitution' doth express ...

Thes. 296. This differenceth a Law from a Judgment: A Law doth Instrumentally constitute the Right by way of Regulation: The Judgement doth but Determine of it when Controverted by way of decision, or in order to execution.

Thes. 297. As *Debitum vel Jus*, Due or Right, is the Common nature of Morality (directly, as *injustum* indirectly) so is it the essential *terminus* of a Law.

Thes. 298. The common word 'Obligation' is a tolerable substitute of 'Constitution of Due' which I willingly use, but choose the other in a Definition rather; 1. Because Obligation is but a Metaphor. 2. And defective of fit expressing the whole essential Act of Laws ...

Thes. 299 The Due that is constituted by Law is twofold: 1. What shall be the subjects duty, that is, the *Debitum officii*. 2. What shall be Due to him upon obeying or disobeying, or otherwise, for the ends of the Law; that is, the *Debitum præmii vel pænæ*; or the *Jus habendi vel ferendi* ...

Thes. 300. Lastly, it is only the *Debitum subditorum* as such, that is constituted by a Law; and so it is distinguished from Rulers acts about their owns or aliens duty ...

Thes. 301. The will of the Law-giver doth alwayes attain its nearest end; which is, To oblige, or to make Due; but its ultimate ends depending on the Subjects will, are often frustrate ...

Thes. 302. Laws are the Rule of Duty & of Judgement ...

Thes. 303. As the Soveraign Power maketh Laws, so may it Abrogate, or correct those Laws ...

Thes. 304. It belongeth to the Soveraign Power to make a stated universally-obliging Interpretation of the Laws . . .

Thes. 305. It belongeth to the Soveraign to dispence with Penal Laws, by pardoning offences: and also to dispence with Positive Laws about Duty, when the End and Reason of the Law requireth it: Because his Laws are to bind the subject, and not himself . . .

Thes. 306. A Law being the Instrument of Government, and the Rule of Duty and Judgement, the Law-giver by making it doth oblige himselfe, ordinarily to Govern by it; So that he is engaged in point of Prudence and Fidelity, for his Honour, and for the Common good, not rashly to pardon crimes, nor dispence with Laws; but still upon grounds of security as to their ends . . .

Thes. 307. He that dispenceth with a Law upon just occasion, doth not thereby become a Lyar, nor make the Law speak falsely: because it speaketh but *de Debito*, and not directly *de Eventu*, as it is a Law . . .

Thes. 308. As no Law-giver can dispence with Gods Laws, nor with the necessary means of the common safety, so neither may he dispence with his own Covenants, nor deprive any causelesly of their Right, nor ordinarily or causelesly dispence with his own Laws, nor when the ends of Government forbid it . . .

Thes. 309. It belongeth to the Soveraign to grant Priviledges; which he may reverse, unless he have expresly or implicitly disabled himself thereto . . .

Thes. 310. To blot out infamies (as in case of bastardy) and *aperire asyla*, and other inferiour *Jura Majestatis*, are reducible to the greater, and need not be enumerated . . .

Thes. 311. As the Power of making Laws is the first and most eminent part of Soveraignty; so the Power of appointing all Inferiour Magistrates is the second: there being no Governing Power in the Commonwealth, but what is derived from the Soveraign . . .

Thes. 312. It is a matter of exceeding moment to the safety and welfare of the People, that Inferiour Magistrates be men fearing God, Prudent, just, of publick spirits, and couragious, hating impiety, vice and all injustice: And therefore next to the making of Good Laws, it is the Soveraigns principal work to be exceeding carefull of his choice of Officers, and to keep out insinuating unworthy men . . .

Thes. 313. Princes should be very circumspect and sollicitous to find out the worthiest persons in the Land, and advance them to Magistracy and Trust, and to resist such as by flattery, nearness, friends, or bribery, seek advancement . . .

Thes. 314. The Soveraign hath Power to be Judge in his own cause; ordinarily, as having no superiour judge; so the controversie be not with the body of the people, about the very ends of Government . . .

Thes. 315. It belongeth to the Soveraign to be Judge of all inferiour Judges . . .

Thes. 316. The last Appeal is to the Soveraigns Judgement, and his sentence is final; so that from him there is no Appeal but unto God . . .

CHAPTER 12

Of due Obedience to Rulers, and of Resistance

Thes. 317. It is the Command of God the universal Soveraign, that every soul be subject to the higher Powers, and resist them not; and this not only for fear of punishment, but for conscience sake, Rom. 13.1 to 7; Tit. 3.1; 1; Pet. 2. 13,14,15.

Because the right understanding of these commands of God, is of great use for our guidance in these weighty points, I shall stay a while upon the search of that Rom. 13 which saith most; and if we understand that, it will be the easier to understand the rest.

Many occasions concurred to make this document of the Apostle necessary to the Romans. 1. There were Hereticks crept in among them that abused the doctrine of Christian Liberty, and perswaded them that subjection to the Rule of Magistrates was against their Liberty. 2. And the weaker Christians were the easier induced to entertain this doctrine in part, because they were Heathen Magistrates that they were under. And the Christians, being (justly) prohibited by the Apostles to go to Law about personal injuries, before Heathen Judges, but to agree them among themselves, they were the readyer to have low thoughts of such Judges as useless or burdensom, or not fit to be the Governors of Christians. 3. And especially because many of the Christians had been Jews, that were hardly brought to any but a forced submission unto Gentile Rulers; and were ever prone to rebell against them, thinking it an honourable vindication of their holy state and Church, which they thought no Heathen had right to Rule over. The first Hereticks rising from the Jewish Christians, and Judaizing so palpably in this and other things, and the weaker sort of the Jewish Christians being so prone to hearken to them, gave great occasion to the Apostle thus to press the doctrine of subjection.

Where note, that the main question here resolved, is, Whether Magistracy, and Heathen Magistrates should be submitted to as Gods Ordinance for conscience sake? And so it was about the very state of subjection: which among us Christians is a matter past doubt; though we are not all agreed about obedience in some particular cases.

The Precept it self is laid down in the first verse, 'Let every soul be subject to the higher powers.' The first moving Argument is drawn from the efficient cause, which is God. 1. In general Magistracy is his Institution 'There is no power but from God.' And so it is he that sets up Magistrates, and they are subordinate to him, and have a power derived from him 'The Powers that be are ordained of God.' The conclusions hence inferred are v. 2 that therefore 1. Whoever resisteth the power, resisteth Gods own Ordinance, that is, both breaks his Law, and resisteth a Power derived from him, and consequently resisteth God. 2. And so great a sin as resisting Gods Officers and ordinance, deserveth a grievous punishment. In the third verse, the Apostle doth conjunctly bring in his second Argument, (from the end of Government;) & also answer an objection which thence was brought against it. 'What can be expected from Heathens (might the Christians say) but acts of enmity? They will still be persecuting us.' The Apostle at once answering this, and arguing *à fine* for subjection, tells them, that Magistrates have their office to be a terrour to evil works, and not to good: And therefore let us do good, and if the office be used but according to its instituted nature, we shall have praise from Magistrates, and need not fear them. For it is for our good that God hath appointed them. Here the Apostle conjoyneth his two Arguments, from the Author and the End, 'He is Gods Minister for thy Good.' Its possible a wicked man may abuse his office: but this is the End for which God hath appointed Magistracy in the world; and this even Heathen Magistrates profess that they intend; and such vice and vertue as they are acquainted with, they do in some measure deal with accordingly. But if men do evil, then they have cause to fear the Magistrate; 'for he is Gods Minister, a Revenger to wrath, to inflict punishment on him that doth evil': But men must blame themselves and not the Magistrate, if they suffer for ill-doing. Hereupon the Apostle repeateth the Conclusion, that there is a necessity of subjection, not only to escape punishment, but to obey God, even for conscience sake; And hence infers a further Conclusion, that for conscience sake also we must pay them tribute, because they are Gods servants, employed in his work for our good: And therefore on these grounds Tribute, Custom, Fear, Honour must be given to all to whom they are due. Where he sheweth that it was the Governors in actual possession then that he commanded subjection to, when he argueth from their actual Labour for the Subjects good . . .

> Thes. 318. A Christians subjection to Magistrates must be parti-
> cipatively Divine, that is, to Magistrates as Officers authorized
> by God the Universal King.

He that obeyeth upon any other account excluding this, doth not obey a Magistrate as a Magistrate, but as an Idol, or as one that is able to do him good or hurt: and so it is himself that he serveth in his obedience; and there is no Divine obedience in it. But a Christian understandeth that God is the Alpha and Omega, the first and last; and that of him, and through him, and to him are all things, Rom. 11. 36. And therefore he intendeth God in all, and dependeth on him in all; and doing all for him and by his command, all things are sanctified that he doth, and from God he shall receive his reward: Our Obedience is principally denominated and estimated from the principal Authority. In the last Resolution all the Obedience of a Christian to whomsoever is Divine: and all the Obedience of a wicked man is to an Idol, or to carnal-self; to which he subjecteth even God himself.

> Thes. 319. All persons, even Pastors of the Church, are bound
> to this subjection to Magistrates, as I have before proved, and it
> is a double wickedness and treason for them to exempt them-
> selves, that should Preach the doctrine of obedience to
> others . . .
>
> Thes. 320. Rulers must be obeyed in all lawful things . . .
>
> Thes. 321. Kings and Magistrates must be obeyed, even about
> the Worship of God, in all lawfull commands . . .
>
> Thes. 322. About the circumstances of Divine Worship, much
> more about secular things, if the Prince command one thing (not
> contrary to Gods Law) and the Pastors of the Church command
> the contrary, we must obey the Prince before the Pastors . . .

Thes. 323. We must obey Magistrates, though we know not that their Commands are lawfull, as long as they are so indeed, and we have no sufficient Reason to believe them unlawful . . .

Thes. 324. Many things are sinfully comanded, that are lawfully, yea necessarily to be obeyed . . .

Thes. 325. It is lawful for subjects to swear fidelity and obedience to Soveraigns . . .

Thes. 326. It is the subjects Duty to defend their Prince with their strength, and hazzard of their lives, against all foreign and domestick enemies that seek his life or ruine . . .

Thes. 327. It is a most impious thing for Popes to pretend to disoblige Christians from their Oaths and fidelity to their Soveraigns, and to encourage their subjects to rebel and murder them . . .

Thes. 328. It is a great Controversie, whether a subject may fight at a Princes command when he knoweth not the cause to be just, or when he knoweth it to be unjust? Answ 1. If he know it to be unjust, he may not; (except Accidentally *aliunde* some further prevalent Reason warrant it.) 2. If he know it not to be unjust, when it is so, because he doth not his duty to know, he is bound to do that duty, and knowing to forbear. 3 If he know it not to be unjust, because he hath no capacity to discover the unjustice, nor to judge of it, then he may bear arms.

1. The guilt of blood is so heavy a thing that no man should draw it upon himself or his Prince: unjust war is murdering: And no man should murder in obedience to a Prince, when God condemneth it. 2. The Accidental exceptions *à fine*, &c. I shall speak of among the Affirmative Propositions. 3. Wilful ignorance will not excuse a man from the guilt of murder, though a King command it. But the person is at once obliged to use means for his better information, to lay by his errour, and to forbear the sin. 4. But when the sin or unjustness of the war is not notorious, nor within our reach to know it, then we must obey our Rulers that are the Judges or discerners of the case: For, 1. Rulers may not open all causes of a war to all the Souldiers: Sometime the case requireth such secrecie and expedition, as will not consist with that. 2. Subjects by reason of distance and disacquaintance are usually incompetent Judges of such cases. 3. And if

they should never fight till they know the Justness of the cause, they would neglect the Necessary Defence of their Soveraign and Countrey.

Yet, if there be not competent knowledge that it is a good cause, men should not thrust on themselves, nor go to war without some kind of Necessity.

> Thes. 329. The same answer serveth to that other Controversie, Whether a subject may execute an unjust Sentence of a Prince or Judge?

If it concern the Common-wealth directly (or nearly) he must suspend his execution till he have competent satisfaction: As if he were commanded to put to death some persons of great Eminency and Interest in the Common-wealth. But if it be but against a private person (as the hanging a man condemned for felony, the shooting to death a Souldier condemned for mutiny) here if the unjustice be not notorious, and you see no great cause to suspect it, and be not negligent in doing what concerneth you in your place, for due information, you may do execution, if you are commanded. But not, if the unjustice be notorious, or such as you may well discover, without transgressing your bounds in the enquiry. In such cases, Princes should find no Executioners: And the Executioners are guilty of the crime: For God is to be obeyed more then man. Doeg was cursed for slaying the Priests at King Saul's command. It cost the Captains and Souldiers their lives that would have surprized Elias, at the Kings command. Obadiah is blessed that saved the Prophets; and so are the Aegyptian Mid-wives that saved the Israelites children, whom the King commanded to destroy. Many that have been Executioners in the Martyrs death, have had exemplary plagues. Its the Legal way of restraining Kings from unjustice, to punish their Executioners that are subjects, that others may fear obeying them in wickedness.

> Thes. 330. A Soveraign that is an Heretick, or wicked man, yea Infidel or Heathen, must be obeyed in all lawful things: but with an Obedience answerable to his Authority.

I shall open this together with the next Thesis.

> Thes. 331. He that hath no such Right to Govern, as will justifie himself for it before God, may yet be such whom we are obliged to obey.

We have here one of the weightyest and difficultest cases about Obedience, before us. It is very hard to conceive how an Infidel or Heathen can have any Right of Government, because they deny the Universal Soveraign from whom they must derive their Right, or they can have none: And how can a Rebel receive Authority? And why should we obey him that hath no Authority? Nay is it not impossible, when *Authoritas Imperantis* is the formal object of Obedience? Also will it not follow that the Pope should be obeyed that is no Infidel or Heathen?

And yet Christ, and Paul, and Peter have so plainly decided the case, that the Heathen Magistrates that were in their daies were to be obeyed, that we must needs take that for a certain truth. And therefore we have only to consider upon what ground, and how far they are to be obeyed, and to answer the objections ...

The Truth, as I conceive, lieth thus. 1. If the Infidelity of a Prince be not notorious, he is no Infidel to you and me, and then there is no doubt. As in the Ministry, so in the Magistracy, if he be in the place, and not a notorious Usurper, he is an Officer to me: The Benefit of the subject from Magistracy (and Ministry) is first considerable: They are means to our good. The Duty is in order to the Benefit. We have Title to the Benefits of the office, though an Usurper be in the place. And having right to the Benefit, must do the Duty.

2. If the Ruler be notoriously an Infidel or Heathen, yet he is supposed to own a God, even one highest God, that is most perfect in Power, Wisdom and Goodness, and to profess himself a subject of God, and an Officer under him to punish evil doers, and encourage well-doers: This the Heathens did profess. But withall they knew not the Redeemer, nor the True God aright, with a saving knowledge, but dishonoured him by worshipping many Idols in conjunction with him. And in the execution of their offices, they persecuted Christianity, though they encouraged Moral Vertue. What then must we think of such? 1. It is better for the world to have such Governours then none. And therefore they did more good then hurt. There never was among those Heathens so bloody a persecutor, that did not save the lives of many from persecution, for one that they destroyed. For it is the rabble rout of the Vulgar that are the bloodyest persecutors: Where the Emperours killed an hundred Christians, had they but turned loose the vulgar rabble, they would have killed a thousand, or

made an end of them. We should have ten thousand Persecutors for one, if there were no Rulers to restrain the Serpentine Malignant enmity that is in the multitude of the ungodly. 2. Seeing therefore that we have preservation and benefit by them as Governours, we owe them duty as Governours. 3. They are Analogically Rulers, having an Analogical Authority *imperfecti generis*. As they own a God, and profess to worship God, and to preserve peace and order in the world, and punish vice, and promote vertue, according to the Law of Nature, so they are *in tantum* truly Magistrates. But as they deny the Redeemer, and corrupt the doctrine of the God-head, so they fall short of that dependance on the fountain of Authority; that should make them fully men of power. 4. They are accordingly to be obeyed with obedience proportioned to their Authority, and no more. 5. How far an Atheist or Infidel is to be rejected, I shall mention anon under the Affirmatives. 6. Even those that by Atheism, or doing more hurt then good, do nullifie their Magistracy, may yet be materially, though not formally obeyed to avoid evils that else would fall upon our selves, or upon the Church or Common-wealth. 7. And private men may not lay hands on them, as long as God and the Common-wealth (or body of the Nation) forbear them. If a justice of Peace renounce the King, and yet go on to execute the Laws, and if the King be one that can seize on him at his pleasure, and willingly forbeareth him, the subject must let him alone, and obey all that he commandeth according to Law, till the King lay hands on him, or forbid obedience to him. 8. Such persons therefore have no right *Coram Deo* to govern, which will justifie them against the accusation of Usurpation or Treason against God: But yet the people may be bound to obey them (though they know this) not as so Authorized, but as being in the seat or place of Government, and commanding in Gods name by his voluntary permission. If a Traytor come and charge me to obey the Kings Laws, I will obey them as the Kings, though formally I obey not him; But if he be one that the King permitteth in a place of power, I will obey him also, so it be not against the King. So is it in this case, about Infidel and Heathen Governors.

And now the objections need no further answer. The grand Objection (that they are Traytors against God, and have no Power from him, because they deny him) is answered in this that hath been said. The other Objection (that this would infer obedience to the Pope) is easily answered: The Office it self of the Papacy is erected by man against the will of Christ. An Infidel King is in an Office of Gods institution, though the person be half unfit: But the Pope is in an Office that God condemneth, whatever the person be. And therefore a sinful office may not be obeyed by us at all.

Thes. 332. To obey a man that is known to have no Power; is not of it self unlawful, so the office or thing commanded be not forbidden ...

Thes. 333. Private men disjunctly are not made Judges of the Title of their Princes, and therefore must obey them that are in Possession and Administration, unless their Usurpation be so notorious as to be past controversie ...

Thes. 334. If Usurpation be notorious, yet if it be not to the injury of another, the body of the Nation may lawfully afterward Consent, and having consented, are obliged to obey, though still the Usurper is accountable to God for unjust procurement of their consent ...

Thes. 335. It is the subjects Duty to submit to suffering, and not resist the Power of their Rulers, in cases where they may not lawfully obey ...

Thes. 336. In many cases where Officers may be resisted, it may be unlawful to resist the Soveraign himself ...

Thes. 337. In many cases when it is Lawful forcibly to resist a Prince, in some one particular cause or act, we may yet remain obliged to honour and obey him in all things else, and not to depose him, or hurt his person ...

Thes. 338. Every breach of Oath or Covenant by the Prince, will not warrant the people to depose him, or disobey him ...

Thes. 339. When it is notorious that a man hath no right to Govern, the people are not bound to obey him, unless by accident ...

Thes. 340. If a Lawful King be limited, if he Command the subjects beyond his Limits, in matters exempted from his power, or else in matters that the nature of his office extendeth not unto, that command is not an act of power; and therefore it is not a resistance of Power to disobey it.

The Resistance of a person in power, in a point wherein he hath no Power, is not to resist Power, (that is, *Jus regendi*) but the will of a private man: For he is a private man in all things exempted from his Power. 1. A School-master hath nothing to do to command his Scholars in matters about their trades and callings in the world, but only in matters of learning and manners, because it belongeth not to his Office. A Captain hath no Power (as such) about mens estates, but only about the manners and military actions of his Souldiers, in order to his military ends. If a Judge of one Court step into another without Commission, *in alieno foro*, his Sentence is null, and no man bound to obey it. So if the Minister presume to command in things belonging to the Magistrate, and not to him, his act is private, vain and null. So if a Soveraign will turn Physitian, and command all men to take this or that Physick only, not in order to publike good, but private health; or if he will turn Pastor and do things proper to a Pastor of the Church, his acts are private and null, as being without the verge of his vocation.

2. And where his Covenants with his people limit him, he hath no power in the excepted points; e.g. if he be restrained from raising Taxes without the peoples consent, if he yet command the payment of such taxes, he doth it not by Authority: For neither God nor man did ever give him Authority thereto. If the Constitution restrain him from raising war without the consent of the Senate, and yet he undertake to do it, it is not an act of Authority, for he never had Authority thereto.

Object. Who hath Power to limit a Prince, when he is the Officer of God?

Answ. 1. God hath limited him. 2. God hath not determined in Nature or Scripture of the species of Government, nor of the person or family that shall Govern: The People therefore being his Instruments or means, may limit their Soveraigns in things that God hath not determined of. 3. His own Covenants may limit him. And the people having strength and liberty, may force him to such Covenants as are necessary to their security, before they choose him to be their King. No man or family hath Originally more right to Govern a Nation then the rest, till Providence and Consent allow it them. Few Princes will plead a successive Right of Primogeniture from Noah. If the people then say, 'We choose you, (and your family successively) to Rule us on these and no other terms; Accept these terms, or we accept not you.' If he thus accept them, he obligeth himself, and all his successors, that will Rule on that foundation. And therefore he hath no more Authority then another man, in the excepted points.

> Thes. 341. He that thus commandeth beyond his bounds and without Authority, may be lawfully Resisted in those Commands, unless the Law or Constitution forbid such Resistance: Provided that the Honour and Authority of the Ruler be preserved, and he be obeyed in all lawful things.

Not obeying, is the first and chief Resisting; And that is proved lawful before, which proveth this also. He Resisteth not Power or Authority, that Resisteth only the will of a man, that (in that) hath no Authority: Indeed if the Constitution should be (which is not to be imagined) that the Prince shall have no Power in this or that, and yet if he assume it, none shall resist him, then men are restrained from resistance. Otherwise in those points he is a private man. Yet accidentally Resistance may become a sin or a Duty. If it cannot be done without the common loss and hurt, by dishonouring and deposing the Governour, it is a sin by accident. If it be necessary to restrain his usurpation, and to secure the publick good, it will be a duty, and no indifferent thing.

If I be bound to obey or not resist, where there is no Authority to require my obedience, then it must be somewhat distinct and separated from Authority that I am bound to: And what that is, must be discovered. It can be but Accidental: and that's nothing to the point.

> Thes. 342. No Law can oblige us to Punishment but for disobedience; And therefore where the Obedience was not due, the disobedience is inculpable, and the punishment not due: And where it is not due, I am not obliged to it by that Law, though possibly some other Law, may bind me to submit to undue sufferings . . .

> Thes. 343. Inferiour Rulers have no Authority but what is given them from the Soveraign Power; and therefore in all other things the subjects are not bound to obey them; but may forcibly resist them, by the Consent of the Soveraign . . .

> Thes. 344. No humane Soveraign hath Authority to forbid what God commands, nor to command what God forbids; but their Laws that are notoriously contrary to the Laws of God, are nullities, and cannot oblige to obedience or punishment . . .

Thes. 345. To speak properly, no Law obligeth any man to suffer, but only to submit, and not resist: And therefore we are allowed to fly to escape undeserved suffering.

Christ himself alloweth his Disciples to fly in case of persecution, unless when accidentally the confessing of his name requireth them to stay. He that flyeth doth not obey, or suffer: and yet offendeth not, because he doth not disobey a Command of Authority, but of usurping Will, nor doth resist to the disturbance of the common peace, nor to the discouragement or disparagement of Governours. And if flight, then any other lawful means may be used to avoid unrighteous sufferings, as by intreaty, and by mediation of friends, or as Paul by an Appeal; and why not by forcible escape out of prison, or the inferiour officers hands? The Apostles went out of Prison when the Angel let them loose; and the fear of the People often rescued Christ and them. Basil was violently rescued from the Tribunal by the multitude, and many antient Bishops have so escaped: This is Resisting, and violent Resisting: but when it is but an escape from the hands of persecution and injustice, and is no injury to the Governour, nor a disturbing of publick order or peace, it is not the resisting that God forbids, nor any resisting of Authority.

Thes. 346. In many cases it is lawful to Resist the Officers and Instruments of a King, though against his will.

1. As to their persons, they are subjects, and have not themselves the Soveraign Power. 2. Every man that saith he comes in the Kings name, is not to be believed. 3. Unlawful commands should have no Executioners, if they may be known to be unlawful: And therefore the Executioners deserve punishment, and not obedience. 4. A King may be limited himself, and then cannot give the Power to his Officers that he hath not. And when they are sent by meer Will without Authority, they may be dealt with as private invaders of our rights. Elias destroyed two Captains and their Companies with fire from Heaven, that came to command him to come to the King, 2 King. 1.9, 10. Though the manner was extraordinary by Miracle, yet the matter (destroying the Kings Souldiers) was the same as if it had been done by war; and was done by his voluntary Resistance. Every souldier is not the King: and the command of obeying the higher Powers, obligeth us not to obey them that have no Power high or low; but are the meer Instruments of will and Arbitrary invasion, and

not of Power. A Kings will cannot justifie his own acts that proceed not from Power but usurpation: Much less his Officers or Souldiers acts.

> Thes. 347. A King must not be obeyed that commandeth a subject to kill him, or unjustly to kill another, or to do any evil that is or may be known to be such . . .

> Thes. 348. It is the Duty of a Woman to Resist a King that would ravish her; and the duty of others to assist her.

For 1. To ravish her is no act of Authority, and therefore to Resist is no Resisting of Authority, but of lust. 2. Else the Woman should be guilty of Adultery, being bound by God, to preserve her chastity, and so should those that being bound to assist her, do neglect it.

> Thes. 349. Much more should a Nation preserve themselves, or their Representative Body, from the unjust endeavours of a King, that would destroy them.

The Reason is most evident; 1. *A fortiore*: If the life and chastity of a single person may be rescued by force from the Will and Instruments of a destroying and unchast King, much more may a Nation or Parliament be so rescued.

2. We have a concurrence of many greatest obligations to such a rescue. 1. Parliaments we call out about our work, and trust them to secure our Interest, and therefore to forsake them to the will of the unjust is to betray them. 2. There is the highest Reason for Natural self-preservation, to preserve a whole Nation. 3. The honour and interest of God, is most concerned in publike interest. He that thinks a Parliament or Nation should lay their necks upon the block, or quietly perish whenever a King would have it so, hath lost so much of humanity, that he is unfit to be *Civis*, a member of a Commonwealth. Jonathan was not more worth than a Parliament of faithful Patriots, or than a Nation.

> Thes. 350. The destruction of the Body of the People, or of the Common good, can never be an act of Justice in their King or other Governours (except they had a special command for it from God:) And therefore no Justice can be pretended for it . . .

> Thes. 351. No Warre can be lawfull in King or Subjects that is against the common good: except as aforesaid, when a Nation is

devoted to destruction by God, the Universall King, or their wellfare is inconsistent with the more desireable wellfare of the Nations round about them.

1. No King hath any power, but what is for God and the common good: therefore he hath no power to make warre against the common good. His Office essentially is to Govern for the common good. Therefore it is not only besides, but contrary to his Office to fight against it therefore he can give no such power to his Souldiers: therefore it is no Resisting of Power, but of Injustice, to fight against him and his Souldiers in that case, in defence of the Commonwealth.

2. Every subject is by nature, and Relation, bound to preserve the Commonwealth in his place, as well as the King: and therefore none of them can be his instruments against it.

3. If warre be just, either as a meanes, or as an end: The latter no man is so void of reason as to pretend (that is fit for us to dispute with.) If as a meanes, it is either as a meanes to the common good, or to something better, or to something worse: If warre be a meanes to the common good, or else unlawfull, then have we that granted which we seek: then the warre is sinfull that is against the common good. If it be undertaken for a lesser good, it must needs be sinfull: for a greater good is not to be cast away in order to a less. Reason will cry shame on this. Though it were the Right and Prerogative of the King, it cannot be justly preferred before the common good: For even his Prerogative, as his Office and Government it self, are the meanes to this.

Two things indeed are above the common good of a Nation: One is the Interest, Pleasure and Honour of God himself. The other is the good of the world; or of many and greater Nations round about. And the welfare of these (and of the Church universal) may be a higher end then a Nations good, but nothing else.

> Thes. 352. Though a Nation wrong their King, and so *quoad meritum causæ*, they are on the worser side, yet may he not lawfully warre against the publike good on that account, nor any help him in such a warre, but *propter finem* he hath the worser cause.

The Reason it is plain in what is said: 1. If not only his Rights, but his very Office and Administration be *propter bonum publicum*, then may he not plead or, defend those Rights *contra bonum publicum*:

But the Antecedent is past controversie: therefore so must be the consequent.

2. An excessive penalty beyond the proportion of the offence, may make that cause bad, that else would have been good; The danger or ruin of the Commonwealth, or its felicity is such a punishment. If a King be wronged, he must be righted according to the proportion of his wrong: whatever is against the Commonwealth, especially in the great matters of its safety and felicity, is incomparably above the proportion of his wrong: It is more injustice to seek the destruction of the common good, for a real injury to a single person, then it was in them to do that injury.

> Thes. 353. A warre raised against the Body of a Nation, is by them to be construed to be against the common good; No warre therefore against the Body of a Nation, by any of its members; Prince or people, can be lawfull: At least except in the two fore-excepted Cases, viz. the Command of God, and the Interest of the many Nations near them.

Reasons of the Antecedent: 1. The very miseries of a warre do hazzard all the safety and felicity, yea the being of the Commonwealth.

2. He that raiseth warre proclaimeth hostility with them he warreth against. He that proclaimeth hostility against the Nation, deposeth all friendly Relations, and is supposed to be one that will deal as an enemy. An enemy is to be supposed to be one that intendeth not the good or felicity of the Commonwealth.

> Thes. 354. It is not professing in words, that the warre is raised against a rebellious Party only, or that the King intendeth by it the common good, that should make the Nation take it as warrantable, and for their good, if they be the Party that it is actually raised against . . .

> Thes. 355. Though some injury to the King be the occasion of the War, it is the duty of all the people, to defend the Commonwealth against him; yet so as that they protest against that injury.

This is a plain consequent of the former.

1. They resist no true Authority, in resisting him that warreth against the Commonwealth, which is the end of Government.

3. It being the end, no meanes can be pleaded against it.

4. *A simili.* If my own Father or Mother wrong another by a foul word, and the injured person seek their ruine for it: I must not forbear defending my parents, because they were offenders; so be it I protest against their wrong doing.

2. A Lawyer at the Bar may plead against an excessive mulct or penalty, that would be imposed on a culpable Client. If his Client have done a trivial wrong, and another would therefore take away his estate or life, the party that had the worse cause *quoad culpam*, hath the best *quoad pœnam*, and the Lawyer may defend him: And so must a Subject the Commonwealth from hurt and danger.

3. If your own King had wronged the Pope or King of Spain, or a savage Indian King; and a War begin, upon it; If it be justly supposed that the enemy if he should prevail, would destroy the happiness of the Commonwealth, we may and must all fight against them, for the defence of the Commonwealth; but not for the justifying of the Princes cause, which we may possibly be called to protest against. Every wrong that's done by a King, doth not forfeit the peoples happiness, nor warrant the enemies to invade it, nor exempt them from defending it.

> Thes. 356. If a Nation regularly choose a representative Body, of the most noble, prudent, interested members, to discern their dangers and the remedies, and preserve their liberties and safety, the people themselves are to discern those dangers and remedies, by their eyes, and to judge that to be against the common good, which their Trustees do rationally and regularly acquaint them to be so.

Proved. If they must discern their danger either with their own eyes immediately, or with others; it is not necessary that it be by their own immediately. For Countrymen are unacquainted with State-affairs, and with enemies contrivances at home and abroad: And nothing more easie then to bring them past all remedy, before they can see the evil themselves. And what need they Trustees, if themselves immediately were capable. If it must be by others, either by the King, or their Trustees. If they do trust the King absolutely and entirely, they must stand to it: But then what need they choose Trustees. Kings being much trusted against strangers, our case supposeth, that the people do not absolutely trust him, but that in the Constitution, they have provided, that the publike peace and felicity shall be held by reasonable security, and not meer trust in the Princes will: And that Parliaments are appointed to that end. And if so, they are to be trusted accordingly.

And as the Constitution and our Choice requireth it, so their Interests require it; they being many; and their Interest great, and not lying so much within the temptation of an opposition to the peoples interest, as the Princes doth: And it is supposed that the Constitution of the Government, appointeth them for this very end, to secure the people from the usurpation and tyranny of Kings: and therefore in that case Kings are not by the people to be credited before them; for them they should not appoint or choose them.

> Thes. 357. If the said Parliament or Trustees be also legally the Kings chief Council, and so have a double capacity of discerning the dangers of the Commonwealth, the people are the more to see their dangers by their eyes.

For 1. This supposeth them in fullest capacity to discern them. They that are legally the Kings chief Council, are to be supposed acquainted with State-affairs, and how things stand between him and the people. 2. And the King himself having not his office for himself, but for the people, is to see their danger and remedies by the Council, which the Constitution doth appoint him. The Law therefore supposeth them to be the most credible Judges.

> Thes. 358. If the King raise War against such a Parliament, upon their Declaration of the dangers of the Commonwealth, the people are to take it as raised against the Commonwealth, till it be notorious that the Parliament have deceived them and betrayed them.

The Reasons are plain: 1. Because the dangers of the Commonwealth were first declared by competent Judges, and credible Witnesses. 2. Because all their own dangers and oppositions is justly supposed to be for the sake of the Commonwealth. 3. Because they are the Commonwealth, or people Representative. 4. Because being the only legal Trustees appointed for the Nations security from tyranny, when they are conquered, our security is conquered, and the very Constitution overthrown.

> Thes. 359. If a Parliament be moreover the supreme Judicature, by the Constitution enabled to censure and punish Delinquents

and enemies of the Commonwealth, and to raise the power of the Nation against them, if they resist, the King himself having no Authority in that case to pardon or protect them; then is it just for such a Parliament to raise Arms against such Delinquents, to bring them to due punishment, and to prosecute them, though they have the word or will of the King on their side.

This case is plain: For 1. It is Subjects here that the War is raised against. 2. It is in a legal execution of Justice. 3. It is against no Authority: For it is in a case, where it is supposed that the King hath no power to pardon or protect, it's supposed that his protecting power is restrained unto certain cases, of which this is none. 4. If all Delinquents or enemies shall scape, that will but rise in Arms for their security, Commonwealths are destroyed, and Justice and Judgement are idle names, when a few Thieves may easily kill the Judge. And if Kings shall have power to pardon all Delinquents without limitation, the common good is wholly intrusted to their wils, where the King is absolute and above all Laws, he may protect all offendors. But where the Laws are above the King, they must be obeyed though his will be against it, and he forbid it: For his will is not his Authority.

Thes. 360. If in the fundamental Constitutions, any rights by contract be reserved to the people, and the King obliged to maintain them, the people may lawfully defend those Rights, (by means proportionable to their worth) against the King that violateth them, unless they have also consented to be restrained from such defence.

1. If the Rights be but such as are needfull *ad melius esse*, or the loss of them be tolerable, the defence of them must not be by deposing the Prince, but by gentler meanes: Though as Thieves are hanged for robbing one man, so divers Subjects may be destroyed for robbing the Commonwealth at the Kings command, of its Rights and Liberties. 2. But if people to avoid a civil War, have expresly tyed themselves not to resist a King or Subjects, that by his command do deprive them of their Liberties, then they are wholly at his will. 3. But such a Consent or Obligation is not to be supposed, unless it be expressed. For 1. The very Covenanting for our Rights importeth, that we secure them, and leave them not meerly to the Princes will. 2. And in Covenanting for them, we exempt them from his power; so that in invading them he is but a private man; and in resisting him we resist not

Authority, but Will. For if he have power of our excepted Rights, it is either immediately from God, or mediately by Consent of men. Not the former: For we suppose it to be in cases that God hath left undetermined. The people can have no Right to that which God himself takes from them: Not by man. For it is supposed that the people have excepted these things from the Princes power, and he consented.

> Thes. 361. The Oaths of Kings, and the Charters or Laws in which they have expressed their Consent to Govern on such and such termes, together with the ancient Customes of the Nation, are the discoverers of the Princes limits, and the Peoples Rights.

Though every breach of Covenant forfeiteth not the Crown, yet every Covenant or Consent of the Prince doth shew the limits of his Power. If he (that naturally had no more right than other men) do accept the Government on such and such termes, or afterward Consent to them, he hath no power beyond or against those termes: and therefore he may not break his Oaths.

> Thes. 362. It is lawfull to resist either King or Subjects that are his Instruments, by Law-suits, or by force, where the Laws allow it, if he be not above Law, and do not Repeal them.

I spake before of the peoples Rights reserved from the Kings power: I speak now of the allowance of the Law. If the Law be above the King, then may be do what the Law alloweth, though against his will. If it allow us to sue the King in his Courts of Justice, we may do it: If it allow us to sue his Agents, as subjects that have broke the Law, though by his command, we may do it. If the King bid a man murder another, I may sue him, and hang him against the Kings will, if the Law allow it. If the Kings Tenant keep an unjust possession against me, it is lawfull for me to sue him at Law, and at last, if he forcibly resist, the Sheriff may raise the Power of the County to eject him, though against the Kings will, when the Law alloweth it. And if the Law allow us to resist his Armies, we may do it: and so doing, we Resist no Power, but strength and will. But where the King is Absolute above the Laws, as being meerly his own Acts, there we may Resist, till he repeal the Law, or forbid us, and no longer (on that account.)

> Thes. 363. Where the Soveraignty is distributed into several hands, (as Kings and Parliaments,) and the King invade the

others part, they may lawfully defend their own by warre, and the subject lawfully assist them, yea though the power of the Militia be expressly given to the King; unless it be also exprest that it shall not be in the other.

The Conclusion needs no proof; because Soveraignty as such hath the Power of Arms, and of Laws themselves. The Law that saith the King shall have the Militia, supposeth it to be against enemies, and not against the Commonwealth, nor them that have part of the Soveraignty with him. To Resist him here, is not to resist Power, but Usurpation, and private will. In such a case, the Parliament is no more to be Resisted than he; because they also are the higher Power.

> Thes. 364. Names are not the only notes of Soveraignty: If a King have the Title of the Supream head, or only Soveraign of his Dominions, and yet a Senate have an essentiall part without the Names, they lose not their part, nor is it to be judged of by the Name.

A people may give an honorary Title to the Prince, and not give the same to others that have part in the Soveraignty: and this is ordinary: sometimes for the Nations honour, which they would have to be abroad conspicuous in their Prince: and sometimes to please him instead of fuller power. Those therefore that will judge of the power of Princes by their Titles or Names, and thence fetch Arguments to resolve mens consciences, know not what a narrow foundation they build on: Of which see Mr. Lawson against Hobbs his Politicks.

> Thes. 364(*sic*). Where the Soveraignty is in several hands, and so the Constitution supposeth their agreement, the dividers are the dissolvers, and upon a Division barely among themselves, in which the Commonwealth is not concerned, the Subjects should obey neither of them against the other, as having no power against each other: but should be against them, that in obedience to either part do raise the War.

The Reason is plain: Because though they are many natural persons, they are all but one civil person; and because that all the power of Arms here is either defensive against Enemies, or vindictive and punitive against offending Subjects. But none in soveraignty while such, are to be taken as enemies: And neither part that have the

Soveraignty, as such, can be offending Subjects; for they are no Subjects. Indeed in such a Senate, the persons considered disjunctly may be Subjects: but it is conjunctly as a house or body, that they have the Soveraignty. Moreover, all lawfull War is for the common good: But the dissolution of the fundamental Constitution, is not to be taken for the common good, but grievous hurt and ruine, though when necessity dissolveth it, the best parts must be first secured from perdition.

> Thes. 365. Upon such a division among them that have the highest power, if some Subjects will unlawfully begin as instruments of the divisions, the rest are then obliged to stand up, and that for the safety of the Commonwealth, more then for either of the parties, and for that party that is for it; and against them both, if they be both against it.

1. It is notorious to the Nation, when the King and Senate (that are now supposed to be sharers in the Soveraignty) do disagree, and fall into hostility and open War, that the frame of the fundamental Constitution is dissolved. And when the ship is split or sinking, it's time for the passengers to save themselves and their goods as well as they can: When the house is on fire, we must shift for our selves and that we have: When the Government dissolveth itself, they that possessed it turn us loose to rule ourselves, and defend our selves. If a man fight against himself, he is to be held as a distracted man: And so should King and Senate be in such a case, being but one civil person: But if any will rush in, and help one hand against the other, the people must either fall on them, or otherwise secure themselves. In this case the Prince hath no offensive power against the Senate, nor the Senate against the Prince: and therefore we should so obey neither, nor help neither, as such: But if we see that all will not be so wise or honest, but some Delinquents will adhere to one of the parties, and some foolish people to the other, we must then look to the Commonwealth.

And here if one party have the juster cause *catéris paribus*, we must adhere to that part; not as authorized primarily against the other, but as justly defending themselves against them. But *si catéra non sint paria*, that is, if the welfare of the Commonwealth lie on one side more then the other, yea though that side had at first begun the wrong, (much more if that party were just and innocent) we must joyn with that part: yea or against both, if the safety of the Commonwealth require it. For then we go not against Authority; neither King nor Senate having Authority (unless to defend themselves and the Nation) against the other. And surely whether we may save the Commonwealth against Authority or not, there is no doubt but we may save it without any governing Authority, when it is not against it. Nature that alloweth self-preservation to all, that forfeit not their lives, doth eminently require a Nation to preserve themselves; their common welfare being a thing that can be forfeited to none but God, and neighbour Nations; not to any within themselves. It is not the falling out of King and Parliament that forfeiteth the Nations happiness, or can make it unlawfull to preserve it. If you suppose them both to be guilty of an unjust War, as having no power against each other, then may the people defend themselves against the Souldiers of both, as being but *prædones & grassatores*: Or make use of either to further their defence. But if one of them as a defender, or on other accounts have the more righteous cause, the people may joyn with them so farre as it is righteous, securing still the Commonwealth. A King may have cause to blame a Parliament, when he hath no cause that will justifie raising a War against them; and a Parliament may have cause to blame a King, and yet none to raise War against him. In this case, when one is originally in the fault, or it's ten to one, both of them in some fault before a War, but neither of them in such fault as will warrant a War against the other, (which is a dissolving of the Government it self, and is an injury to the Commonwealth, more then to themselves) the people may joyn with neither of them as offenders against the other, but must first look to themselves and the common safety which the contenders do forsake, and next consider what use may be made of either to that end; and in subserviency to it, rather to defend the innocent then the guilty: The Law knowes not a Division, but supposeth an Unity; and therefore it hath nothing to do in directing any of the Subjects to fight against either King or Parliament: When it comes to this, the business is resolved into the fundamental Lawes of God and nature, antecedent to all humane Lawes. The Defender may have a just War against the Invader, by the grounds of nature: But neither of their causes is to be preferred to the Commonwealth. And if *finis gratia* for the common safety, the people should take part with the more culpable side, not as owning their original causes, but as joyning with them for the common safety; this maketh not the people guilty of the ill beginning or cause of those they joyn with. e. g. As I said before, if the King abuse the Pope or Turk, and they raise War against him for it, the people taking his part to prevent the Nations overthrow, do not thereby engage themselves in the original of the quarrel, nor become guilty of his fault, nor of any unlawfull War; for they manage it but as defensive, against such as would take unjust revenge of the innocent. And so if a Parliament should somewhat dishonour or abuse a King, (when yet neither of them should go to War for it) the people joyning with the Parliament, are not guilty of that abuse; nor of an unlawfull War, while they interesse themselves only in the business of their own preservation, and not in the original of the difference. The Law of nature stands, when men do sinfully dissolve the Commonwealth.

> Thes. 366. If in case of such division the Constitution (foreseeing it) have determined which side we must adhere to, then that part becomes the Soveraign, which we must obey against the other.

If it be said in the fundamental Contracts, that in case the King and Parliament differ, the Subject shall adhere to King against Parliament, or to Parliament against King; then in that case the other loseth his Authority, or rather had but a diminutive part, which might be resisted. But this is a case that seldom happens: For were there such a determination, that one must not be obeyed, they would not enter into the contention, unless by force to make a change.

> Thes. 367. If the Senate besides their part in the Soveraignty, have a just offensive War against delinquent Subjects, and profess no War against the King unless defensive, and also be the Trustees of the people for the security of their liberties and happiness, and suffer danger, and enter into War upon no account of their own, but the peoples; then are the people bound to adhere unto them by many obligations.

This is most evident from all that is said before, and needeth no more proof. But I suppose some will say here, that then the case is hard with Kings that have Parliaments to joyn with them in the Soveraign power: for the people must alwayes take part with the Parliament, though they do the wrong, because it is they that are their Trustees and Representatives, and so Kings must ever be at their mercy.

I answer, 1. Where this is the Constitution, it is supposed that a King must never fight against his people, or Parliament: and if he receive the Crown on these termes, he meeteth with nothing but what he consented to; he might have refused it, and may leave it when he will. He must never expect upon any pretence of self-preservation, to have the peoples consent, that he shall have power to destroy them, or make War against them or their Trustees.

2. But yet there are cases in which we all must take part with a King against a Parliament: As 1. If they would wrong a King, and depose him unjustly, and change the Government, for which they have no power, the body of the Nation may refuse to serve them in it, yea may forcibly restrain them. 2. If they notoriously betray their trust, not in some tolerable matters, but in the fundamentals, or points that the common good dependeth on, and engage in a cause that would destroy the happiness of the Commonwealth; it is then the peoples duty to forsake them, and cleave to the King against them, if they be enemies to the Commonwealth: But this is not to be suspected till it be notorious. But Parliaments are indefectible: Should they ever be so corrupt as to seek our ruine, we should not think our selves obliged to obey them or defend them. They may forfeit their power as well as Kings: But no such thought must be entertained of either, till necessity force it.

> Thes. 368. If a King deliberately and obstinately engage himself in the change of the Constitution in the substantials, to the destruction of the safety and happiness of the Nation, he may not only be resisted, but ceaseth to be a King, and entreth into a state of War with the people.

1. 'Tis not a change in smaller matters, but the substantials of the Government that we speak of. 2. It is not a sudden passionate act, but a setled endeavour that we speak of. 3. And so the case is plain. For 1. In Contracts each party is conditionally obliged: And we are bound to him, on condition he be true to us. If one party shall remain bound, though the other violate their fidelity, the Covenants are vain. In other Relations it is so, and therefore in this. 2. He dissolveth the Government: and then he can be no Governour. 3. He becometh an enemy, and therefore can be no King. A destroyer cannot be a Ruler and Defender. He proclaimeth hostility, and is not to be trusted.

Thes. 369. It belongeth to the people to discern among competitors and contenders for the Government, whose cause is best, and to resist usurpers and enemies to their Peace.

That the Nation is thus to have a *Judicium discretionis* is evident: 1. Because it is their interest that is principal in the business: the good or hurt will be principally theirs. 2. If they do not judge (discerningly) they cannot execute: And then the people must not help their Soveraign against usurpers. But if they must, (and who else shall) then must they discern whose cause is right, that they may know whom to help, and whom to resist.

Thes. 370. Though an Infidel or Heathen King have a Power *secundum quid*, and may be the Head of an Infidel or Heathen Commonwealth, yet may he not be voluntarily chosen the Head of a Christian Commonwealth.

Not only because the Commonwealth cannot be called Christian when the Head is a Heathen, but because it is treachery against God and the Redeemer, for a People that have their free choise of their Governours to choose such as are enemies to the Universal Soveraign: They should hereby be guilty of some degree of a National Apostacy: The Kingdoms of the world should be the Kingdoms of the Lord and of his Christ: therefore they must not be given up to Infidelity. But if a Nation be not free to choose their Governours, but are by the Sword or otherwise forced to submit, then whether they should submit to an Infidel to avoid destruction, is a case that I am not now to determine: But it is to be decided, not by the personal present suffering which the Nation by such submission may avoid; but by the interest of their posterity and the Nations round about them. If the present spoil and ruine of a Nation might prevent the captivating of posterity or neighbour Nations more considerable to perpetual Infidelity, or tyranny of Infidels, it should be born: But if they can make better terms for themselves and posterity (without greater hurt to the Christian cause and Nations) by such submission, then without, I see not but they may submit to the Government of Infidels: And if they submit and promise obedience, they must obey in lawfull things, and be faithfull to them: But if Christians live (as the primitive Christians did) in a Commonwealth where Prince and people are Infidels, there they owe obedience whether they promise it or not: For their being subjects, and members of the Commonwealth containeth their obligation. While they have the protection, they owe obedience.

> Thes. 371. The chief part of the common good, or happiness, is the enjoyment of the meanes which God hath made necessary to salvation: It is therefore as lawfull for a Nation to fight for the preservation of these meanes to themselves and posterity, as for their worldly goods and liberties, at least: though for neither, without just Authority and License.

The Liberties, Goods, and other accommodations of the flesh, which worldlings so much value and contend for, are dung and dross in comparison of the things of everlasting life. If therefore we may not fight for Religion, much less for Liberties or Lives that are contemptible in comparison thereof. It is therefore either confusion and ignorance of the state of the Question, or palpable errour, in them that maintain, that it is unlawfull to fight for Religion. It is one thing to fight to make others Religious, and another thing to fight to preserve our own Religion, and to preserve the meanes of Religion to us and the Nation and our posterity. They grant themselves what they deny, when they say that we may fight for our Lives and Liberties: For though all that fight for their Liberties, fight not for their Religion; yet all that thus fight to preserve Religion, do fight for their Liberties also. Persecutors will take away our Lives or Liberties, if we worship God according to his will, and use the necessary meanes of salvation. In fighting against this persecution, we fight principally and ultimately for our own and posterities salvation, and next for the necessary means thereto, and proximately for our lives and liberties.

And it is but a delusory course of some in these times, that write many volumes to prove, that subjects may not bear Arms against their Princes for Religion, As if those that are against them did think that Religion only as the end, yea or life or liberty, would justifie Rebellion? Or that the efficient authorizing Cause were not necessary as well as the final? It's as true that subjects may not fight against their Princes for their Lives or Liberties, as that they may not for Religion.

There are other things necessary to warrant an action besides the final Cause. All things are not a means to a good end: nothing can be a means that's against the end: but many things may be unwarrantable, and no just meanes, which by man are intended to the best end. No man may do anything against his salvation, nor against the publike good, especially in matters of their salvation: But yet all is not lawfull that men do with an intent to further their own or other mens salvation. Where bearing Arms against Princes is warrantable *quoad fundamentum*, this will warrant it *quoad finem*. No better end, but there must be a good ground also.

And yet as to the end, it is not every matter of Religion, much less every erroneous conceit of men, that is sufficient. If men that are Equals, yea or Superiours, should think indifferent things to be necessary, or those that are necessary only *ad melius esse*, to be simply necessary; or those that are evil to be good, and hereupon shall force them by fire and sword on other men, they shall answer for their errour, arrogance and cruelty together. If Papists will first believe their fond opinions to be articles of faith, and necessary to salvation, and then will think that the salvation of men, and the publike good dependeth on them, and therefore will propagate them by the sword, or rebell against Princes to maintain them, their errour will not justifie their wickedness. It must be truly the cause of God, and the truly necessary meanes of life, and of the common good, and not mistakes or smaller matters, that must be the sufficient end of Warre, even in Princes themselves, that fight for Religion: Much more in people; of which in the next.

> Thes. 372. In a Christian Commonwealth, where Rulers in their Oaths or Covenants have obliged themselves to maintain the Christian faith, and necessary meanes of the salvation of their people, and have taken the Government on these termes; if after this they break these Covenants, and cast off Christianity, or cast out the meanes of salvation, which they bound themselves to defend, it is lawfull for the body of that Nation to resist them, and defend their welfare: Much more if those that have but part in the Soveraignty, do this.

Note here 1. That I speak not of an Infidel Nation, where the people never make such Covenants with their Princes, but would doubly persecute, were they not restrained: There an Infidel Prince may be a protection and blessing to those few among them that believe. Whereas in a truly Christian Nation, either no Governour would be better then a persecuting Infidel, (the people associating in Communityes) or at least, they may easily choose a better. 2. I speak not of those Christian States and Nations, that have already promised obedience to known Infidels. But of those that have limited the power of their Princes, in these things: And if the Constitution limit them, their Acceptance of the Government is an implicite Consent and Covenant though there were no more. 3. I say not yet that every private man may resist, but that the body of the Nation in this case may. And the Reason is evident: because 1. They are naturally bound to preserve the common good, especially in the greatest points. 2. And in so doing, it is no power, but arbitrary usurpation which they resist. For God giveth Kings no power against himself; and it is here supposed that the People have excepted this power from their Princes: And therefore in this they have no power, and to resist them is to resist no power.

And to break the Covenants, and reject the termes on which they did receive their Crowns, is to disoblige the people to whom they Covenanted, and cast away their Crowns, and turn into a state of enmity, if it be habituate, and if it be in the Essentials of the Covenant; and especially if they prosecute it by a Warre. What man can pretend to be so independant, and above the God of Heaven, as to have an Authority against him, and consequently not from him, which no men may resist. But if the Cause be Gods, and the Prince disabled to oppose it by the Constitution, the case is then most clear.

Here I shall again annex a Caution, and then answer some Objections.

If private men in doubtfull cases will take on them to be judges of their Governors, and conclude them to violate their Covenants, or their Constitution, or the Common safety when it is no such matter, they grievously sin against the Ordinance of God, and the publike Peace. And in case of a private or less publike injury, it is rebellion to make a publike resistance, by raising a warre. A woman may by personall private resistance defend her Chastity against a King; but she may not raise a warre to defend it. The Priests did lawfully (Azariah with fourscore more valiant men) withstand Uzziah the King when he went into the Temple to burn incense; and told him it belonged not to him, and bid him go out of the Sanctuary: yea when the Leprosie rose upon him, they thrust him out, 2 Chron. 26. 16, 17, 18, 19, 20. But if they had raised a warre against him for this, they had done ill.

And when a people are necessitated to a defensive warre; if thy will proceed beyond a just defence, and depose their Kings or Governours that have not deposed themselves, nor notoriously made themselves uncapable, they will be Rebels in deposing them, though their defence was just.

A Civil warre doth hazzard the happiness of a Nation, and therefore is not to be enterprized for any smaller crimes, or for the avoiding of any tolerable evil, but for that which is notoriously more dangerous to the Nation than the warre it self.

Indeed where all the Nation agree (as in the defence of Jonathan against Saul) or so many that there is no party to make warre against them, then if the King would break his Covenants, or violate their Liberties in a lower case (as Jonathans death was) they may as one man say, This shall not be: and hinder the execution of the evil, without a warre; yet so, that they nevertheless obey and honour the King in all things else.

And now concerning a Peoples defence of their happiness and safety against a King, that was restrained by the Constitution or his Consent; I must answer some of the Learned Hadrian Saravia's Objections, *de Imperan. author. & Obed.* li.4. cap.4[24] He argueth from the state of Marriage, 1. That many Covenants about Dowry, Joyntures, &c. may be violated, without dissolving the marriage. 2. That the essential conditions may be violated without such dissolution. 3. That no stipulation can be made that will warrant the offended party to separate.

To these I answer: 1. I grant him, that till a King do actually cast away his Government and become an Enemy, or else habitually make himself incapable or be made so by God, the people may not depart from their subjection. It is not casting off subjection in state, but resisting in a particular case that is now in question.

2. The case of Marriage and Civil Government so much vary, that the Objection is of no force. For 1. God hath already stated the power of Husband and Wife, and subjected the Wife to the Husband by his Laws, and that for all alike; so that they are not left at liberty to make any alterations, nor several Species of Husbands, as Commonwealths may have several Species of Government. God hath not determined in his Word, whether this or that Nation shall be governed by a Monarch, by the Optimates, or by a mixt Government. He hath left it free to them to put the Soveraignty into the hands of

---

[24] Hadrian Saravia, *De imperandi authoritate, et Christiana obedientia, libri quator* (London, 1593).

one, or two, or an hundred, or a thousand; and to make the division equall or unequall: much more to limit Rulers in the things that God hath left to their prudentiall determination. 2. Moreover God hath determined that Marriage shall be for life, and not for a limited time; and that it shall not be dissolvable on any terms but those of his description: But he hath not done so by Governours. He hath no where made it necessary that Kings shall be for life, and unremoveable: A Dictator for a year, or two year is not forbidden: A King for seven year, is not contrary to Gods Word. If a people that are free, may choose whether they will have a King or none, then may they say, If you will accept the Crown for seven years, we will subject our selves to you, else not. If they resolve to have Kings by Rotation as Rome had Consuls, that every year or seven year they might have a new one, though I think it not fit, yet it is not against any word of God. And if they may absolutely stipulate with them, to be Kings but for such a time, then may they conditionally stipulate to be Kings no longer then they do so or so. e. g. To forfeit their Crowns, if they shall raise War against the Nation, or if they introduce a forraign power, or if they set up infidelity, or banish the Gospel, or if they dispossesse the people of their Proprieties. There is liberty for such contracts here, when there is none in Marriage, which God hath not left so much to the will of man.

3. And yet even in the case of marriage, I deny his conclusion, that the violation of the essential Conditions doth not warrant a separation. He confesseth that Adultery and wilfull desertion, are just Causes of divorce: and these are the violations of the essential Conditions. An obstinate perpetuated *negatio congressus*, is a desertion. His instances of sterility, morosity, and adventitious impotency, are not instances of a violation of the essential Conditions. A scold violateth not the essential Conditions and voluntary sterility, and impotency subsequent were never Covenanted against. Voluntary self-debilitation (yea involuntary) in many Christian States, is allowed as a just cause of Divorce. But if it be not so, yet

4. The case differeth in this: A Nation must needs have Government: But a man or a woman are not in such necessity of marriage: If a Husband be impotent, the woman may lawfully live without his use. But a Nation may not live ungoverned: And therefore if a King fall distracted, or statedly incapable, they must be governed by others.

5. And lastly I answer, That even about Joynture, and Peace and outward Priviledges, though a Woman may not be divorc't for injury

206

in these, yet hath she her remedy from the Magistrate, who is superiour to her Husband. By your similitude then, you should allow a Nation their remedy, in as great and much greater cases, which yet will not warrant a divorce, or withdrawing of their subjection.

There is somewhat *in exercitio*, that is essential to Governing; and somewhat that pertaineth but to better Governing. As he that useth not the former is no Governour, so he that is uncapable of it, is uncapable of Governing. If the essential qualifications be wanting, or the essential conditions violated, and the essential ends be statedly subverted, the Government is nullified: Or else the essence is not the essence. If that part of the happiness of the people be subverted that is next to the essential end, they may retain and exercise the power of seeking a due Remedy.

The commonest remedy that Nations have thought meet to use in this case is, to keep all Subjects under the known Laws, and Courts of Justice, that they may not dare to execute unlawfull Commands, and to restrain Kings from pardoning or defending such malefactors as do endanger the Nations Rights and Peace: And so to let the Person of the King alone, and to punish the Subjects that break the Laws, though he command them. This is a resisting the Lusts, and the Wills of Princes, but not them, as to their Persons or their Power . . .

> Thes. 373. A notorious Atheist, and Enemy to the Essentials of Godliness, that sets himself to root it out, is an open Traitor or Rebel against the God of Heaven, from whom all Power must proceed: And therefore as he is a Magistrate but *secundum quid*, so it is but an answerable obedience that we owe him, as one that is tolerated by God in his Rebellion, for the maintaining of external Order among men, for the common good.

> Thes. 374. If a Prince that hath not the whole Soveraignty, be conquered by a Senate that hath the other part, and that in a just Defensive Warre, that Senate as the conquering part, cannot assume the whole Soveraignty, but must suppose the Government *in specie* to remain, and therefore another King must be chosen, if the former be uncapable.

I here respect the Senate as the remaining Soveraignty, and not as the Peoples Representative: And so the case is plain: Because, 1. They conquered not the Species, but the Individual. 2. They conquered not the People, but the Prince: And therefore they have no

Power to change the Constitution, which was formed by Contract with the People. The Commonwealth hath not forfeited its form of Government when a Prince hath forfeited his Interest: And therefore *Rex non moritur*: The Constitution remains good; and the Conquerours have no power to change it, without the Peoples Consent.

> Thes. 375. If the whole Family with whom the People were in Covenant be extirpated, or become uncapable, the People may new forme the Government as they please, (so they contradict not the Law of God:) not by Authority, but by Contract with the next chosen Governours; nor as Subjects, but as Free men, the Government being dissolved.

When one party in Covenant is dead (naturally or civilly) the other is free: Subjects as such, have nothing to do to change the Government: nor Subjects while such, unless they expresly reserve that liberty. But when a whole Royal Family is extinct, or all that they were in Covenant with for succession, they are disobliged, and may offer the next, what terms they please, that are consistent with the Laws of God. But they cannot settle the new Government, either as Subjects, or as Rulers, but by Contract: For they can command no man to become their Governour, and submit to their terms; but they may offer it to any that is fit, who is as free to accept it, or refuse it.

> Thes. 376. Where there are not Assemblies Representing the People, or some Trustees enabled to be the Preservers of their Liberties, it will be hard to imagine how a Warre can lawfully be raised for their Defence, in any of the forementioned Cases, unless where they are almost all of a mind.

For it must be some private men that must be the beginners, whose actions are not the actions of the Nation; nor can they know whether the Nation approve of them, and would concurre: so that the Possibility and Lawfulness of Defence will be questionable, where there are no Trustees.

> Thes. 377. Though too many lay their Religion and Salvation at the feet of Princes, because they have first laid them at the feet of their fleshly interest and lusts, yet most men have more need to be called on to obey their Rulers, then told how farre they may disobey or resist: And in doubtfull cases, it is safest to suffer, rather than resist.

Every man is naturally selfish and proud, and apt to break the bounds that God hath set us, and to be Kings and Laws unto our selves. This Rebelling disobedient disposition, therefore should be first resisted and subdued, as a greater enemy to the peace of Nations (at least of many) then the faults of Princes are.

> Thes. 378. The proud censoriousness of Subjects, that think themselves capable of Judging of all their Rulers actions, when they are so distant as never to know or hear the Reasons of them, is the common Cause of sinfull murmurings and Rebellions.

The most ignorant Country people are exceeding prone to pass their censures upon the actions of Kings and Parliaments, and shoot their bolt before they ever saw the Mark. How confidently will they blame and reproach their Superiours, as if they were able themselves to Govern better, or at least were so much honester then their Rulers, that their honesty would supply their lack of wit. In all ages, murmuring against Superiours, and ignorant censuring them, have been the common sinne of the people: Though alas, Princes have given them too much occasion and provocation.

> Thes. 379. The most excellent Policy is true Piety: and the principal way for Princes to oblige the Subjects to them, and remove all fears of Seditions and Rebellions, is heartily to devote all their Power and Interest to the Cause of God, and the common good.

This will engage the Lord to own them, that is the King of Kings, and the disposer of all, in whose favour alone their safety lieth. And this will endear them to all that are good, and cause them to be as zealous in loving and honouring them, as children to their Father. Yea, it will breed much Reverence in the minds of common and ungodly men, who will speak highly of Godliness in a Prince, though they like it not for themselves. And when they see that Princes are Fathers of their Countreys, and seek not themselves, but the common good: it is the most excellent means to procure them common Love and Reverence.

> Thes. 380. A Prudent, Godly, Righteous Prince is so rare, and so great a mercy, that the People that enjoy such, are bound exceedingly to Love, Honour and Obey them, and daily pray for them, and cheerfully pay the Tributes they demand, and willingly venture their lives for their Defence.

Oh how few Joshuah's, David's, Josiah's, Constantine's, Theodosius's, &c. have the Kingdoms of the world enjoyed! At this day alas, how few are the Princes that have any zeal for God, and preferre his Kingdom and Interest before their own! How many are fighting their own warres, arising from the lusts that warre in their members, and making havock of the Church of God? But how few are studious to promote the Gospel, and the union of the Churches, and Peace of Christians, and the Conversion of the unbelieving world! Let them that God enricheth with so great a mercy, value it highly, and take heed of murmuring and ingratitude, or of neglect of those earnest prayers, and cheerfull obedience, by which so great a mercy may be continued and improved. How sad a blow was it to England that Edward the Sixth was so soon taken away! How many would have after redeemed his life with the dearest price, that before too much undervalued their happiness! One serious thought of the state of most of the Nations of the world, should turn the murmuring humour of too many into hearty Praise, and earnest Prayers to God for our Superiours. If that Nation that is most happy of any upon Earth, in a Government suited to the highest Interest, and to Gods Description, (Rom. 3. 3.) should yet murmure and despise that Government, it would be a most hainous sin, and a terrible Prognostick, especially to the guilty souls.

CHAPTER 13

Of the late Warres

Having laid down these fore-going Grounds, it would not be here unseasonable to render a publick account of my own actions, in answer to that Question, which I have been urged with by so many, 'By what Reasons was I moved to engage myself in the Parliaments Warre?' But (though I have not leisure to render so full an account to each particular Quærist, as may be satisfactory, and therefore could be content to dispatch it here at once for all, yet) it will require so long a History of my own affairs, and also so many ungratefull recitals of the abuses and evils of those times, that I shall not undertake so unpleasant a task, till I am called to it by such necessity, as will excuse these inconveniences: but only cursorily shall cast in these following brief accounts instead of a fuller Declaration.

§. I. The malignant hatred of seriousness in Religion, did work so violently in the rabble where I lived, that I could not stay at home with any probable safety of my life. My life was sought before I went away: Sober, pious men of Neighbour-Parishes, that thought the rabble had been upon my head in a tumult (when indeed I was out of Town) were knockt down in the streets, to the hazzard of their lives, when they went among them to look after me; and meerly because they were accounted Puritans. And all this was but on a false rumour, that the Churchwardens were about to obey the Parliaments Order, in taking down the Images of the Trinity about the Church. The Warre was begun in our streets before the King or Parliament had any Armies. The hatred of the Puritans, and the Parliaments Reformation, inflamed the ignorant, drunken, and ungodly rout, so that I was forced to be gone even before the Warres; but when I returned, and the Armies came among us, I could then stay no longer; nor had I any place of safety from their rage, but the Armies and Garrisons of the Parliament: And multitudes of my Neighbours as well as I, were forced into Garisons to save their lives, that else would have lived at home in peace. And I only propose it, Whether those Subjects, that are utterly undeservedly deprived of the protection of Magistrates and Laws, are not discharged of their obligations, and turned out of their Relations to them, and are put to seek for other Protectours?

§. II. A Parliament (as farre as I have been able to learn) hath all these four or five capacities 1. It is a Representative of the People as free. 2. It Representeth the People as Subjects. 3. By the Constitution they have part in the Soveraignty. 4. They are the Kings chief Councel. 5. And they are the Kings chief Court of Judicature.

Of the Antiquity of their Power, and its Extent, I referre you to Mr. Bacons Treatise of Parliaments, and Mr. Prin's Book of the Power and Priviledges of Parliaments[25] (to pass by others.) But it is no way necessary to the cause in hand to prove the Antiquity of their Being, or their Power. When ever they were established in that Power, it was by an Explicite or Implicite Contract, between the Prince and People, there being no other Ground that can bear them, except an immediate Divine Institution, which none pretend to. And the Prince and People have as much power in this Age to make such a Contract, and alter the Constitution, as they had three thousand years ago. And therefore if I find them in possession of the Power, and can prove but a Mutual Consent of Prince and People, I need no other proof of their Power.

§. III. When I say that the Parliament Representeth the People as free, I take it for undeniable, that the Government is constituted by Contract, and that in the Contract, the People have not Absolutely subjected themselves to the Soveraign, without reserving any Rights or Liberties to themselves; but that some Rights are reserved by them, and exempted from the Princes power: And therefore that the Parliament are their Trustees for the securing of those exempted Rights, and so Represent the People as free; not as wholly free, but

---

[25] Nathaniel Bacon, *An Historical Discovery of the Uniformity of the Government of England ... Continuation ... Until the End of the Reign of Queen Elizabeth ... Being a Vindication of the Ancient Way of Parliaments in England* (London, 1651); William Prynne, *The Sovereigne Power of Parliaments and Kingdomes* (London, 1643).

as being so farre free as that exemption signifies. The Rights and Freedom of the People as a People, are in order of nature before the Constitution, and excepted, and so established and secured in it. 1. And this is the first Capacity of Parliaments, To Represent the People as a People, to secure their Liberties as Trustees. If any man deny them this Capacity, he makes us absolutely subject to an unlimited arbitrary power, contrary to all Law, and our long possessions, and to all reason. To have no rights, and to have none but what are wholly at the Princes will, and which we have no security for, is in effect all one.

2. The Parliament as they Represent the People as Subjects, can do nothing but humbly manifest their grievances, and Petition for Relief.

3. The Parliament as having part in the Soveraignty by the Constitution, hath part in the Legislative power, and in the final Judgement.

4. As it is the Kings chief Councel, he is ultimately to hear them in cases that concern the safety and Peace of the Commonwealth.

5. As it is his highest Court of Justice, they have power of judgement and execution, over all the Subjects; so that from them there is no Appeal: The King being to judge by his Judges in their several Courts, this is his highest Judicature; yet so as that the Power of Judging was not equally in both Houses.

The Disputers that oppose the Parliaments Cause, do commonly go on false suppositions, about the very Being and Power of Parliaments, and take it for granted, 'That the Soveraign Power was only in the King, and so that it was an Absolute Monarchy, and not a mixture of Monarchy, Aristocracy and Democracy; and that the Parliament had but the proposing of Laws, and that they were enacted only by the Kings Authority, upon their Request, and so that the Power of Armes, and of Warre, and Peace, was in the King alone; and therefore they conclude, That the Parliament being Subjects may not take up Armes without him, and that it is Rebellion to resist him; and most of this they gather from the Oath of Supremacy, and from the Parliaments calling themselves his Subjects.'

But their Grounds are sandy, and their Superstructure false, as I shall manifest.

1. The Oath of Supremacy secureth the Kings Title against all forrain claim, either of the Pope or any other, and consequently against all home-bred Usurpers: But the Name of Supream, or Sov-

eraign, given peculiarly to the King, is no sufficient discovery of the constitution of the Commonwealth, nor any proof that it is an absolute Monarchy, and not a mixt Government, and that the soveraign Power is wholly in him: When the contrary is known in the Constitution, the Name or Title is no disproof. It's usual to honour the Prince with the Title of Soveraign, (for divers weighty Reasons) when yet the Senate or Nobles have a part in the soveraign Power. Such Oathes therefore bind us only to acknowledge the Kings Soveraignty as it is in the constitution, implying the Power of the Parliament, and they cannot be interpreted to be against the Constitution: Politicians and Lawyers commonly warn us to take heed of judging of the Power in the Commonwealth by meer Titles.

2. That the Parliament are Subjects is confessed; but as they are Subjects in one capacity, (both in their personal private states, and as the Representative of the Subjects as such) so have they part in the Soveraignty also, in their higher capacity, by the Constitution, as shall be proved. The same Persons may have part in the Soveraignty, that in other respects are Subjects.

3. Some go further, and would prove from Scripture, the full Soveraignty of the King, as from 1. Pet. 2. 13, &c. As if the Species of Government were universally determined of in Scripture; and so all forms of Government made unlawfull, except absolute Monarchy. If they could prove this, they might dispatch many Controversies in Christian States about their Constitutions, and all must be reduced to one form: But there is nothing in Scripture against other forms, but somewhat for a mixt Government in Israel. God hath not told us whether England and all other Nations shall be Governed by One or Two, or four Hundred: but where the King is the Supream, it is the will of God that the people should obey him, which is all that Peter requireth. The Romans hated the Name of a King: It was neither the intent of Peter here, or of Paul, Rom. 13, to determine whether the Emperour or the Senate were Supream: much less to determine that Kings must have the full Supremacy through the world.

This folly possesseth the Democratical party also, (that call themselves Commonwealths men:) they imagine that God himself hath given the Soveraign Power to the people; and consequently that no Government, but Popular is lawfull. Whereas it's certain, that God hath not tyed the Nations of the world to Monarchy, Aristocracy, Democracy, or any one form, but left that free to their own choice, under the Direction of his general Rules, and the ordering of his Providential disposals:

And as the Objecters Grounds are manifestly rotten, so that their superstructure is unsound, and that indeed the Parliament hath a part in the Supreamacy, I shall undeniably prove.

1. Legislation is the most principal eminent part of the Soveraigns Right: But Legislation belonged to the two Houses of Parliament as well as to the King: therefore the Right of Soveraignty belonged to the Parliament in part, as well as to the King.

The Legislative Power, is not only essential to Soveraignty, but is the one half of its essence, and the first and chiefest part. He that denyeth this, renounceth Policy and Reason. But that the Parliament had a part in the Legislative power, (even of Enacting, and not only of proposing,) is undoubted. I will not run to Records, or to Writers for proof, because here a contradicting wit may find some work; but I will give you two proofs, that nothing but immodesty can contradict. The first is, Common Experience *de facto*. Parliaments do make Laws: the King was sworn to Govern by those Laws, *quas vulgus elegerit*: the Lawes expressly speak their Authors, 'Be it Enacted by the Authority of Parliament' or 'by the Kings Majesty, and the Lords, and Commons in Parliament Assembled, &c.' It is not 'upon their Petition or Proposal' only, but 'by them', or 'by their Authority'.

2. The King himself (by the advice of his delinquent Council in the time of his separation from Parliament) doth confess as much as I desire: '1. That the Government of England is mixt of Monarchy, Aristocracy, and Democracy. 2. That it is not an Absolute Monarchy. 3. That the Ballance must hang even between the three Estates. 4. That the King, the Lords, and the Commons, are these three Estates: 5. That the Laws are made in England by a King, by a House of Peers, and by a House of Commons chosen by the people joyntly. 6. That the House of Commons are an excellent Conserver of the Peoples Liberties. 7. That they are solely entrusted with the first Propositions concerning the Levies of Monies, the sinews of Peace and Warre; and the Impeaching of those that violate the Law. 8. That the King is bound to protect the Law. 9. That he may not make use of his power to the hurt of those for whose good he hath it. 10. That the Commons are to Advise him for the Protection of the Law. 11. That the Lords are trusted with a power of Judicature. 12. That they are a Screen or Bank between the Prince and people, to assist

each against the Encroachments of the other and by just Judgement to preserve the Law, which ought to be the Rule of every one of the Three. 13. That the Parliament have a Legal power, more than sufficient to restrain the power of Tyranny. 14. That the encroaching of one of these Estates upon the others power, is unhappy in the effects to all'. All this you shall have in the Kings own words in his Answer to the Parliaments 19 Propositions.

[There being three kinds of Government, Absolute Monarchy, Aristocracy, and Democracy; and in all those their particular conveniences and inconveniences; the experience and wisdome of your Ancestours hath moulded this out of a mixture of these, with the conveniences of all three, without the inconveniences of anyone, as long as the Ballance hangs even between the three Estates, and in their proper channell (begetting verdure and fertility in the meddows on both sides,) and then overflowing of either on either side, raised no deluge or inundation: The ill of Absolute Monarchy is Tyranny: The ill of Aristocracy is Faction, and Division: the ills of Democracy are Tumults, Violence, and Licentiousness. The good of Monarchy is the Uniting of a Nation under one Head; to resist Invasion from abroad, and Insurrection at home. The good of Aristocracy is the conjunction of Councils in the ablest Persons of a State for the publique benefit. The good of Democracy is Liberty, and the courage and industry which Liberty begets.

In this Kingdome the Laws are joyntly made by a King, by a House of Peers, and by a House of Commons chosen by the People, all having free Votes, and particular Priviledges; the Government of these Laws are intrusted to the King; Power of Treaties of War and Peace, of making Peers, of choosing Officers and Counsellors of State, Judges for Law, Commanders for Forts and Castles, giving Commissions for raising men to make Warre abroad, or to prevent or provide against Invasions or Insurrections at home, Benefit of Confiscations, power of pardoning, and some more of the like kind are placed in the King. And this kind of regulated Monarchy having the power to preserve that Authority, without which it would be disabled to preserve the Laws in their force, and the Subjects in their Liberties, is intended to draw to him such a respect and relation from the great ones as may hinder the ills of Division and Faction, and such a fear and reverence from the people; as may hinder tumults, violence, and licentiousnes. Again, that the Prince may not make use of this high, and perpetual power, to the hurt of those for whose good he hath it, and make use of the name of publick necessity for the gain of his private Favorites and Followers, the House of Commons (an excellent Conserver of Liberty, but never intended for any share in the Government, or the choosing of them that should Govern)* is solely intrusted with the first Propositions, concerning the Levies of Moneys (the sinews of Peace and War) and the impeaching of those, who for their own ends have violated that Law, which he is bound to protect, and to the protection of which they were bound to advise him. And the Lords being trusted with a Judicature power, are an excellent Screen or Bank, between the Prince and People, to assist each against the Encroachments of the other, and by just Judgements to preserve that Law which ought to be the Rule of every one of the three – since therefore the Legal power in Parliament is more than sufficient to restrain the power of Tyrannie – since the encroaching of one of these Estates upon the power of the other, is unhappy in the effect to all.]

You see here all the Parliaments capacities acknowledged: 1. That the Commons are chosen by the people, as Trustees for their Liberties, (and that they represent them as Subjects none deny.) 2. That they are the Kings Advisers. 3. That the Lords have the power of Judicature, as the Commons of impeaching, &c. 4. That the Legislative power; (that is, the Soveraignty) is joyntly in King, Lords and Commons as three Estates; and so that the Government is mixt of Monarchy, Aristocracy and Democracy. And thus far we are agreed of the Constitution.

3. And if it were not thus confessed, we might prove the Parliaments interest in the Supremacy, by some Judicial Instances, with the restraints of the King; (but that it's needless to debate a confessed thing.) ...

§. IV. I was satisfied by Reason, and consent of Lawyers, even those that are most zealous for Monarchy, and most judicious, that in many Cases a King may be resisted ...

§. V. The Laws in England are above the King: Because they are not his Acts alone, but the Acts of King and Parliament conjunctly, who have the Legislative (that is, the Soveraign) Power. This is confessed by the King in the forecited Answer to the 19 Propositions.

---

* He meaneth the executive part.

§. VI. The King was to execute Judgement according to these Laws, by his Judges in his Courts of Justice: and his Parliament was his highest Court (as is said) where his personal will and word was not of sufficient Authority to suspend or cross the Judgement of the Court, except in some particular cases submitted to him.

§. VII. The peoples Rights were evidently invaded: Ship-money, and other impositions were without Law, and so without authority: The new Oath imposed by the Convocation, and the King: the ejecting and punishing Ministers for not reading the Books for Sports on the Lords Daies, for not bowing towards the Altar, for preaching Lectures, and twice on the Lords Day, with many the like, were without Law, and so without authority. If Bishops *jure Ecclesiastico* might have commanded them, yet could they not lay any corporal penalties or mulcts for them, nor should any man have lost his temporal livelihood or liberty, which Ecclesiasticks have no power over. Many thousands have suffered, or been forced to remove out of the Land, upon the account of illegal impositions.

§. VIII. The Parliament did Remonstrate to the Kingdom, the danger of the subversion of Religion, and Liberties, and of the common good and interest of the people, whose Trustees they were. And we were obliged to believe them both as the most competent Witnesses and Judges, and the chosen Trustees of our Liberties. We are our selves uncapable of a full discovery of such dangers till it be too late to remedy them: And therefore the constitution of the Government having made the Parliament the Trustees of our Liberties, hath made them our eyes by which we must discern our dangers. Or else they had been useless to us.

§. IX. The former proceedings afforded us so much experience as made the Parliaments Remonstrance credible. We had newly seen a general endeavour to change the face of things among us. Many new orders in the Church; abundance of the most painfull Preachers (though peaceable) cast out: Abundance of ignorant, idle, scandalous Readers kept in; and practical serious godliness made the common scorn, though found in the conformable to all the legal Orders. I will forbear to rake any further into those calamities. Only I shall say, that I suppose my Reader to have been acquainted with those times, and with the course of the High Commission, and the Bishops Courts, and to have read the Articles in Parliament against Bishop Laud, Bishop Goodman, Bishop Wren, Bishop Pierce, &c. and the charge against the Judges about Ship money; and Mr. White's Centuries:[26] and Mr. Prin's Introduction, or Works of Darkness brought to Light; and his Canterburies Tryal, and his Popish Royal Favorite, and his Romes Master piece; and especially the sworn Articles of the Spanish and French Match.[27]

§. X. It was time for us to believe a Parliament concerning our danger and theirs, when we heard so many impious persons rage against them; and when the Army then in the North was (by the confession of the chief Officers) about to have been drawn up towards London; to what end is easie to conjecture: when so many Delinquents were engaged & enraged against them, who all took refuge with the King. And when we say the odious Irish Rebellion broke forth, and so many thousand barbarously murdered; no less (by credible testimony) then an hundred and fifty thousand murdered in the one Province of Ulster only: I suppose him that I dispute with to have read the Examinations by the Irish Justices, and Mr. Clarks Persecution of the Church in Ireland[28] else he is incompetent for the debate. If you say, What was all this to England? I Answer, we knew how great a progress the same party had made in England, and it was them that we were told by the Trustees of our safety, that we were in danger of, and the fire was too near us to be neglected; and our safety too much threatened, to be carelessly ventured in the heat of the peril; or to be wholly taken out of our Trustees hands, when thousands were thus suddenly butchered by the Papists in our own Dominions, and those Papists likely to have invaded England, when they had conquered Ireland, and their Friends were so powerfull about the Court, & through the Land, and the Parliament hated by them for opposing their attempts (the Irish professing to raise Arms for the King, to defend his Prerogative & their own Religion against our Parliament) I say, in such a time as this, we had reason to believe our entrusted Watchmen, that told us of the danger, & no reason to suffer our lives and liberties to be taken out of their Trust, & wholly put into the hands of the King. We had rather of the two be put

---

[26] John White, *The First Century of Scandalous, Malignant Priests* (London, 1643).

[27] William Prynne: *Hidden Workes of Darknes Brought to Publike Light* (London, 1645); *Canterburies Doome* (London, 1646); *The Popish Royall Favourite* (London, 1643); *Romes Master-Peece* (London, 1643).

[28] Samuel Clarke, *The Persecutions of the Church of England, from the First Planting of the Gospel, to the End of Queen Mary's Reign* (London, 1652).

upon the inconvenience of justifying our defence, then to have been butchered by thousands, or fall into such hands as Ireland did: For then complaining would have been vain. It would not have made dead men alive, nor recovered England out of their hands, for the survivors to have accused them of perfidiousness or cruelty. It was then no time to discredit our Watchmen.

§. XI. We saw the King raise Forces against the Parliament, having forsaken them, and first fought to seize upon their Members, in a way which he confest a breach of their priviledge.

Obj. The Tumults at Westminster drove him away.

Answ. Only by displeasing him; not by endangering him, or medling with him.

Obj. The Parliament was not free by reason of them.

Answ. The Parliament knew best when they were free. If the major part had thought so, why did they not Vote against those tumults, and forbid, and bring the rude Petitioners to Justice? The disorders on both sides among the tumultuary, were unexcusable: but no just cause to cast the Nation into a Warre. A Prince may not raise War against his people, because Apprentices shew some rudeness in their behaviour.

Object. But the Parliament began the War.

Answ. For my part, I am satisfied of the contrary: but the cause dependeth not on that. And the debate is not easily managed to satisfaction on either side, because we agree not what was the beginning of the Warre. If the Apprentices tumultuous petitioning were a Warre, then it was begun long before on the other side, when the Army was to have been drawn up towards London, and by other waies; as when the King set a Guard on them against their wills, when the Lord Digby raised Forces near the City; and the King afterward in Yorkshire, the Parliament had no Army: so that if actual raising force was the beginning of the Warre, it seems he begun. But yet he saith, Their Commissions were dated before his. It may be so: (I knew nothing of that.) But Forces may be raised before they have any written Commissions. It was long before that the Lord

Digby wrote to him to withdraw into a place of safety, to these ends which he pursued. If you say, that those began the War that gave the first occasion; 1. We must follow that so high as will make the discovery difficult, and the debate irksome. 2. And when we have done, no doubt (as in most fallings out) we shall find that both sides were too blame, though not equally too blame.

§. XII. All the Kings Counsellours and Souldiers were Subjects, and legally under the Power of the Parliament. They had Power to try and Subject, and judge them to punishment for their crimes. The Offendors whom they would have judged, fled from Justice to the King, and there defended themselves by force.

Object. But the Parliament would have injured them.

Answ. Who should be Judge of that, if not the Supream Court of Justice? The Laws are above the King.

Object. The Parliaments Souldiers were Subjects of the King, as well as the Kings Souldiers to the Parliament.

Answ. True: but if Subjects break the Laws, the King is to judge them by his Courts of Justice, and so the King can do no wrong.

§. XIII. If inferiour Courts of Justice may prosecute the execution of their sentences, in several cases against the Kings Will, and the Sheriff may raise the Power of the County to assist that execution, much more may the Highest Court do thus: But the Antecedent is commonly acknowledged to be true: Therefore.

§. XIV. The Parliament did not raise War against the Person or Authority of the King; nor did I ever serve them on any such account: but their cause was, 1. To defend themselves and the Commonwealth from evil Subjects, that flying from Justice, had made up an Army by the Kings consent. 2. To bring Offenders to a Legal Trial. 3. And consequently to Defend themselves against the Kings misguided Will. So that their War was directly against Subjects, but remotely against the Will of the King, but not against his Authority or Person. And Subjects cease not to be Subjects, when they get into an Army, and procure his consent to their illegal enterprise. Unless every one of his Souldiers was a King, or some of them at least, I know not that I ever fought against the King. Nor really do I believe that every man is against him, that is against a Subject that hath His Commission, when by the Law which is above the Will and Commission of the King, he is a Subject still, and answerable for his offences.

That it was Subjects that the War was raised against, and not the King, appeareth, 1. In all the Parliaments Declarations of their Cause (though his misdoings they alledge as the occasion of their necessity.) 2. In their Commissions to their Souldiers. All that ever I saw were for King and Parliament: Yea it was the common word of their Souldiers, if they were asked, 'Who they were for?' to say 'For King and Parliament.' 3. We had two Protestations, and a Solemne League and Covenant imposed on the Nation, to be for King and Parliament. And if Declarations, Professions, Commissions, and National Oaths and Covenants will not tell us, what the Cause of the War was, then there is no discovery. I refer the Reader that would know the Parliaments Cause, to their *Remonstrance of the state of the Kingdom*; and *A Declaration of the Lords and Commons assembled in Parliament, setting forth the Grounds and Reasons, that necessitate them at this time to take up Defensive Armes, for the Preservation of his Majesties Person, the maintenance of the true Religion, the Laws and Liberties of this King-dome, and the Power and Priviledges of Parliament.* (August 3. 1642.) These fully tell you the Parliaments Cause, being their profession of it.

§. XV. When the Parliament commanded us to obey them, and not Resist them, I knew not how to Resist and disobey them, without violation of the Command of God, Rom. 13. 'Let every soul be subject to the Higher Power', &c. And without incurring the danger of the Condemnation there threatned to Resisters. I think none doubts but that Command obliged Christians to obey the Senate as well as the Emperour. When it was confessed by the King, that the Legislative Power was in the three Estates conjunct, and the State was Mixt, and consequently that the Parliament had a part in the Soveraignty, I thought it Treason to Resist them, as the Enemy did, apparently in order to their subversion, and unlawfull to disobey their just Commands, such as I thought these were.

§. XVI. When the Subjects were in doubt of the sense of the Law, (into which most of the Controversie was resolved) I took the Parliament to be the Highest Interpreter of Lawes that was then existent in the Division. And therefore that it was Law to us, which they declared to be Law, so it were not directly and clearly against our own Knowledge, or against that truth which in our callings we might well attain the Knowledge of. I knew no higher Judge of the Law then to appeal to. If in case of Ship-money the Judges of inferiour Courts did satisfie the King, then in case of the safety or danger of the Commonwealth, I thought the Judgment of the highest Court should satisfie me.

§. XVII. I had great reason to believe, that if the King had conquered a Parliament, The Nation had lost all security of their Liberties, and been at his Mercy, and not only under his Government: and that Warre is an act of Hostility: and that if he had conquered them by such persons as he then imployed, it had not been in his power to have preserved the Commonwealth if he would: His impious and popish Armies would have ruled him, and used him as other Armies have done those that entrusted them. And therefore when Ireland was so used before our eyes, and the Papists there so strong, and the Queens, and the Earl of New-castles forces (besides others) so many of them Papists, and the common Souldiers of the King were commonly known, where ever they came, by horrid Oaths and Curses, being called Damn-me's, because 'God damn me' was their common word, and when a man was used by them as a Traitor, that was but noted for a Puritane, or was heard to read the Scripture, or to sing a Psalm in his Family; I say, when these were they that were imployed to conquer us, I knew that the safety of the Commonwealth lay in resisting them, and that they could have conquered the King, when they had conquered us.

§. XVIII. I had sufficient ground from what is cited before from Grotius[29] (and more such like) to conclude that the Parliament having a part in the Soveraignty, might defend their part against any that invaded it: and exercise it upon any Subject. And that their part was invaded, the fore-mentioned evidences, with what is in their Remonstrances shew: And the very intermission and almost extinction of Parliaments sheweth it yet more. The King was entrusted with the Calling of Parliaments, on supposition that called they must be: The seasonableness which he was entrusted with, was but a circumstance; and if under pretence of seasonable calling them, he will call none, or to no purpose, or break them up before they can do the work to which they were appointed, this is but to betray the trust of the

---

[29] On which, see Richard Tuck, 'Grotius and Selden', in J.H. Burns (ed.), *The Cambridge History of Political Thought* (Cambridge, 1991), pp. 499–529.

Commonwealth. Parliaments by Law were to be held yearly, and say some, before the Conquest twice a year. They that trusted the King to call a Parliament, thereby expressed that they were to be called, & it was not in his power to extinguish them, by not calling them.

§. XIX. I knew, that as the Parliament was the Representative Body of the People of the Commonwealth, who are the subject of the Common Good, so that the Common Good is the Essential End of Government, and therefore that it cannot be a just War that by their King is made against them (except in the fore-excepted Cases): And that the end being more excellent than the means, is to be preserved by us, and no means to stand in competition with the End. And therefore if I had known that the Parliament had been the beginners, and in most fault, yet the ruine of our Trustees and Representatives, and so of all the Security of the Nation, is a punishment greater, than any fault of theirs against a King can from him deserve; and that their faults cannot disoblige me from defending the Commonwealth. I owned not all that ever they did; but I took it to be my duty to look to the main end. And I knew that the King had all his Power for the Common Good, and therefore had none against it; and therefore that no Cause can warrant him to make the Commonwealth the party, which he shall exercise Hostility against. And that War against the Parliament (especially by such an Army, in such a Cause) is Hostility against them, and so against the Commonwealth; all this seemed plain to me. And especially when I knew how things went before, and who were the Agents, and how they were minded, and what were their purposes against the people.

§. XX. When I found so many things Conjunct, as two of the three Estates against the Will of the King alone; the Kingdoms Representative and Trustees assaulted in the guarding of our Liberties, and the highest Court defending themselves against offending Subjects, and seeking to bring them to a Legal Tryal, and the Kingdoms safety, and the Common Good involved in their Cause (which may be more fully manifested, but that I would not stir too much in the evils of times past.) All these, and many more concurring, perswaded me, that it was sinfull to be Neutrals, and Treacherous to be against the Parliament in that Cause. These were my apprehensions, and on such grounds as these here briefly hinted. And it somewhat moved me to see what the Parties on both sides were, of whom I will now say no more, but that it were a wonder if so many humble honest

Christians, fearfull of sinning, and praying for direction, should be all mistaken in so weighty a case, and so many Dam me's all in the right. But yet this was not the Rule I went by, but some Motive on the by.

So that the Cause of the Parliament which they engaged us to defend, 1. Was not the Sovereign Power of the People, as above the King, and the Original of Authority; as if the State of the Commonwealth had been Democratical. 2. Nor was it to procure a change of the Constitution, and to take down Royaltie, and the House of Lords, but clean contrary, it was the Defence of the old Constitution against the changes which they affirmed were attempted. 3. Nor was it the altering of Laws, which is not to be done by force, but freely by the Law-givers. And therefore it was not to procure a cessation of the Magistrates Power in Religion, for encouraging well-doers, and restraining intollerable Deceivers, which some call Liberty of Conscience. 4. Nor was it to offer any violence to the Person of the King; but to rescue him from them that had seduced him into a War against his Parliament, to his peril. These were the Grounds that we were engaged on, and I knew no other.

And therefore whereas some Pamphlets now flie abroad, that would defame the Parliament and their Adherents, as having engaged in a Treasonable Cause, and make that Cause to have been, 1. The Changing of the Government into Popular. 2. Or the Defence of it as Popular already, as if the People had been the Sovereign Power. 3. The deposing or destroying of the King. 4. The vindicating of an illegal or unlimited exemption from the Magistrates Power in matters of Religion, which they call, Religious Liberty; these need no further confutation then the reading of the Parliaments *Remonstrance* and *Declaration* aforesaid, and the rest of their published Professions, and Oaths, and Covenants. The clean contrary to these they openly professed: As, 1. That King, Lords and Commons in Parliament were the Legislators, and so had highest power. 2. That it was the Peoples Proprieties and Liberties, (and not their personal Sovereignty) that they defended. 3. That it was the Defence and not the destruction of the Laws that they endeavoured. And, 4. That it was former connivance at Popery that they were offended at, and not a Liberty for Popery that they fought for; and that Heresie and Popery were Covenanted against by them, is well known; though the Liberty of Truth and Godliness they defended. And, 5. That they intended no hurt, but preservation to the King. This was their professed Cause.

I know Grotius in the fore-cited passages goeth higher, That a King may lose his own part in the Sovereignty in a War, in which he invadeth the part of those that had a share with him: And I know that he concludeth that Hostility is inconsistent with Government; and that other Learned Politicians conclude, That if a King will make himself the Enemy of the People, and engage in War against them, he deposeth himself, and may be used by them as an Enemy. But these things belong not to the Old Cause of the Parliament; nor, for my own part, have I ever interested my self in any such Cause, and therefore am not to be accountable for it. Every man must answer for himself. It is only that Old Cause that I have been engaged in. And many things that since have been done, my soul lamenteth and disclaimeth.

Yet must I add, That though I own not all the ways of men, that have had a hand in our Changes, 1. I am confident that these that have been cast down, had great cause to acknowledge the Justice of God against them, especially for their encouraging the scorn of Holiness through the Land, and the persecution of multitudes fearing God, which the righteous God would not put up.

2. That I am bound to submit to the present Government, as set over us by God, and to obey for Conscience sake, and to behave my self as a Loyal Subject towards them. For, 1. A full and free Parliament hath owned it, and so there is notoriously the Consent of the People, which is the evidence that former Princes had to justifie their best Titles. They that plead Inheritance and Law, must fetch the original from Consent (Though, as I have shewed before, that Consent doth but specifie, and then design the Persons, on whom God himself doth confer the Power.) . . .

I have made this Confession to the world of my former actions, and the reason of them, 1. At once to satisfie the Many that demand satisfaction. 2. That if I have erred, I may not die without Repentance, but may be recovered by their advice.

And therefore I will further confess how I stand affected to these actions in the review, 1. The experiences of War, and the evils that attend and follow it, hath made me hate it incomparably more than I did before I tried or knew it: and the name of Peace, much more the Thing, is now exceeding amiable to me. 2. I unfeignedly believe that both Parties were too blame in the late Wars: The one Party in the things forementioned:* and the other in too impatient under-goings the Prelates persecutions, and some in too peevish scrupling and quarrelling, where there was no cause, or not so much as was pretended. But who can be free from some causeless scruples, that hath any Faith of his own, and is not careless of his soul. 3. I think that all of us did rush too eagerly into the heat of Divisions and War, and none of us did so much as we should have done to prevent it: And, though I was in no capacity to have done much, yet I unfeignedly Repent that I did no more for Peace in my place, then I did, and that I did not pray more heartily against Contention and War before it came, and spake no more against it than I did; and that I spoke so much to blow the Coals. For this I daily beg forgiveness of the Lord, through the precious blood of the great Reconciler. 4. The hatred of Strife and War, and love of Peace, and observation of the lamentable miscarriages since, have called me oft to search my heart, and try my ways by the Word of God, Whether I did lawfully engage in that War or not? (which I was confident then was the greatest outward service that ever I performed to God:) And whether I lawfully encouraged so many thousands to it? And the issue of all my search is this, and never was any other but this, 1. The case of blood being a thing so dreadful, and some wise and good men being against me, and many of their Arguments being plausible, and my understanding being weak, I shall continue with self-suspicion to search, and be glad of any information that may convince me, if I have been mistaken; and I make it my daily earnest prayer to God, that he will not suffer me to live or die impenitently, or without the discovery of my sin, if I have sinned in this matter: And could I be convinced of it, I would as gladly make a publick Recantation, as I would eat or drink: And I think I can say, that I am truly willing to know the truth.

2. But yet I cannot see that I was mistaken in the main Cause, nor dare I repent of it, nor forbear the same, if it were to do again in the same state of things. I should do all I could to prevent such a War; but if it could not be prevented, I must take the same side as then I did. And my judgement tells me, That if I should do otherwise I should be guilty of Treason or Disloyaltie against the Sovereign

---

* See the Life of Mr. Herbert Palmer in Clarks *Martyrology*, pag. 438, about the Kings Death.

Power of the Land, and of perfidiousness to the Commonwealth, and of preferring offending Subjects before the Laws and Justice, and the Will of the King above that safety of the Commonwealth, and consequently above his own welfare; and that I should be guilty of giving up the Land to blood (as Ireland was) or too much worse, under pretence of avoiding blood, in a necessary defence of all that is dear to us.

And it were too great folly, by following accidents, that were then unknown, for me to judge of the former Cause. That which is calamitous in the event, is not alway sinfull in the enterprise. Should the change of times make me forget the state that we were formerly in, and change my judgement by losing the sense of what then conduced to its information, this folly and forgetfulness would be the way to a sinfull and not to an obedient Repentance. Nor can I be so unthankfull as to say, for all the sinnes and miscarriages of men since, that we have not received much mercy from the Lord: When Godliness was the common scorn, the prejudice and shame most lamentably prevailed to keep men from it, and so encouraged them in wickedness: But through the great mercy of God, many thousands have been converted to a holy upright life, proportionably more than were before, since the reproach did cease, and the prejudice was removed, and faithfull Preachers took the places of scandalous ones, or ignorant Readers. When I look upon the place where I live, and see that the Families of the ungodly, are here one, and there one in a Street, as the Families of the godly were heretofore (though my own endeavours have been too weak and cold) it forceth me to set up the Stone of Remembrance, and to say, 'HITHERTO HATH THE LORD HELPED US.'

And now I must say (to prevent the Cavills of malicious Readers,) That though I have here laid down the Grounds upon which I think my Engagement in the late War to have been justifiable, yet I intend not that every one of these distinctly, is a sufficient Medium to inferre the Conclusion: But all together shew you on what Grounds I shall proceed with any man that will ingenuously dispute the Point. I must profess, that if I had taken up Arms against the Parliament in that Warre, my Conscience tells me I had been a Traitor, and guilty of Resisting the Highest Powers. And such Writings, as the (pretended)

French Discovery of the Scotch and English Presbyterie,[31] abound with so
much Ignorance of our Cause, or Serpentine malice, that they are
much uncapable of changing mens judgements that know their vanity.
But the Reading of such Books doth make me lament the misery,
of the World, through the partiality of Historians: This Book, and
Sanderson's History,[32] and many more that I have lately seen, upon
my knowledge do abound with falshoods, and delusory omissions,
and are (in my judgement) as unfit to give Posterity a true Information
of our late affairs, as the *Alcoran* is to tell them the right way to
Heaven. I know I shall highly offend the Authors with saying so; but
not so much as they offend God and wrong Posteritie by their
falshoods. The foresaid (pretended) French Anti-Presbyterian, takes
it for granted, that the total Sovereignty was in the King, and upon
that, and many such false suppositions, he makes the Presbyterians
the odiousest Traitors under Heaven; So that I do not wonder that
Forreign Nations do spit at the very name of an English Protestant,
as at the name of the Devil: And that Papists make their Ideots
believe, That the Protestants in England are run stark mad, and
turn'd such Rebels as can never more for shame upbraid them with
their Laterane Decrees, their Powder-plot, or their murdering of
Kings: And what have those Protestants to answer for, that by odious
lies do feed these reproaches of the ways of truth, and of the innocent
servants of the Lord? Yea the said (English) French Calumniator,
most palpably contradicteth himself, and telleth all the world that he
lieth: When he hath charged the Presbyterians with Hypocrisie and
Treachery in their Oaths and Covenants for the safety of the King,
the Priviledges of Parliament, &c. he proves by the breach of those
Covenants, that they were false in making them: And yet confesseth,
that it was other men that broke them, and pull'd them down, to
enable them thereto. Our only comfort is, That malice and lying shall
not carry it at last, nor pass the final sentence on us.

If any of them can prove, that I was guilty of hurt to the Person, or
destruction of the power of the King, or of changing the Fundamental
Constitution of the Commonwealth, taking down the House of Lords,
without Consent of all Three Estates that had a part in the Sover-

---

[31] See Pattinson, *The Image of Both Churches*.
[32] William Sanderson, *A Complete History of the Life and Reign of King Charles* (London, 1658).

eignty; or that I violated the Priviledges of Parliament by imprisoning or excluding the Members, and invaded the Liberties of the People, I will never gainsay them, if they call me a most perfidious Rebel, and tell me that I am guilty of far greater sin than Murder, Whoredom, Drunkenness, or such like. Or if they can solidly confute my Grounds, I will thank them, and confess my sin to all the world. But malicious railings of them I take for Rebellions themselves, I shall not regard.

Meditations

April 25, 1659

When I had gone thus far, and was about to proceed a little further, the sudden News of the Armies Representation, and of the dissolving of the Parliament, and of the displeasure against my Book against Popery, called, *A Key for Catholicks*, and some other passages, interrupted me, and cast me upon these MEDITATIONS and LAMENTATIONS following.

SECT. I

God is not the God of Confusion, but of Order: Wonderfull! Whence then are all the wofull disorders of the world! Why are they permitted, while infinite Wisdom, Goodness and Power is at the Stern! He loveth and tenderly loveth his People: Why then are they tost up and down the world, as a Sea-rackt vessel, as the football of contempt! His Spirit is the Spirit of Love and Peace! And his servants have learn'd to be meek and lowly, and his Disciples are all humble, and teachable, and tractable as little children: How comes it to pass then that their habitation is in the flames? And that they are hurried about the world with tempests? And dwell so much in the stormy Region? And that his Lambs must be sent forth among Wolves? Nay that *Homo homini Lupus*, is turned to *Christianus Christiano Lupus*! Surely a word, a beck, a will, of him that ruleth over all, is able to compose this raging World, and still these waves, and bring all into perfect order: How easily could he dispell our darkness, and reconcile our

231

minds, and heal our breaches, and calm our passions, and subdue corruptions, and bring us into the way of pleasant Peace? And can Infinite goodness be unwilling to do us good? Astonishing Providence! That the Vessel should be so tost that hath such a Pilot! And the Kingdom so disordered that hath such a King! And the Patient so almost deplorate that hath such a Physician, that is able to cure us when he will! O what a wound is it to our souls, that the Churches enemies of all sorts stand by, and laugh at our folly and calamity, and hit us in the teeth with our God, and our Reformation, and our Godliness, and our Hopes! With our Fasting and Prayer, and all our pretended brotherly love! And thus it hath been from age to age! And while we glory in the hopes of better days, and thought that Charity was reviving in the world though it cooled when iniquity did abound, new storms arise; our hopes delude us; we find our selves in the tempestuous Ocean, when even now we thought we had been almost at the shore! What Age, what Nation hath so followed Holiness and Peace, as to overtake them? Doth the most perfect Governour of the world delight in impious confusion?

Oh no! his works are glorious, and bear their share of the impress of his excellency. Shall we presume to call the heavenly Majesty to account? Must he render a satisfactory reason of his ways, to every worm? Is it not enough to assure us that they are the best, in that he is their Author who is infinitely good? We that are in the Valley of Mortality, and the shadow of death, are yet uncapable of seeing that, which on the Mount of Immortality we shall see to our satisfaction. We see but pieces of the works of God, both as to their extent and their duration. As all the Letters make one word, and all the words do make one sentence, and all the sentences and sections and chapters make one Book, & the use of the letters, syllables, words and sentences, cannot be rightly understood or valued, if taken separated from the whole: no more can we rightly understand & value the works of God, when we see not their relation to the whole. We parcel Arts and Sciences into fragments, according to the straitness of our capacities, and are not so pansophical as *uno intuitu* to see the whole; and therefore we have not the perfect knowledge of any part. As the whole Creation is one entire frame, and no part perfectly known to any, but the comprehensive wisdom that knoweth all; and as the holy Scripture is an entire frame of holy Doctrine; and the work of Sanctification is one new man; so also the works of disposing

Providence, are perfectly harmonious, and make up one admirable Systeme, which our non-age hindereth us from understanding. We must learn the Books of God by degrees; word by word, and line by line, and leaf by leaf; but we shall never be ripe Scholars till we have learnt all: And then we shall see that Nature and Grace, Scripture and Creatures, Physicks and Morals, and all the works of God for man, do constitute one most perfect frame, which we shall admire for ever. The knowledge of method, is necessary to our knowledge of several parts: They borrow much of their sense from their aspect on that which goeth before and cometh after; and the first hath some connexion to the last. The Wheels of a Watch considered separatedly, are useless toys: but in the Frame the smallest Pin is usefull. God seeth all his works at once: were it possible for us to have such a sight, it would answer all our doubts at once. The works of Providence are yet unfinished, and therefore not to be seen in their full beauty: six days sufficed to the Work of Creation; but almost six thousand years have not ended the disposals of this present World. Had we seen the Creation after the first or second or third days Work, we should not have seen it in its full beauty: But on the seventh day God rested in it all as very good. A scrap or broken parcel of the most curious picture containeth not the beauty of the whole, nor is seen in its own beauty but as joyned to the rest. One string of this Instrument maketh no great melody. But when we are perfected, we shall have a more perfect knowledg of the Providences that now we do but spell. What Christ is doing in planting and pulling up in all these disorders of the world, we know not now, but hereafter we shall know. The day makes haste, when all those actions shall be opened at once to a common view: when the men that make this bussle in the world are dead and gone, and Prince and people, Parliaments and Armies are off this Stage, and appear undrest before the Lord, and have received their everlasting recompence, from him that is no respecter of Persons, then Judge of these present ways of Providence: The end will expound the actions of this day.

Till then, as we know they are the ways of the most wise, so we must consider how many minds he hath to govern! Every man hath an understanding and will of his own! And, O how different! When so many thousand millions of men are of so many minds, or are principled and tempted to so many. We may wonder that such order is preserved in the world. Especially considering that their Interests are almost as various as their minds. Where they should agree they differ; where they are uncapable of a joynt possession, they agree in the desire of that which is impossible. How many have a mind of the same Crowns, the same Honour or Office, or Land, or other bait of worldly vanity: And how easily might Satan set all the world together by the ears, by casting such a bone among them, if God were not the universal King. Mens interests engage them against each other: And their vices are suited to their carnal interests: When humane nature is so corrupt, that vices swarm in the hearts of the ungodly, as worms in a Carrion; when ignorance, self-conceitedness, unbelief, sensuality, pride, worldliness, hypocrisie, and passions of all sorts abound! When so many hearts are blinded and byassed: and all men by corrupted nature are enemies to a Holy Peace, & honest Unity must be attained by crossing the very natures and interests of so many; when the best have so much of these corruptions, and grace that must overpower them is so weak; when the tempter is so subtile, diligent and uncessant, our temptations to evil, and hinderances to good, so many and so great, how wonderfull is that overruling Providence, that keepeth up so much order in the world! And preserveth us from utter confusion and Inormity? It is infinite power that so far uniteth such incoherent matter, and that, so far restraineth such corrupted souls: that every Nation are not Cannibals, that every Prince is not a Nero, or Dionysius, and every person is not a Cain, is all from the wisdom and mercy of our Almighty King. Let God therefore have the honour of his transcendent Government; He attaineth his ends by that which seems to us Confusion. He is a perfect Governour that perfectly attaineth the ends of Government! His ends are known to him, but much unknown to us. The night is usefull as well as the day, and darkness is no dishonour to the Creator. Nor is it dishonourable to him that there are Toads and Serpents on the earth, & that he made not every worm a man, or every man a King, or an Angel: Much less that wicked men do wickedly, when he hath resolved to govern the world in a way consistent with the Liberty of their wills. If sin were perfectly restrained, and the world reduced to perfect order, we should not have the benefit of persecution, which must be expected by those that will live godly in Christ Jesus. How should we ever express and try our patience & self-denial and contempt of all for the sake of Christ, if we had all things here as we would have them? It argueth too carnal a frame of mind, we are hearkening after felicity, or too great things on earth, and with the Jews would have a Kingdom of this world, and a Saviour that should make us great on earth: Should we not expect that God in equity and wisdom should keep a proportion of our comfort to our duty, and cause our prosperity to be answerable to our fidelity? If we have lesse here than we expect, and suffer after our faith and diligence, eternity is long enough to make amends for all: But that a sinfull, careless, hypocritical world, should yet be a prosperous world, is utterly incongruous, unless we would have our portion here. While the world is wilfully so vile, no wonder if it be so miserable. When sinne makes the greatest breach of order, and divideth our hearts from our Creatour, what wonder if lesser disorder do attend it, and we be all divided from each others? And whose conscience will scruple rebellion, resistance, or disobedience against the higher powers, that is hardned in rebellion, resistance, and disobedience against God?

It is a great mistake to expect perfection of so excellent a thing as holy order here on earth. If we are sure that there will be no perfection of knowledge, charity, self-denyal, patience, and all other graces necessary to our perfect order, how then can that order be perfect that must result from these? Can ignorant, froward, imperfect men, make up a perfect Church or Commonwealth? Or can we be greatlyer mistaken, then to ascribe to earth the Prerogatives of Heaven? Have we daily experience of imperfections and corruptions in our selves and others? Is not every soul imperfect and disquieted, and disordered? And every Family so too? And every Parish, Corporation, and society so? And can it then be better in a Commonwealth? Can it be perfect and ordered aright, that is composed of imperfect disordered materials? The whole cannot be gold, where all the parts are stone or iron. Unbelieving souls! Repine not in your ignorance against the Lord! When you come to Heaven, and see the perfect order of his Kingdom, and look back with better understanding on the affairs of the world that now offend you, then blame the Lord of imperfection in his Government if you can? All mercies on earth are but hatching in the shell: None are here ripe! We must know what earth is, that we may the more thankfully know what Heaven is. We must sow in tears, if we will reap in joy. We must know what sinne is, before we find what grace is, and what grace is, before we find what glory is. If sinne were not suffered to shew it self in the world, and play its part, it would not be sufficiently hated: nor Grace, or Christ, or Heaven sufficiently valued. We love the godly much the better, because the neighbourhood and tryal of the ungodly, sheweth us the difference. We are the more thankfull for our own grace, because of the experience of our corruptions. Holy order will be the sweeter to the Saints, because of the odious confusions that stand by. And as it is necessary that Heresie arise, that those which are approved may be made manifest; so is it necessary that Warres, confusion, and rebellions arise, that the meek, and peaceable, and obedient may be manifest.

They are good works as from God, and as to the finall issue, which he accomplisheth by bad Instruments. And when the work is rough, and below his upright ones, he useth to leave it to polluted hands. Even evil Angels are oft his Instruments in afflicting: and God can do good by the Devils: But when there is such a difference between the principal cause and the instrument in the work, and each worketh as he is, and bringeth somewhat of his nature to the effect, no wonder if there be a mixture of order and confusion in the world: and that be sinfull and confusion as from men, that is good and orderly as from God. If there were nothing in the world but what is of God, there would be nothing but what is good. But when Satan hath got so great an Interest, and is become a Prince that ruleth in the Children of disobedience, shall we wonder to find the works of Satan? Or shall we dare to impute them to the Lord? Or blame his Government because the enemy makes disturbance.

It is the reckoning day that sets all straight. Many are now triumphing whom God laughs to scorn, because he sees that their day is coming. Till then we must live a life of Faith. If fleshly props be taken from us, and we be left to live on God alone, our comforts will be the more pure, as having little of the creature to defile them. A sensual life is a beastial life. If God were not resolved to hold his servants to a life of Faith, with little mixture of sensible evidence, we should not have such seldom Messengers from the other world; and from age to age have scarce any more then Faith to tell us of the invisible things. When all men that we trusted to are gone, we shall comfort ourselves only in the Lord our God. And is he not enough for us alone? How apt are we to draw out from God to men? But when some prove insufficient, and others treacherous, and their friendship is as the waves and weathercocks, we shall cleave the closer to the Rock of Ages, and retire our selves with mortified and Heaven-devoted souls to God. And the more we converse with him, and see him in all the Creatures and their Products, the more we shall perceive his order in their confusions, and their confusions making up his order. But O when we see his blessed face, and behold the glory of the universal King, how sweet an harmony shall we then perceive in the concord of all the motions and affairs that now seem only tumultuary and discordant. We shall see how all these distant lines do meet in God, and in him we shall find all Providences reconciled, and making up one beauteous frame.

SECT. II

But it is not the disorder that is so much offence, as the quality of the persons from whom it doth proceed. Shall the work of God be hindered by them that seems his most resolved Servants? Must the cause of Christ be abused by its Friends? and his Church distressed by its Members? These are works that better beseem the enemies, even Satan himself then the Servants of the Lord. Shall we be guilty of the impenitency of the Churches enemies, while we seem to justifie their actions by our own? Must we receive these wounds in the Houses of our Friends? Did we once think that the Gospel must have suffered so much by them that were so zealous for it? Our familiar friends, that took sweet counsel with us, and went with us in company to the House of God? Yea still it is professedly for God, that God is abused and dishonoured: It is for Christ that Christ is so much resisted: It is for the Gospel that men have liberty to deny the Gospel, and dispute against it; and for the Scripture that men have leave to revile and argue against the Scripture, and draw as many as they can into the same condemnation: It is for the Church, that the Church is wounded and torn in pieces, and that the Pastours of it are by license vilified. It is for the godly that the godly are cast out: and it is for the interest of the Saints that liberty is granted to draw men from the waies of sanctity: It is for mens salvation, that liberty is granted to tempt and draw the people to damnation. And it is for the security of the Nation, our Religion, Peace and common good, that the Trustees of it are so used, and our security seized upon, as they have oft been: It is for Authority that Authority hath been brought into contempt: and made the football of the world: And if God were not wiser and faithfuller then man, the Church would be utterly destroyed in order to its preservation: and our common good would be procured, as the Irish did procure the Peace of Ireland: 'Our Brethren that hate us, and cast us out for the Lords Name sake, say, Let the Lord be glorified', Isa. 66.5 O lamentable case, that God also must be called upon, and engaged in the Causes which he so abhorres! That he is feigned to be the Author of Satans works? That Prayers are engaged against Prayers? And so many Parties fast and pray, and cry to God from morning until night, with greatest fervency, that he would direct them in his way, and acquaint them with his Truth and Will, and own his cause, and help them in his work against their Brethren: and all rise up with strengthened confidence, that their cause is right, and are by Prayer animated to their contrary wayes, which in some of them must needs be very evil. Alas, that the ungodly should be thus tempted to scorn the Prayers of the Saints; and weak ones tempted to suspect their force.

But did we not know till now that offence must come? And that it will be woe to the world because of offences? (And to them also by whom the offence doth come?) Is it such a wonder for purblind men to stumble? Or for children in their hasty running to catch a fall? May not friends fall out and hurt each other in their passion? Friendship is not seen, nor Judgement seen, when Passion is up; but a friend doth seem a very enemy, and a man of Reason seemeth mad. Much more if passion turn to phrensie! What wonder then if the dearest friends have foul words and blows from the distracted? Especially if they are loose and armed. The remnants of ignorance will have their effects, according to the matter that we are imployed in. So far as corruption remaineth unmortified Satan hath so much interest in us: and therefore hath somewhat to make use of, and may easily make men Instruments in his work, when he gets the advantage against their graces. But instead of being scandalized with my God, or with his holy Truth and Work, let my soul be jealous of it self, and from all these things receive Instruction.

1. And first, I see here what Man is! How unmeet a Pillar for our confidence? Too fickle to be a certain Friend: too feeble to be a sure Support: too frail to stand in strong temptations, without relief from the Almighty strength: too vile for us to glory in: too blind, too selfish, sinfull, and infirm, to be the Guardian of the Church! Were Godlinesse chiefly entrusted in such hands, and did the Cause and honour

of the Lord, depend most on their wisdom, fidelity and innocency, how soon; how certainly would all be lost; and prostituted to the enemies scorn? 'Cease then from man, whose breath is in his Nostrils: for wherein is he to be accounted of?' Isa. 2. 22. 'Thus saith the Lord, cursed be the man that trusteth in man, and maketh flesh his arm, and whose heart departeth from the Lord. For he shall be like the heath in the desert, and shall not see when good cometh, but shall inhabit the parched places in the Wildernesse, in a salt Land, not inhabited. Blessed is the man that trusteth in the Lord, and whose hope the Lord is: For he shall be as a tree planted by the waters, and that spreadeth out her root by the Rivers, and shall not see when heat cometh, but her leafe shall be green, and shall not be carefull in the year of drought, neither shall cease from yielding fruit', Jer. 7.5, 6, 7, 8. Though grace do elevate the soul, and tend to its perfection, yet being imperfect, it leaves man frail, and meeter to be our trouble then our Rest.

2. How dangerous a thing is it to have a mistaking Judgement, in practicals of greatest moment? How lamentably will it misguide their Prayers, their Speeches, and their Practices? And the greater is their zeal, the forwarder will they be to prosecute that evil which they take for good. While they are pulling down the Church, supposing that they are building it, how resolutely will they proceed? Let but a zealous mans understanding be deluded, and it will engage him in a course of hainous sinne. He will distort all that he readeth or heareth, to the strengthening of his sinne. Sermons and Prayers, and Providences, shall all be prest to serve him in his evil way. How earnestly will he beg of God for assistance in his iniquity, when he thinks it is his duty? How joyfully will he give God thanks for prospering him in doing mischief? What evil will not a man do, if you can but make him think it good? If he kill the holiest Servants of the Lord, he will think that he doth God service by it, and that his peoples blood is an acceptable Sacrifice. Were it the killing of Christ, the Lord of life, they would not stick at it, but say, 'Let his blood be on us, and on our Children.' It will drive back all the motions to Repentance, and confirm them in impenitency, and make them angry with all those that approve not of their transgressions, and will not be as bad as they: It will cause them to misinterpret all Gods Providences, and misapply his Promises and Threatnings; and their hearts will rise, with zealous indignation against all those that would recover them:

Reproofs, though most necessary, they will call Reproaches: and those will be taken for sensorious railers, that tell them of their crimes, though with the tenth part of the plainnesse and seriousnesse as the case requireth. In a word, the disease is strengthened, and secured from the power of all Remedies. Let us therefore beg of God, that he would not leave us to a deluded mind, nor give us over to the errour of our hearts. O what cause have we to be jealous of our understandings, and diffident of our selves, and to prove our way before we make too much hast in it; lest the faster we go, the further we go out of our way! What cause have we to hearken to the Judgements of the wise, and to be much in learning, and diligent in the use of holy meanes to increase our knowledge? What need have Babes to know their weakness, and keep their due dependance on the strong, and those that lack wisdome, to ask it of God, and withall, to seek for it as silver, and dig for it as for a hidden Treasure, and to be fearful of falling into forbidden paths?

3. How dangerous a thing is Pride of heart? When once it grows to an enormeous height, it will make men swell with self-conceit, and think none so fit to govern Countries and Nations as they: Nor any so fit to teach the Church: Nor any so meet to judge what is good or evil to the Commonwealth. They will think that God hath qualified them to hold the reines; and if he bring them within the reach of a Crown, or lower Government, they will think he offereth it them. How despicably look they on the Judgements and Counsels of men much wiser then themselves? Pride makes every Constable a Justice, and every Souldier a Commander, and every man a King, a Parliament, and a Pope in his own eyes. O what cause have we to watch against this tumifying deluding vice, and to learn of Christ to be meek and lowly, and to behave our selves as Children in his School, and to suspect our understandings, and walk humbly with our God? What Slaughters, what Scandals, what Breaches in the Church, what Triumphs for the Devil, hath Pride wrought in the Earth, and that among them that professe the Faith? And it fortifyeth and defends it self: It will not see it self, nor bear with the means that should disclose it. It hateth faithfull necessary plainnesse, and loveth foolish daubing flattery. With humble words, will men be proud: with formal confessions and daily reprehensions of the Pride of others, and complaints of the abounding of Pride in the world; with high applauses of the humble, and zealous exhortations to humility, will men be proud and

not observe it. When they read their condemnation in the Scripture, as that God abhorreth the proud, and knoweth them afar off, and humbleth them that exalt themselves. When they read the Prohibitions of Christ, against sitting down at the upper end, and seeking honour of men, against despising of Dominion, and speaking evil of dignities, and resisting the higher Powers as set over them by God; they read all this as if they read it not: They perceive not the sense of it: They know not that it speaks to them: But as the ignorant unrenewed soul doth hear the substance of the Gospel, but as a lifelesse empty sound, as not understanding or favouring the things of the Spirit, so usually do Professors hear or read Texts that condemn the sins that they are guilty of.

4. How dangerous a thing is it, to grow strange at home? And so unacquainted with our own hearts, as not to know their errours and enormities? If we should but long neglect our Watch, and grow unobservant of our hearts, how vile will they be, when we think they are upright? And how hypocriticall, when we think they are sincere? and what horrid things may we attempt with good pretences?

5. How deceitfull a thing is the heart of man? When after so much light and means, after so much teaching and enquiry, after so long self-observancy and use of means, and so many discoveries and confessions of sinne, most odious sinnes should so easily creep in, and be indulged and undiscerned, yea befriended and maintained, as if they were the holiest Works? How deceitfull is that heart, that cannot discern the most ugly mountainous transgressions? Yea that entitleth them, the Work of God?

6. How dangerous is it for men to lean to their own understandings, or to hear none but those that are engaged in their own Cause? And to loose and reject the advice of impartial standers by, that have had better opportunities of knowledge then themselves.

7. And how dangerous is it to live under strong temptations? And to have a potent carnal Interest before them! What a byas will such an Interest be to the understanding, when it should try the good or evil of their wayes? After great Victories, Renown and Honour is become mens Interest: and how odious is any word or way that would eclipse their honour? If some of the Victories of Alexander or Caesar had been obtained by perfidious Rebellion, how hainously would they have taken it to have been told so, and called to Repentance, for that which was the matter of their Renowne, and to have their acts of

highest Honour numbred with the most odious crimes? What cause have we daily to pray, that God would not lead us into temptation? When Honour, and Dignity, and Command and Wealth, are become a mans Interest, what will he not believe, and do to serve it, if wonderfull grace do not preserve him? Any cause shall seem righteous that promoteth that Interest; & any Arguments shall seem valid that do maintain it: Gain shall become Godliness: For nothing shall be Godliness that suiteth not with their gain, or other ends: and Paul and Peter should not be godly, if they crosse their Interest, and especially if they do it plainly and faithfully. And the Herod that hath reverenced John Baptist, and heard him gladly, will yield to the cutting off his Head, if Herodias be once dearer to him then the Lord. How excellent and necessary is self-denial? How dangerous a standing have the Rulers and Commanders of the world? What a folly is it to envy them, or desire to be in their Condition? What wonder, if few of the great and rich are saved? And if it be 'as hard for them to enter into Heaven, as for a Camell to go through a needles eye', how little cause have the low and poor to murmur at their condition? Experience hath taught me to resolve, that I will never put confidence in my nearest Friend, nor the best man that I know, if once he have a potent carnal Interest, and dwell among great and strong temptations. Though I doubt not but God hath his humble ones, whom he preserveth even in such assaults, yet how rare is it for Cedars long to stand, on the tops of Mountains? 'Man being in honour and not understanding, is like the beasts that perish', Psal. 49. 20.

8. How dangerous a thing is it to be once engaged in a sinful way? The further they go, the more their engagements will increase: How hard will it be to return, when once they have set foot in a course of sinne? Their interest then will lead them to impiety, and even to persecution it self; and to take Christ, and Scripture, and faithfull Ministers for their enemies. For all these are ingaged against sinne, which the guilty soul is ingaged in; Christ and Scripture do condemn it: Ministers must (as they have a Call) reprove it; and faithfull Christians must disown it: and this will enrage the guilty soul. The guilty have not the patience of the Innocent. Had I wrote that to the view of ten thousand that are Innocent, which hath so exasperated the guilty, it would not so much as have offended them. As Seneca saith, 'It hurteth them that have sores, to think that they are touched, though you touch them not.' Fear makes them complain as if they

were hurt: the sick and sore are impatient and querulous. And all that defendeth them in the sinfull way that they are ingaged in, they like and own: And so they go on from sinne to sinne, deceiving and being deceived. And if God have so much mercy for them, as to recover them by Repentance; How dear must it cost them, in comparison of what a prevention would have done?

9. How dangerous is it for uncalled men, to dream that every opportunity is a Call, to meddle with things above their reach, and seize upon Offices which they are unfit for? When men that have not had the inward and outward opportunities and helps for holy knowledge; which Ministers of Christ must have, will invade the Office upon a proud conceit of a fitness which they have not; or will be more peremptory in their judgement in Theological difficulties, then is suitable to the proportion of their knowledge; and when men unacquainted with the true Principles of Government, will be rashly condemning the actions of their Governours, and turning them besides the Saddle, that they may get up themselves, when ever they have a conceit that their Governours erre, and that themselves are wiser, and can govern better; what an Ocean of iniquity doth this presumption plunge them into?

10. What delusions doth a galled Conscience betray men to? When they have done evil, in stead of Repenting, they would fain bring others to approve their deeds, and fain have them justified before the world? And what if they were? Doth this conduce to their Justification before God? Is this any salve to a wounded soul? Will God absolve them, because men do it? What figg-leaves are these, that will not hide their nakednesse from Posterity, much lesse from God.

11. How abundantly hath experience satisfied me of the blessed-nesse of Peace, and the mischiefs of Warre, from the ordinary effects of them upon the soul. In Peace when we live in quiet Neighbour-hood, and in Church-order, men are esteemed among us according to their real worth: A poor Christian that is of excellent parts, and of a holy exemplary life, is he that bears the Bell among us, and the scandalous are presently discovered, and noted to their just contempt and shame, (Psal. 15.4. 2 Thess. 3.14) and froathy, wrangling, proud Professors, that know nothing but dote about words that gender strife, and edifie not, are looked upon as the spots in our Assemblies: so that Humility, Innocency and Edification here, bear all the glory and the sway. But in the Armies, some of our hopefull Professors turn'd

Drunkards (and when they came home, we could scarce recover them;) some turned away from Ministers, Ordinances, Scripture, Godlinesse, from Christ, and from common Sobriety and Civility: Some that sped best, lament their coolings, distempers, and discomposure of soul, and are other men in Peace, as to the beauty and integrity of their lives, than they were in Warre. And (which is the thing I aim at) true Godlinesse and Vice are seldom rightly estimated in Warre. A slip into excesse is excused there as a necessary evil. A railing word, or rude behaviour and unseemly carriage, is accounted not much unbeseeming Souldiers for the most part: A great deal of humility and real worth in a private Souldier is buried, and too little observed or operative on others: When an half-witted Officer, or one that is notional, and empty, and ignorant, may be heard and regarded, as if his erroneous words were Oracles. So great is the Interest of Commanders in their Souldiers, that those have been there honoured and followed as men of notable parts and piety, and born much sway, that when they have returned to their Trades, and lived among their able, humble, upright Neighbours, have appeared to be of the lowest forme. I doubt not but Armies, have persons of the highest worth: But I have seen that ignorance, pride and errour, have far more advantage to gain reputation, and play their game, to leaven others, and rule the rost in a military state, then they have in peaceable Church-state.

12. I see more and more, how impossible, it is, that honest, plain, and faithful dealing, in Ministers or others, should ordinarily find acceptance in the world! We must expect to displease God or men, when men will swerve from the wayes of God: God or the guilty will condemn us: Conscience or engaged galled persons will censure us, and swell against us. While their Doctrines or Practices are unreconcilable to God, our Doctrine and reproofs will be offensive unto them. And whose pleasure and favour shall I chuse? Not mans, but Gods: For thy pleasure, O Lord, was I created: In thy favour is life: Or if men be permitted to deprive me of my life; thy loving kindnesse is better than life. Men are corrupt: and honesty will not alway please, when they pretend to honesty: They are giddy, and will not be long pleased with one thing: And I cannot change as fast as they. Their Interests call for that to please them, which is against the Interest of Christ, the Church, and my own, and others souls. And shall I sell all these for the favour of man! Of a lump of dirt, that shortly will

be loathed by those that now flatter them? Men are so many, and of so many contrary Interests and minds, that I cannot possibly please all, or many: and which then shall I please? Nay one mans mind is so contrary to it self, that if I please him in one thing, I must displease him in another. The holiest Apostles and Pastors of the Church, have not pleased them. Christ did not please them: God doth not please them: and how should I?

My God! I am satisfied! May I but please thee; I have enough. How easily may I spare the favour of man, whose breath is in his nostrils, if I have thy favour? He that cannot be satisfied in thee, will never be satisfied. I covenanted not with thee, for the favour of the best of men; when I became thy servant: but that thou shouldst be my God in Christ. Let me have this, and I declare to all the world, that thou hast made good thy holy Covenant, and I have that which I agreed for. O that I had more faithfully pleased thee, though I had displeased high and low, Princes and Armies, and all the world. The favour of man cannot continue my soul in life: I must be sick, and die, and rot in the grave, if I have the favour of all the world. But if God be for me, who shall be against me! All things shall work together for my good: Because Christ liveth, I shall live. The wounds of my soul are not for displeasing men, but thee! The frowns of the greatest leave no sting behind them in my heart: But who can bear the frowns of God? My God! It is not earthly men, that I must live with long! How long have I looked for thy Call! It is thee that I must live with for ever. And therefore, how little doth it concern me, whether I be loved or hated here? Those that shall live with me in thy presence, will all be reconciled by the light of thy Face, and the power of thy Eternal Love. The rest are not of my Communion. It woundeth not my conscience that I have honoured thy Providence, which preserved this Nation from so much guilt: nor that I preferred the honour of thy Cause and Churches, before the honour of sinning men. Wisdom and Holinesse in any of thy servants, desire me not to defend their Neighbour enemy; nor to preferre their Honour before thine, much lesse to justifie their sinne, which hath dishonoured thee, and which they must condemn themselves, that they may not be condemned for it. And the demands of Folly and Impiety are not regardable. I thank thee for weaning my soul from man! But let it not now be estranged from thee. I stand to my Covenant! I give up all! For all is nothing: But then let me have thee, that indeed art all!

Forsake me not, that consent to forsake all for thee, and should not
have consented, if thou hadst forsaken me. The darknesse and distance of my soul from thee, is more grievous to me than all the frowns
of men! Alas my God, that I can know thee no more, after so many
and gracious discoveries! That I love thee no more, that by so many
mercies hast testified thy love, and done so much to convince me
that thou art most Lovely; this, this is the prison, the famine, the
sicknesse, and I had almost said the death of my languishing, droop-
ing, fainting soul! That I have thought, and read, and heard, and said
so much of Heaven, the Rest of Saints, and yet my soul can reach
no higher, and get no nearer, and believe, and love, and long no
more; these, Lord are the wounds and scourges that I suffer! I may
not open my brest with Camero, and say, *Feri miser*; but I may submit
with Luther, and say, *Feri Domine, clementer feri*, if I had but more of
the apprehensions of thy love, and more of the tasts of Heaven upon
my soul. I refuse not the stocks of Paul and Silas, nor their scourges
neither, so I might have their heavenly visits and elevation, which
might tune my soul to their delightful melody. Were I but free from
the Prison of my ignorance, unbelief, and other sinnes, how easily
could I bear the imprisonment of my body! Were I with John in
Patmos, so I might also be with him in the Spirit, I would rather call
it a Paradise, than a Banishment. What can it be but thy presence or
absence, that may denominate places and conditions, a Homo, or a
Banishment, Liberty or Imprisonment, Sweet or Bitter, Happy or
Miserable. Were there a Countrey on Earth that had more of God,
and where the Sunne of his face doth shine more brightly, and where
Heaven is opener unto earth, and the Spirit hath more illuminating,
quickning influences on the souls of men; O that I were banished
thither! How cheerfully, how speedily would I go seek that place?
But while I carry my Gaoler and my Prison about me, and am fettered
in my own corruptions and infirmities, alas, in Liberty I am not free;
while I am honoured and applauded, I am ashamed of my self: While
I am Loved of others, I loath my self: Though my body be afflicted
by none without me (but by thy just and gracious castigations, which
I have born even from my youth) yet how can it chuse but droop and
languish, that is animated by an afflicted soul? How oft do my Bodily
pains seem nothing, being over-sensed with my souls more grievous
languishings? So long have I been a Prisoner at Home, that I could
long for a Prison that would but bring me nearer Home. The

darknesse that I live in in the open light, doth make me think that Dungeon happy, where souls are more open to thy celestial Rayes. I wonder not at the Labours and Patience of holy Paul, when I consider what Spirit dwelt within him, and what a sight he had had of Christ, and whither he was wrapt, and what he saw. The sight of Christ in his Humiliation was much; but the glimpse of a glorified Christ was more, though mixt with somewhat of rebuke and terrour. To be taken up into the third Heavens, and there see things to us unutterable, must needs be an effectual Motive, to all that holy diligence and patience, and a reward exceeding all that we can do or suffer. Much more unworthy are the sufferings of this present life, to be compared with the glory that shall be revealed. It will be a small thing to him to be judged of men, that knoweth that there is one that judgeth, even the Lord; and seeth by faith, the Judge even at the door. Were I fully certain that my sinnes could do no more against me, at the barre of God, then all the censures, displeasures, reproaches or persecutions of men can do, how little should I fear that dreadful day! Might I but finish my course with joy, why should I count life or liberty dear? Let me be equal with the most afflicted of thy Saints, so I may but believe, and love as much as the holiest. Might I but have their measure of the Spirit, how gladly should I submit to their measure of persecution! Might I see what Stephen saw, how gladly would I suffer what he suffered! But I dare not, I must not thus capitulate with God! The times and measures of the Reward are in thy hand. Much lower termes are very high. Dispose of me therefore according to thy gracious will. Thy will is the Original and the End, of me and all things. From it I seek for

guidance, safety, strength and happiness.

By it let me be directed and disposed:

In it alone let my soul have Rest.

Not my will, but thy

will be done.

FINIS

Appendix: Preface to
The Life of Faith (1670)

Preface

Let the Reader know, that whereas the Bookseller hath in the Catalogue of my Books, named my [*Holy Commonwealth or Political Aphorisms*] I do hereby recall the said Book, and profess my Repentance, that ever I published it, and that not only for some by-passages, but in respect of the secondary part of the very scope. Though the first part of it, which is the defence of God, and of Reason, I recant not.

But this Revocation I make with these proviso's

1   That I reverse not all the Matter of that Book, nor all; that more than ONE have accused; As e.g. the Assertion that *all humane Powers are Limited by God*: And if I may not be pardoned for not defying DEITY and HUMANITY, I shall preferr that ignominy before the present *Fastnes*, and Triumph, who defie them.

2   That I make not the Recantation to the Military fury, and rebellious pride and tumult, against which I wrote it; nor would have them thence take any encouragement for impenitence.

3   That though I dislike the Roman Clergies writing so much of Politicks, and detest Ministers medling in State matters without warranty, or a certain call; yet I hold it not simply unbeseeming a Divine, to expound the fifth Commandment, nor to shew the dependence of humane Powers on the Divine; nor to instruct Subjects to obey with judgment, and for Conscience sake.

4   That I protest against the judgment of Posterity, and all others, that were not of the same TIME, AND PLACE, as to the (mental) censure, either of the BOOK or the REVOCATION; as being ignorant of the true reasons of them both.

251

Which things provided, I hereby under my hand, as much as in me lyeth, reverse the Book, and desire the World to take it as *non-Scriptum*.

April 15 1670   R.B.

Index

Index

Cambridge Texts in the History of Political Thought

Titles published in the series thus far